To my

Tani.

Carp Reflections

*The chronicle of fifteen years
of fishing for carp*

by Paul Selman

• Laneman Publishing •

A big chunky mirror caught from Hawk Lake.

This book is dedicated with love to
Wendy, Rebecca and Matthew

First published in 1997 by
Laneman Publishing
5 Lyons Court, Dorking,
Surrey RH4 1AB

© Paul Selman 1997

**British Library Cataloguing
in Publication Data**

A catalogue record for this
book is available from the
British Library.

ISBN 1 901717 00 3

Design and production by:
Lane Design.
Telephone: 01306 875154

Illustrations by:
Pete Curtis.
Telephone: 0171 701 9122

All photographs by the
author unless marked.

Printed in Great Britain.

Contents

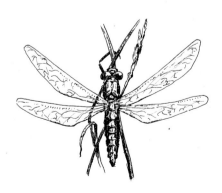

Acknowledgments

My thanks to those who have helped to put this book together.
To Stephen Lane, for his belief in me and for his talented design skills in putting together such a superb-looking book.
To Pete Curtis for his wonderful illustrations, line drawings, cartoons and maps. The book would have been much the poorer without their inclusion. Thanks Pete, even if you did blow-up my fax machine with the constant flow of material!
To the Seal Family, John and Pauline, Richard and Ben, for their moral support, encouragement, proof reading and comments.
To Wendy for the proof-reading as always, the cups of coffee, the late dinners and for putting up with me in the first place.

I'd like to thank a few friends who have encouraged me in my writing generally, and whose support and encouragement in this field, I will always be grateful for.
Tim Paisley, for his friendship, criticism and praise when necessary and for teaching me to write in a professional manner.
Julian Cundiff, for his support and for being a pleasure to work with.
Roger Smith, who pointed me in the right direction.
Kevin Clifford, for his general advice, encouragement and understanding.
Peter Mohan, for his advice and positive support in the early days.
David Hall, Jim Foster and Bob Roberts, for their kind words.
Bill and Skid, for being Bill and Skid.
Les Bamford, for showing me that he is much better at putting a book together than he is at converting buzzers, and for showing me the true value of money.

Introduction

"When are you going to write your first solo book?" has been a question I've been asked many times in recent years. The problem was finding the time. I've been writing and editing with some intensity in my spare time over the last few years and fishing waters where expending time was necessary to have any chance of catching fish. I find it impossible to write whilst fishing, even though I've tried. There are just too many pleasant distractions. I wanted to write a book and the only way I was ever going to produce one was to force myself to sacrifice precious fishing time, since I couldn't renege on writing commitments given to my fellow editors. I started the book in what was the close season of 1996, got a couple of chapters completed, then the fishing season hit and it ground to a halt. It looked as if I would never get it done. I had another good summer and autumn, and, prompted by my good friend Julian Cundiff to instill more discipline into the rather scatter-brained Selman head, I committed myself to complete the book over the winter. I forced myself not to go fishing until the whole process was complete.

I've tried to write a book I'd be interested to read myself. I'm an avid reader of carp literature both old and modern, and I know what I like. I wanted to avoid writing a purely technical book, as there have been so many of these in recent years, often repeating the same information. My idea of a good carp book is that it be part-technical, part-atmospheric, part-narrative - in short, a good read. This is what I have tried to provide - I leave it to you, the reader, to decide if I have been successful. I wrote a series for *Carpworld* - some years ago now - in which I wrote an article about each of the waters I'd fished in recent years. The series was very well-received and I had a sack-load of mail from readers. The concept behind this book was similar. To write a definitive account of the most significant waters I have fished in the last 15 years. I decided not to look at my fishing of the 1970's, as I don't think that the carp anglers of today would be interested in what has quickly become a bygone era. Thus, fifteen years coincides with the beginning of the modern carp scene, the era of the hair rig, boilies and carbon rods.

I've looked at the ten or eleven lakes which have been the most significant both in terms of my fishing and the technical developments that occurred on them. I've fished many more waters than this during this period both home and abroad. Whitley Pool, Lymm Dam, The Ocean, Grey Mist Mere, Farlow's, Shillamill, Horseshoe Lake, Spring Pool and Trench

Pool are other English waters that spring to mind that I also enjoyed success on. But they were not all that significant from a problem-solving point of view when compared to the lakes I've written about.

When writing about lakes one has fished in the past, one relies on memory which is often fallible. Things get forgotten over the passage of time. If I have got the odd fact wrong, I apologise. I have tried to check things out for accuracy where I could.

I've been fishing since the age of four, and I've had a wonderful thirty-six years of fishing for all types of fish. The last 15 years of my carp fishing have been marvellous. I've been very fortunate to have fished so many superb carp waters and have been privileged to fish with so many fine carp anglers. I have such very happy memories - far too many to feature in just one book.

I'd like to thank all my carp fishing friends on all of the waters I've written about for giving me those happy memories. If I've taken the mickey out of one or two of you in this book, please remember that it is with both affection and a mischievous wink that I write.

I hope I'll fish with you all again at some time in the future.

Halsnead Park Lake

Dusk was falling and low rain clouds framed the yellow sunset. A strange sound
caught my ear, as of air blown through a paper tube, a sudden 'russsh'. What could
it be? Looking back I saw the square pool, inky black under its wall of trees....
'Russsssh' the sound came again, louder this time....
Then I saw the heron.
B.B. The Idle Countryman 1944

Hidden away in a heavily wooded hollow lying just a few miles away from the great maritime city of Liverpool there is a small carp lake. Not an ugly, concrete-circled and artificial park pool as its somewhat unfortunate name might suggest, but a carp pool in the classical English tradition: small and intimate, reed and tree-lined, with the little nooks and crannies and characteristics that carp fishermen everywhere look for in a carp water. If one were to set out to deliberately design a carp water it would look like Halsnead. Nature created Halsnead in the place it was meant to be. Unfortunately, the politicians and the planners (who, of course, lived somewhere else) had created a hostile environment which bordered the lake, and which had begun to strangle and periodically rape the beauty and wonderment of the place when I first stumbled onto it, and which continues to do so.

I discovered Halsnead through several chance conversations. My girlfriend's parents had come to accept that I was an incurable eccentric who fished for carp and had remarked on this to a family friend who was a barmaid in a local social club. She said she had met other strange fellows who fished for carp in a local lake which was owned by the social club and that their conversations at the bar were all about mysterious things called buzzers, boilies and bolt rigs. She had agreed to enquire about membership for me, although there were potential problems - it was necessary to be a social club member to join the fishing section, to join the social club it was necessary to work for the major company that owned the social club and the lake. As I didn't work for that company - I wasn't working full-time at all - I thought that would be the end of the trail. By some quirk of fate and not a little skull-duggery, social club membership was bestowed upon me by post one May morning, much to my surprise. I cajoled Wendy into taking me to find the lake to see what good fortune had thrown into my lap. Five hours later, after driving around in circles and not finding anything that resembled a carp lake, with the mainly incomprehensible locals unable to supply any meaningful directions, we gave up and returned wearily home. I put the precious ticket away and forgot about the lake.

One September morning I was fishing a prolific water near Winsford, called The Ocean, and had just landed my first fish when two curious fellows from Liverpool started to make their way round to my pitch. Unbeknown to me, they were to become angling friends for the next few years. They were called Robbie and Bobbie which sounds like a clubland comedy duo and being from Liverpool where everyone has that deeply ironic and somewhat cruel humour they, of course, were.

Now in those days, carp fishing was still a very secretive and mysterious business and although you did talk to people you gave away as little as possible whilst, of course, trying to glean as much information as you could from everyone without it appearing obvious. It was very much a game of cat and mouse. On The Ocean, the locals (like they do on every other carp lake in the universe), gave outsiders like myself a nickname and regarded them with suspicion and often contempt. I had two nicknames depending on which group of Winsfordites we are referring to, because on this particular water there was open hostility and distrust between two distinct groups of locals too! To some I was known as "Mr Mingle Fruit" - because they had supposedly sussed out that I was using Rod Hutchinson's newly released Mingle Fruit bait, which of course, I denied vehemently, even loudly slagging it off as a useless bait when a local enquired. I was using it of course! My other nickname was "Mr Neat and Tidy" which in those days I was - which will come as a surprise to those who know me now! My tackle and set-up was truly ultra-cult and very flashy and the very latest carp fashion accessories gleamed in the sun and everything in the pitch was laid out so impressively. I really was a carp angling dandy in those days. It was this dazzling tackle that attracted Robbie and Bobbie to me like magpies and also my growing reputation on the water as a catcher of carp to which I was not entitled because I didn't live in Winsford.

I hurriedly unhooked the fish I had just landed in the net in the water as they lumbered (particularly in the case of the somewhat rotund Bobbie) around from the next swim down and then immediately cast out before they saw anything. For the next two hours, I cursed under my breath that they would go away as the cast-out rig had no bait on it! I knew that anyone who approached me was only after my secrets - after all, that was the only reason I ever talked to anyone - so I initially regarded them with deep suspicion and coolness. Like everyone in those days, I remained polite and courteous in the conversation that followed but gave nothing away. The conversation mainly focussed on their questions about my tackle. Looking back, I was quite helpful telling them how much such and such cost, and where they could get it from. After a while, they began telling me about a water they fished, which most didn't know about which contained some big commons - Robbie proudly showing me some photos of lovely looking commons up to 19lb - very good fish for the north in those days. Of course, I chanced it, and asked about the water. They revealed the rough location but told me that it was impossible for anyone to get in. It then clicked - it was that very same water I'd acquired a ticket for. Triumphantly, I reached into the rucksack, pulling out the impossible ticket. "Is this the water?" I innocently enquired, "I've got a permit but I didn't think it was worth bothering with." Robbie and Bobbie looked at each other open-mouthed in total shock!

After regaining their composure, they opened up completely about the lake and I was able to piece together a great deal about it. It had been carp fished since the early 1970's when it had been a very weedy and quite difficult lake. It had always held good fish by northern standards and had been fished by some very well-known northern anglers. Some are still legendary today, some have long been forgotten. Geoff Booth, Graham Marsden, Ronnie Pendleton, Jim Hindle and Kevin Clifford were some I recall mentioned. It had produced a 30 pounder and another of 27lb plus and used to contain a legendary mirror known as The Old Boot that had been caught many times and several huge uncatchable commons had been seen. In recent years, it had been neglected by the well-known names who had moved on elsewhere and the big mirrors had disappeared along with them with common carp now coming to the fore, with some twenties. This was very interesting - twenty pound commons were very rare in those days and most experienced carp anglers hadn't caught one. I certainly hadn't come close to one. It was a very good floater water but generally prolific regardless of method used, with many good doubles. All this was very interesting!

There were some negative aspects to their description too. The water was greedily controlled by a faction of match-orientated anglers, who were very anti-carp fishing and who had placed severe restrictions on rod usage. Only one carp rod could be employed until October, but night fishing was still allowed. They also seemed hell bent on trying to turn the classic carp pool into a match fishery by filling it up with "bits" and regularly poisoning what was once luxuriant weed growth at the first signs of any re-emergence. A sprawling council housing estate had been built close by, and its bored younger inhabitants colloquially referred to proudly as "scally-wags" seemed drawn to the lake and its surroundings from time to time, and some alarming difficulties had been experienced by lone carp fishers at dead of night with local punks, glue sniffers and joyriders. Robbie and Bobbie's lurid descriptions of these frightening incursions reminded me very much of my old school history lessons which were made very entertaining by the embellishments of the redoubtable, very large, moustached and one-eyed Miss Taylor. One of her particular fancies was to try to frighten us with horror stories about the heathen barbarian hordes and Attilla the Hun's ravages of civilisation and all things decent - which tended to dwell greatly on the massacre of innocent babies and the ravishing of young virgins. Not that even old Attilla himself would have contemplated ravishing the awesome Miss Taylor!

What seemed straightforward directions to the lake were given and I arranged to meet the pair who would be carp fishing there the following Sunday. Wendy and I set forth on the appointed day (I couldn't drive and relied on the long-suffering Wendy or fishing friends like Peter Ray to ferry me about), and eventually after another tour of the urban environs we found ourselves in the car park right next to a very pretty carp lake whose principal feature was a large island which could be reached by a walkway. It was September, and the leaves were just starting to go to those wonderful autumnal shades of brown, ochre and red. "Pick me up just on dark," was the command. "Fine, but don't keep me waiting," replied Wendy, knowing full well that I would be slow to leave. The anticipation of that last minute carp always delayed my departure - and still does.

The pretty little lake was packed with fishermen of various sorts as it always was on a Sunday. The majority were float-cum-matchmen, sitting on those silly, brightly coloured, plastic boxes daubed with the name of some tackle manufacturer. Mind you, I shouldn't be so disparaging - one of those silly boxes was a feature in my bivvy for several years and was only disposed of after a certain large not-to-be argued with gentleman thought it amusing to keep hiding a live ferret in it. But that's another story... There were probably getting on for 10 carp anglers on the lake, which was very busy for those days, and I wondered if I had really dropped a clanger. It transpired that this was almost the total of carp fishermen in the club and, as they didn't fish anywhere else - with the exception of Robbie and Bobbie - Sunday was the one day a week they all turned out. The first two carp fishermen I came to responded as if I was invisible and took on that distant, silent, Clint Eastwood-type demeanour found on any carp lake in the 1970's and as late on as 1989 on the likes of Darenth Big Lake.

Then the rotund shape of Bobbie came into sight and he greeted me in his customary cheery manner. Swims were at an absolute premium but I spotted one free that looked promising and the paraphernalia was set up in it. I cast out the one permitted rod. Unbeknown to me at that moment this created quite a stir on the lake, for I had settled in a pitch long unfished, which greatly perturbed the regulars. As an experienced and successful carp angler who had fished all over the place - and I had done my best to perpetuate that image - had I seen something that the regulars hadn't by choosing a no-hope pitch? There was a great deal of nervous twitching and for weeks afterwards the pitch was tried out by various anglers. Not a carp was caught or even seen. In reality, I had picked out that pitch because it had two large bushes on either side of it. This meant no-one could see what I was up to, but I could plainly see what everyone else was up to! Carp fishing watercraft.

From my hidey-hole, I was able to identify two distinct groups of carp anglers fishing the lake. The first group, were slightly older and more experienced in carp fishing terms than the second group but more blinkered and hanging on to cherished beliefs. They were still fishing like everyone fished in the late 1970's. Link-legered balls of softish paste baits on longish hooklinks with small leads. One of this group was also optimistically using an anchored floater - a dog-biscuit derivative, so presumably this was the warm water method. The second group could be termed the young thrusters - kids by comparison - with the Clint Eastwood scowls. Although clearly a backwater in carp fishing terms, some of the new methods had begun to filter through, as the side-hooked boilie on the large hook, short hooklink, heavy fixed or semi-fixed lead was evident. No one was using the hair rig, which had just started to filter out and had reached the ears of a small group of anglers in the BCSG locally.

The publication of *Carp Fever* was imminent which would make the rig public knowledge. I had been told about the hair rig by local BCSG organiser Dave Powell, who was fishing Ashlea Pool with Kevin Maddocks, although previously I'd heard it mentioned in a whispered conversation at a CAA meeting and, after hours of speculation, worked it out. I had met Dave in the late 1970's at Gorsty Hall, and had also met Geoff Booth and Peter Ray there. They were very experienced BCSG members and Geoff, in particular, was nationally a big name then. They became good friends, and they took the raw Selman under their wings. I was lucky to have such good tutors. I'd tinkered with the hair rig and caught fish on it, but in truth, had not capitalised on it.

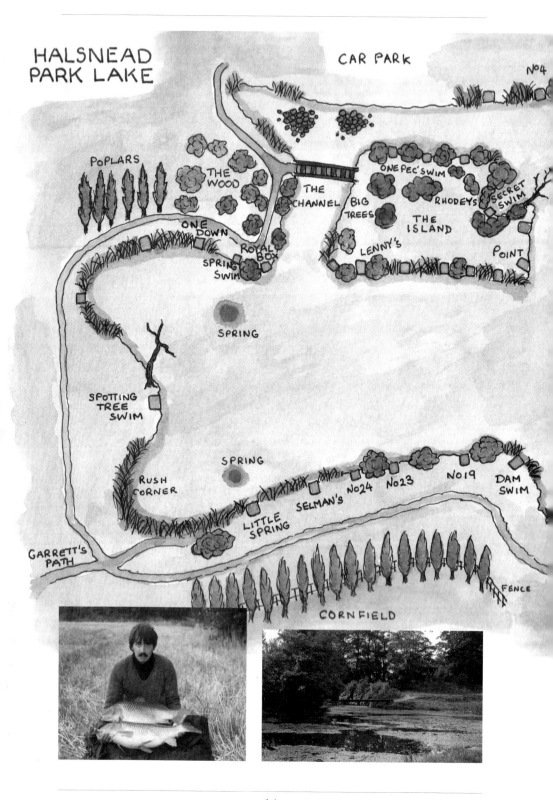

HALSNEAD
PARK LAKE

CAR PARK

N°4

POPLARS

THE
WOOD

THE
CHANNEL

ONE PEC' SWIM

BIG
TREES

RHODEYS

SECRET
SWIM

ONE
DOWN

ROYAL
BOX

THE
ISLAND

SPRING
SWIM

LENNY'S

POINT

SPRING

SPOTTING
TREE
SWIM

SPRING

RUSH
CORNER

LITTLE
SPRING

SELMAN'S

N°24

N°23

N°19

DAM
SWIM

GARRETT'S
PATH

FENCE

CORNFIELD

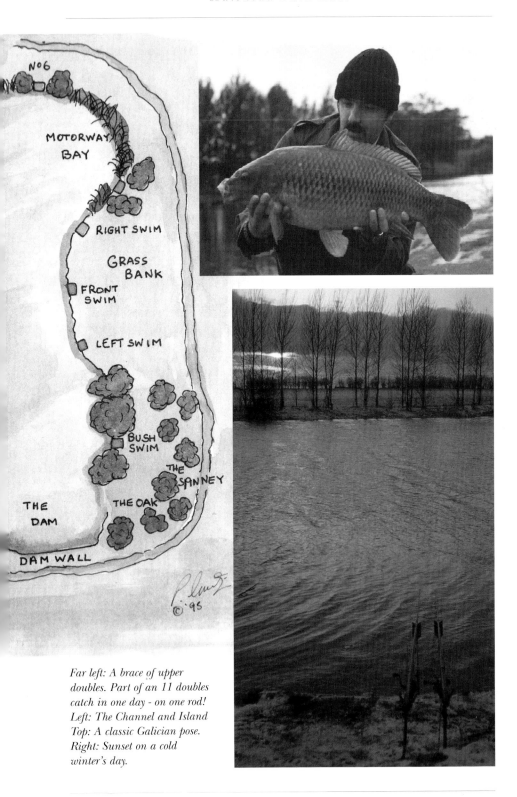

Far left: A brace of upper doubles. Part of an 11 doubles catch in one day - on one rod! Left: The Channel and Island Top: A classic Galician pose. Right: Sunset on a cold winter's day.

I'd been fishing quite easy waters such as The Ocean, Whitley Pool and Lymm Dam which were prolific doubles waters and it was possible to get plenty of runs on the standard bolt rig and even the old link-legered pastes. After years and years on very big hooks you tended to look at the hair rig and the tiny hook and think, I'm not happy with that. Modern day carp anglers won't understand this, but that's how it was. I didn't think I needed the hair rig. I wasn't on any big fish waters - there weren't many locally anyway. I was waiting to get on them, and was fishing waters where the carp were easy to catch in the meantime. I wasn't alone in this, for a lot of established anglers knew about the hair for a year before they began to use it regularly. One or two anglers locally, were bagging up on the big fish waters on the hair and making a name for themselves, as were one or two in the south.

Back in the hidey-hole at Halsnead....

Bob came around after an hour or so - he could never resist a good chinwag and fishing was always secondary to a good gossip for Bob, who found it difficult to keep secrets. Watercraft. The old generation of carp anglers fishing the lake Bob revealed, were all umbilically attached to the local specimen group run by the quite well known and somewhat abrasive character known as Ronnie Pendleton. I had heard of him - he was referred to often, somewhat disparagingly as "Fat Ronnie" or "Rockin' Ronnie" in a gossip column in one of the few commercially available magazines that featured specimen hunting. I knew he was fat but I was not sure of his or the group's angling prowess. From observation, they were of the '70's school and struggling to compete on the water with The Thrusters, who had started to use the bolt rig this very season. Bob told me a story that one of the group had told off one of the successful young lads for tying a two ounce fixed lead three inches above the hook. "That'll never work," was the sarcastic remonstration. Half an hour later, the same purist was seen trying to fix one of his little bombs to the line at the same distance from his soft paste bait moulded around his crust pad (remember those, older chaps?), after the youngster had caught a good double on the no-hope set-up!

Top bottom bait on the water the previous season had been the chick-pea, presented on longish hooklinks, which had taken the water apart and the top surface bait had been a cat food bait which was no longer available called Felix Meaty Crunch. Bob said there had been a feature about the success of FMC on the water in the Angler's Mail, and one of the members, Lenny, had contacted the company on hearing of the withdrawal of the floater from the market and had pleaded with them to sell him the remaining supply! The fish were either on the bottom or the top according to the conditions, and tactics were deployed accordingly. The standard opening enquiry on the water had been "On the Pea?" until it had begun to slow down and, inevitably, the tench had got onto them with gusto. With the demise of the chick peas, one or two of the lads had begun to experiment with boilies, which initially were dogfood/catfood based but fairly recent developments had been with birdfood and semolina based baits flavoured with fruity flavoured Angel Delight blancmange mix. What sophistication!

The water was a backwater not only in terms of rigs in use, but baits too. No high protein? No concentrated flavours? No peanuts yet? This would be a pushover! Then Bob revealed something that made my ears prick up. There were two other carp anglers on the water who were really doing well and who had experienced a few run-ins with Fat Ronnie's group due to their successes, for whilst they were of the same generation they were using the new methods. They were known as the "Two Pete's" and I knew straight away that these were two well known BCSG members called Pete Barker and Pete Dumbill. These guys did know about quality bait and how to use it, so I knew then with certainty that milk proteins were catching. Were they yet on the hair rig? This was less certain, because they were two crafty blokes who wouldn't want to risk giving it away and who would probably reserve it for their quieter big fish waters. That was my guess, and I later found out that it was the correct one.

After a couple of hours, Bob lumbered off to go and talk to someone else for a few hours, like he always did.

As dusk started to fall, a young, blonde haired lad fishing opposite and to the left in a good-looking swim known as The Spring had a blistering run. He struck but made no connection. That was the only action of the unproductive day. I packed away my kit and started to make my way round to the car park as I had no desire to stay on after dark to see if the legendary night-time goings on were really true or just a ploy to deter would-be carp angler club members. In any event, Wendy had sounded the car horn over an hour ago. One thing that did strike me on packing up, was the huge number of rats which emerged of all shapes, colours and sizes, all over the water. They were swimming all over the lake - which I've never seen anywhere else. They were up in the bushes and trees and scurrying around the banks. I have never fished a water with so many rats, before or since. That alone was sufficient deterrent to leave it alone after dark for me. No wonder one of the local after-dark hobbies was rat hunting at Halsnead with a torch taped to the barrel of an air gun!

But I vowed to return. I was having a lot of success from The Ocean and catching lots of doubles but one of the few twenties in the water had thus far eluded me. I decided that once I had caught my Ocean twenty pounder I would begin to fish Halsnead for one of those twenty pound commons and enjoy anything else that came my way in the meantime.

I loaded up the car and, as I quietly closed the boot, had one last look over my shoulder at the darkening lake. As I did, I noticed a heron flap its silent and stately way across the lake and fall onto a far deserted bank. Little did I know, at that moment, that he would be an occasional and sometimes regular welcome companion of mine for the next ten years or so.

....

By the end of October, I'd caught a clutch of nineteen pounders and a twenty-one pound mirror carp from The Ocean. I suspected the nineteens were occasional twenties, depending on who caught them. I knew there was one fish a little bigger than the twenty-one - a twenty-three pounder - but I reckoned my chances of catching it were slight. It was one fish amongst hundreds of lesser fish and the water had become less pleasurable to fish due to a change in bailiffs. There had always been an official ban on night fishing on the venue but as the bailiff was an accomplished carp angler himself, he turned a blind eye to night fishing providing one was a serious carp fisher - discreet and well behaved. After all, he night fished it himself from time to time. Unfortunately, the chap became a little disinterested, and an individual marginally less extreme than Hitler was appointed to beef-up the policing. Mr Mingle Fruit's number was up.

I'd bumped into Robbie and Bobbie a couple of times on The Ocean since I'd visited Halsnead and they kept me posted on the fishing which had been steady but unspectacular. One of the two Pete's had caught a twenty pound common, and another had been caught by a float boy. Having caught my twenty, I decided to keep to plan and leave The Ocean and the barbed wire and searchlights that had sprung up and fish Halsnead for the remainder of the season.

At that time in my neck of the woods, most carp anglers didn't fish in the winter at all. Some turned to pike or chub, others hung up the rods with the first frosts. Those of us who carried on, tended to fish short sessions of a day or a day and night duration. Winter fishing wasn't as comfortable then as it is now. My standard winter kit was a 45" nylon brolly, a bedchair with extended legs, two cheap sleeping bags and a plastic dustbin liner pulled over the end of the bedchair to cover the bit that stuck out in the event of rain or snow! A lot of the clothing, proper bedchairs and bivvies which we take for granted now just were not available then. They were just starting to come in. I don't think people realise how significant an invention the Optonic indicator was in terms of efficient winter carp fishing when used in conjunction with modern methods. Throughout my winter fishing of the late 1970's, I used the old Heron antenna indicator which Dick Walker had been developmentally involved in. They were state of the art then but they were a real pain at times as they were very susceptible to false bleeps due to wind and, with the twitches that were experienced then by both nuisance fish and carp on soft pastes and boilies, they were constantly going off. Once they sounded, they continued to and it was necessary to manually re-set them, or you could adopt my approach, which was to throw something at the buzzer in the hope it stopped sounding off! Antenna-type buzzers were an absolute pain in the winter and you could be up and down all night re-setting them - sleep was a rarity in carp fishing in the 1970's. The solutions were to place sponge foam in the butt ring or have them set so they only sounded when the angler got a screaming run, which was quite rare on the waters I was fishing, so these methods were inefficient. A "butt-ringer" or a "half-way-up" was more common, which is why we placed the bedchair right next to the rods for instant striking. We even used to paint our bobbin needles in one inch graduations to measure the length of those frustrating twitches! The Optonic was in a different class to the Heron which still gave off false indications even with the heavy leads and tight lines which were to follow. Efficient buzzers like the Optonic, and, of course, the invention of the bare hook rigs which converted twitches into runs, helped to make winter carp fishing much more comfortable for the angler, just as much as the modern bivvies and clothing did.

The good side of cold water carp fishing then, was that lakes weren't anything like as crowded as they are today and so it was possible to get a good productive winter swim virtually always, so it wasn't necessary to fish long sessions. If the fish fed at night, you fished at night, packed up, and fished the same swim the following night. Same for day-only fishing. So there was not the same need to sit it out then as often is today on the popular waters.

So it wasn't surprising when I turned up at Halsnead at 8pm on the second Saturday in November, to find the place to myself. I settled down in the Spring Swim, which looked a likely spot and set up the rods. Yes, rods, as it had been decided by the club, that two rods could now be permitted from the first of November. Grateful for small mercies! This would be the first occasion when I would use the hair on the water, and as far as I have ever been able to establish, the first time that this revolutionary rig had ever been cast into the water.

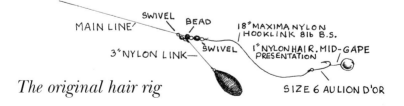

The original hair rig

The version I used that day resembled closely the original rig as devised by Len Middleton and Kevin Maddocks. It looks rather different to the conventional hair rig set-up used today. A short bomb link runs down to the lead: these had been very long in the mid-'70's but by the end of the 1970's were becoming shorter but were very much still in use, particularly on the silt lakes. The hooklink is still quite long, as is the hair. The original concept was that the hair would be above all a confidence rig. It began as a solution to the problem of line-shy fish. The bait was presented much more naturally than when it was mounted on the hook and it behaved more like any free offerings. The carp, which had become adept at testing baits to see if there was an element of risk involved, were simply fooled into thinking that the hair rigged bait was a free offering and in it went confidently back to the throat teeth.

Just how much confidence could be inspired in pressured carp by the use of the hair rig was clearly illuminated on this particular day. I cast out both rods in instinctive fashion, not really knowing what I was fishing over. After ten minutes or so, I wasn't confident about the placing of one of the rods and I was not sure about whether the rig had tangled too. I've always been paranoid about tangles and so there was only one action that could possibly follow - I picked up the rod. As I did so I felt heavy resistance - a fish was attached - but it had given me no indication whatsoever. It was my first Halsnead carp - a mirror of 12lb. I caught four more carp that day and only two gave me full blown runs. The others were just caught like the first, following no indication.

The hair rig's life as a confidence rig was short-lived. Unfortunately, it followed the development of the very successful bolt rig and so very quickly the hooklink was shortened and heavy bombs, either fixed or with a stop a few inches up the main line, were placed directly on the line with no bomb link being used. The rig became a much more deadly version of the bolt rig, the only difference being a hair was now used. This eventually, was to create a rod for our own backs.

The action began to slow down earlier than it might have done had we not abandoned the original confidence rig idea so quickly. There was much more mileage in the original concept than we allowed it. Added to the bolt rig, the hair made carp very, very easy to catch for a couple of years and most of us had previously unheard of catches.

The bait I used that day and for the remainder of the winter was a very simple one. It was a carbohydrate-based bait that relied entirely on its smell as the source of attraction rather than its food value. It was very similar to a lot of baits in use at this time:

6 oz Semolina

2 oz Soya Flour

1 oz Ground Rice

1 oz Wheatgerm

15ml Glycerin

5 ml Rod Hutchinson Topper Flavour

Red Dye

Baits of this type were sometimes referred to as low protein baits and a few of the most successful anglers of the day were trying to advance the argument that these baits were very effective and were even proving more successful than the high protein baits which had dominated many waters in the 1970's. I don't think this was the reality at all. Low protein/carbohydrate based baits did catch lots of fish everywhere but they caught so well because they were fished on the hair rig and it was the rig that was the key factor and not the bait. The hard boilie created by using these ingredients undoubtedly added to the effectiveness of the hair because the carp had to pass the bait back to the throat teeth in order to crush it. But in truth, anything edible presented on the hair at this time was likely to be successful.

The days of commercially available bait rolling aids were a few years away and so the baits were rolled by hand at, I guess, about 14mm size and boiled for two minutes. Glycerin I had been using for several years to sweeten baits, and although better sweeteners were to follow, I always found Glycerin very effective and it had a consistent effect on a bait. I still occasionally use it in situations where a lot of people on a water are using sweet baits but I want to avoid using the very popular sweeteners sold by bait companies for carp fishing purposes. Don't go looking for the original Topper flavour anymore as I suspect the one I used that day was the last of a batch. This was an effective smell with fruity-type notes, but I found after the small quantity I initially purchased ran out, subsequent batches were slightly different and certainly not as effective. Not receiving identical subsequent batches even though they carry the same name, has been a problem for me with flavours obtained from angling suppliers over the years.

The flavour obviously, is the strong smell that attracts the carp to the bait. Back then, I thought that the individual flavour one used - cream, caramel, Scopex, chocolate malt or whatever, was very, very crucial. I don't believe that to be the case today.

The baits were dyed red, and red dominated the colour of my baits for over ten years. I remember thinking when I made up my first modern fishmeal bait how I was going to make it red! I'd caught so many carp on red baits that I simply couldn't bear to use any other colour. I don't think colour matters a great deal in real terms, although my good friend, Frank Warwick, swears that white baits do give a technical edge, particularly at night. I think the key thing here is the angler's confidence. If I ever cast out a red bait I was very confident of catching, any other colour and my head was in bits. My boilies too, have always been absolutely identical in appearance, weight, size and shape. There are better technical arguments for this feature of my bait-making than using red dye. Identical baits allow for pin-point accuracy when baiting up by catapult or throwing stick and I am very accurate with both because I've spent hundreds of hours practising. They fall through the water at the same pace and in the same direction. They behave identically on the bottom when tested by fish. These are technical aspects but primarily I am more confident in using perfectly round identical boilies than knobbly scrag ends. Confidence is a vital ingredient in carp fishing and if you are not confident in using a particular thing you are half-beaten already.

That first day certainly boosted my confidence and I fished the lake several times more that winter catching every time. In fact, it was a little embarrassing, especially when a few of the regulars were really struggling to catch on the standard bolt rig. One by one, I told them about the hair rig and showed it to them. The twenty pound common eluded me that winter, although I caught a personal best common of 18lb 12oz and a number of doubles to 16lb. I learned a good deal about the carp in that first winter.

It seemed when the water temperature was very cold the carp could be located in certain areas in numbers. There were always fish in the vicinity of the Spring Swim. Here, an underground spring would send up three streams of little bubbles all the time - in fact, when the lake was frozen this was the last place to freeze due to the slight turbulence in the water. Often, a two inch hole would remain and I used to have great fun trying to fire boilies into it!

I'd fished a spring-fed water called Whitley Pool in the late 1970's and it was amazing how many carp you could pick up by casting directly onto one of the bubbling springs. I think all fish, including carp, are attracted by turbulence in stillwater, and the natural springs in front of the Spring Swim at Halsnead were very productive. The water depth in this area was around 5' which was the average for this end of the lake, the one difference being the noticeable attraction of the steady stream of bubbles. This is what attracted the carp.

Another spot where fish would always be present was around a sub-surface snag about twenty yards past the Spring Swim and just to the right of it. What the snag was I never discovered, but if you cast at it ten times you'd get snagged once, and you would have to pull for a break, although usually hooked carp were not lost on it. The fish were stacked up around this.

After the initial session, I started to concentrate on a swim known as No.25, which you can identify on the map. Fishing this swim enabled one to fish the Spring Swim, the aforementioned snag which lay in front of No.25 and it had an occasional spring with a nearby snag close in to the left. One could also cover the Channel entrance, the area in front of the Spotting Tree, and the Island too. A south westerley wind pushed past it into the Spotting Tree. This became the swim which I was associated with, as it offered so many opportunities winter and summer.

These two areas were definitely the spots to fish in winter. It was as if the carp liked the reassurance of the snag and the incoming water and air from the springs. Areas of difference are potential winter hotspots. I've found this maxim very important in the winter carp fishing I've done.

Another thing that is interesting, is that during my concentration on Peg 25, I was accused by the regulars, following some real bagging-up trips, of unfairly casting 80 yards to the Spring Swim and thereby encroaching into another swim. I put it at 50 yards, tops, a contention which was greeted then with derision. I never fished that far across if someone was fishing there unless they were maggot-bashing in the margins. Anglers who have fished just one or two waters get things wrong because their perspectives are based on those limited waters alone. Those critics today would probably agree that the distance I fished at was closer to 50 yards than 80 yards.

The classic example is Redmire. If you read Dick Walker's account of the record fish capture you will see that he claims the distance between the Willow Pitch and the far bank to be around 100 yards, and from the Willow Pitch to the Dam forty yards. When I first fished Redmire I was shocked. The far bank from the Willow Pitch was a gentle lob of perhaps half of Dick's estimate and the Dam wall was much closer than I had been led to believe - with modern carp gear it would be fairly comfortable to fish in the margin next to the famous Climbing Tree from the Dam wall at Redmire!

Come late February/March when water temperatures rose, the Halsnead fish could be caught from virtually anywhere, including the usual cold water spots, but the fish seemed to suddenly be all over the little lake with previously quiet areas such as the Grass Bank producing. This was the winter pattern that first year and it remained so for the next ten years and I suspect, it is still true today. Carp are, above all, creatures of habit and once you understand their behaviour in any lake you can predict with great accuracy where the fish will be under both short term and seasonal weather conditions. The one factor that can change this is extreme angling pressure. Fortunately, the Halsnead carp have never been greatly subjected to this.

I really wanted one of those Halsnead twenty pound commons and at the end of that otherwise successful first winter, I decided to really go for it the following summer until I caught one.

. . . .

I thought a great deal about how I was going to approach the water the following season, and spent a fair bit of time visting the water and observing the fish. Individual fish became quite familiar as a result of my time observing them. As is usual in carp lakes in any close season they were off guard and were more ready to show themselves. There seemed to be three commons around the twenty pound mark and a lot of commons in the 15lb plus bracket. These were good fish for the North West back then. The mirrors were more disappointing; there were a lot of them but the biggest fish seemed to be around 15lb. There was one particular fish that stood out. This was a very long, genuine leather carp that was well known to the regulars, the biggest non-common in the lake at around 17lb and was known to be one of the original fish stocked in the 1950's. It was a highly prized fish for it was known to be difficult to catch. This became one of my target fish. Regulars told me that as far as they were aware the originals were stocked by Leney, but also fish

had been introduced from that source of so many of the fish pictured in this book - The Isle in Shropshire. Wherever they came from, there were certainly a lot of carp in Halsnead at this time - I would estimate probably 200 fish with perhaps 80 doubles - not bad for a two acre lake!

In terms of my approach, I

The old and wise Clever Leather. I only outsmarted him once.

had some serious thinking to do. The hair rig was now out and so my advantage rig-wise was gone. In this situation, I felt that I had to look at my bait more carefully and put together a bait far superior than those already in use. I decided to opt for a Fred Wilton derived milk protein bait. I needed a source of good quality casein as the main ingredient. I spoke at length on the telephone to Rod Hutchinson who was then building up Catchum and he sorted some out for me which Ritchie McDonald kindly dropped off. This was an acid casein precipitated by hydrochloric acid and it had a good track record. The other ingredients I sorted out via various chemists and health food shops.

The base mix was:

4oz Casein

2oz Casilan (Calcium Caseinate)

1oz Soya Flour

1oz Wheatgerm

2oz Complan

plus

5ml Geoff Kemp's Green Zing

1ml Rod Hutchinson Intense Sweetener

This wasn't the easiest mix to roll but it was a mix I was confident would achieve what I wanted it to. I'd used so-called HP baits on and off but not really applied them properly and I'd still used other sorts of baits like fishmeals, catfood based baits, carbohydrates and even a spell on amino acid baits developed by Duncan Kay. So many people had emptied lakes on milk proteins and I thought that Halsnead was the ideal opportunity to apply them properly and to see just how effective they could be, as most of the other anglers on the lake would be on nutritionally poorer baits. Pete Barker and Pete Dumbill were noted milk protein buffs but I felt sure that the sheer amount of time and therefore bait I would be putting in would give me the edge. I included Complan in the bait as a vitamin/mineral source. A lot of people used Equivite - a vitamin supplement for horses - but I never liked it as an ingredient. One or two people like Rod had put out some proprietary vitamin complexes but I wasn't keen on these either. With Complan I got a good spread of vitamins and minerals and another source of nutritional food and I knew because it was for human consumption that it would be fresh and not degraded. This was a very expensive bait and I was not particularly well-off in those days being only in temporary, part-time employment and had to make considerable sacrifices in order to afford it.

I wanted to incorporate a smell that I knew would be unique and had never been used before on the lake. King of the carp flavours scene was then Geoff Kemp and he suggested a flavour he'd had great success with that was just about to become huge. This was the now well known Green Zing flavour. Rod had also suggested I incorporate a new type of sweetener he was launching. This was the Intense Sweetener which was to become so widely used later. When I first made up the baits incorporating these ingredients it was obvious that here was something special. They were good enough to eat - true carp sweets.

One other bait aspect had to be considered and that was what bait to use as a floating bait. I wanted to use the same smell and base mix on the surface to reinforce - in theory - the effectiveness of the bait. I decided to make a floating cake by using the same ingredients in the same quantity but by adding a teaspoon of baking powder and twice the amount of eggs. This was baked in the oven until a nice light brown crust was formed. Again, the smell of this was gorgeous. This would be fished on the rig below.

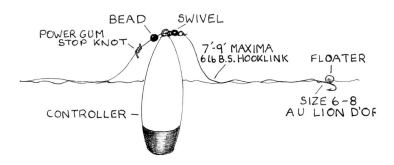

I started pre-baiting in May, introducing a mix three times a week for four weeks and then in the final fortnight of the close season a mix five times a week. It was noticeable that a few others were pre-baiting the lake too - and this was significant in terms of my results too, although I didn't discover why till the following close season. More of this later.

Come opening night - the only night I fished that season - it was obvious that one or two members had overdone the pre-baiting bit. There were hundreds of boilies of all sorts of sizes and colours popping up in the margins!

Opening night, I squeezed in next to Pete Barker on what was a very crowded lake. I tried to ignore the army of rats scurrying all around me. In fact, this was the only all-night session I fished on the lake that season as it was the only occasion I could guarantee company on the water to protect me from the nocturnal antics of the local scallies. Having said that, I still had two drunken and/or drug-crazed skinny dippers, one male, one female, - both unashamedly naked - swim through my lines at 2 o'clock in the morning! Despite the attentions of the bathers, I still sneaked out a couple of doubles, whilst Pete, close by, blanked. He was up to something though, and he was messing about with his rig seconds before casting out, which he did frequently. I spent most of the night trying to work out what he was doing. As it became light, I noticed he had placed a split shot on his nylon hooklink about two inches below his bomb. I thought I'd just ask him straight what it was for. "Oh, that," replied a nervous-looking Pete, " I keep getting tangles, so I've put a shot there to see if it will stop them." I didn't believe a word of it not only because you had to treat everything that Pete ever said with a pinch of salt but he was also a crafty, devious, edge-seeking beggar. If it was to stop tangles, why was he fiddling about with it just prior to casting? Pete was very well-connected in the carp fishing world and he had quite a few friends in the south east of the country which was the hot-bed of carp inventions. Del Romang, in particular, was a good friend of Pete's, and kept him informed of the very latest developments. I suspected that Pete was definitely trying something out that he had been told about, but for the life of me I couldn't work it out. Still, I'd caught and he hadn't, so whatever it was it hadn't worked yet. I decided there and then though, to keep a beady eye on Mr Peter Barker!

What followed for the next two and a half months was the most disciplined and rigorous fishing campaign I have ever undertaken. Funnily enough, it nearly didn't happen, for in June I received a membership card for Wheelock Angling Society who controlled arguably, the best water in the North West at that time - Crab Mill Flash. I nearly tore up my plans to concentrate on Halsnead in the summer due to the temptation of getting amongst those big Crab fish, but, after a great deal of thought, decided to stick with the decision to catch at least one of those twenty pound Halsnead commons. Then I would fish the notoriously difficult Crab Mill.

Halsnead was the target and I attacked it big style. For half of June and all of July and August and early September, I fished Halsnead Park every day from dawn until after dusk except for every other Saturday when a club match prevented fishing. Looking back, this was an obsessive and silly way of fishing and potentially damaging in terms of trying to hold down some vital aspects of everyday living - such as maintaining a good relationship with a partner, eating a reasonable diet and preserving some degree of sanity. I was in the grip of carp fever, which grips me still from time to time, but which I have learned to live with and have learned to balance with the other good things in life. But at that moment, I nearly fell prey to that fever which I have seen completely take over some people's lives. Many friends of mine have been gripped by the fever that disregards everything else in life for the pursuit of carp. Some, like me, have learned to control it, and fish on even today, others have given up carp fishing completely. The fever burned them out.

The routine was up and out of the house at 3.30 am. Wendy would drive me to the lake, to arrive about 4am. Then on to her grandmother's five miles away and then on to work at 9am. I fished hard until around 10pm. Wendy picked me up from her grandmother's and drove home to arrive 10.30pm. Eat dinner collected en-route. 11pm or so, I rolled and boiled two mixes of bait, and made up half a dozen rigs. Bed around 12.30am. Up at 3.30am, hurried wash and dress and Wendy drove to the lake.

This was the routine for 6/7 days a week for me for three months, with Wendy getting a little respite at weekends when she didn't have to work. A woman that demonstrates her love like this, at this period of carp obsession, deserves marrying!

It wasn't surprising, given this amount of application, that I took Halsnead apart. I concentrated my efforts on Peg 25 which, as I said earlier, gave me so many fishing options. My tackle consisted of the old North Western glass fibre SS5 rods and Cardinal 55 reels - state of the art then - and with them there was no area of that particular end of the lake I could not command. Usually, when I arrived at dawn there would be no one but the visiting heron fishing the lake. Only one rod was the club rule of course, but if I was on the lake alone as was normal each day, it was too much of a temptation not to put out a second rod until others started to arrive. Thereafter, the second rod would be hidden on the ground or under a holdall, unless someone got close and could suss-out that I was using two. In those circumstances, I became expert at having a cast-out rod broken down which I would then re-assemble and play the hooked fish on. It was all very silly but caused by the club's own stupid attempt to put carp anglers off. Everyone was pulling strokes because of the silly rule, including many of the non-carp pleasure anglers. If it was obvious I was being watched, or a club stalwart was right on top of me, the "snide rod" was put away and the one

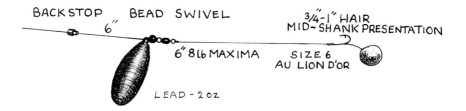

rod rule would be temporarily adhered to. Rig-wise by this time, I'd switched to the bolt rig form of the hair rig using bottom baits (see above) which was very deadly back then. Everything is shorter to the lead which had a back stop placed about 6 inches behind it which created a distinctive run. The rod would be pulled down with force, till the fish ran up against the stop, then an incredibly fast take would occur due to the sheer resistance the pricked carp had to contend with. To heighten the effect, I fished a very tight line, with the line clipped up on a rod clip in front of the Optonic although I did, for a time, adopt a method developed by Pete Barker for achieving the same effect. Pete started using metal ladies hair grips on a piece of cord which were clipped to the line in front of the buzzer.

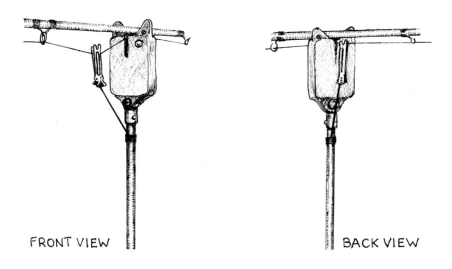

FRONT VIEW　　　　　　　　　　　BACK VIEW

We also played around with them on the other side of the buzzer. The other significant advance was the positioning of the hair which had been re-located from the bend of the hook to a mid-shank position to increase the anti-eject capability. I don't think this was necessary at all, as certainly, on Halsnead, the carp hadn't had the exposure to the original hair to warrant the change. However, they had begun to suss it out on the likes of Savay, Darenth and Longfield, and anglers on these waters were writing about the greater effectiveness the re-positioning provided. The lads on Halsnead and I were reading this and, of course, to keep ahead we all followed the advice - creating an eventual rod for our own backs again.

I kept a fairly detailed diary of captures initially, but to be honest, I was catching so many that each carp became represented by a number with the weight recorded if they looked to be above 14lb. I remember one club member telling me off for not weighing smaller fish and telling me that they didn't count unless I did so! On average, eight fish per day was a fairly typical catch, although there were obviously days when I caught less and also red-letter days when I caught more. What was interesting was the number of mirrors of 9lb or so in the lake - there seemed to be dozens of them in the lake and they looked to be every bit as old as the bigger mirrors. I came to look on these as pests, to be honest. Most of the commons were doubles and these soon started to mount up with the bigger ones starting to come out. Don't get the wrong impression here - the hair rig was at its peak on the water and coupled with a good bait and time and experience, it was very easy to catch fish. It didn't mean that I'd suddenly become the best carp angler in the known universe. Unfortunately, one or two I knew in the early 1980's began to think that they were the best carp anglers in the known universe due to the exaggerated results they had. When things started to slow down, they blew out, never to be seen again.

The twenty pounder came out fairly quickly, but ironically, fell to a piece of my floater cake one July morning. It wasn't a particulary good looking fish and went by the somewhat unkind handle of "Red Belly", due to a natural discolouration it always carried. Ambition achieved, I could then have moved onto Crab Mill but decided to stay put for there were fish I still wanted to catch. I dispensed with the floating cake fairly quickly after that, for although it caught me quite a few fish, I was catching more on good old Chum Mixer and there was so much Chum going into the lake that it was pointless going to the trouble of cooking a floater. The carp were really on the Chum on days when floaters were a good bet. It reminded me of that very truthful Wilton statement that carp will always take advantage of the best available food source. The carp were very easy to catch off the top but you tended to get a higher percentage of smaller fish - particularly those pesky 9lb mirrors - and before long I decided that I wasn't interested in fishing floaters even when the rest of the lads were using them. I was going to catch them purely on my boilies and from August on, I stuck to that. I caught a better average-sized fish because of it, and, because my baits were always going in, results got better and better.

I kept hearing of big fish from Crab Mill, but wouldn't be drawn for the moment. I was enjoying myself and I knew Crab was a much harder water. I was enjoying the satisfying feeling of leaving the water as darkness fell, tired and exhausted after a hard day's successful fish-catching and I knew that session fishing was necessary to succeed on Crab.

The signal to reel in the rods and go home was provided by my friend the heron who arrived as dusk began to fall each day. I used to look out for him. I've always been fascinated by herons. I remember when I first saw one as a young boy, I thought it must have escaped from a zoo for it seemed to be a very un-English, foreign-looking bird. They are wonderful creatures and many of the carp lakes I have fished have been graced by their presence.

There were actually two herons that visited Halsnead although one was in human form. The Heron was our nickname for that young, blonde haired lad I mentioned earlier. John Garrett was his real name and his behaviour was almost as fascinating to watch as the birds. John lived in a house a field away from the lake and a well-trodden path ran from his back garden to the lake. He wandered back and forth several times a day for years. John was basically paranoid about the lake and when he wasn't fishing, he used to worry from his bedroom window about what someone might be catching when he wasn't. He couldn't sleep or concentrate on anything and would have to leave the house and check out what was going on. He'd arrive shortly after dawn or on dark, hence the nickname, either to fish or to check out what was happening. John had two fishing modes: he'd fish every night or every day, depending on his whim, although he was virtually ever-present due to his paranoia. He would wander from angler to angler, and talk in a whispered tone which everyone used to hear as a ...sssssshhhppppppp... sound. He'd get what he could from one bloke, then move to the next, slagging off the previous fellow to the next! One of his favourite ploys was to sniff the landing net to detect whether you'd actually caught one or not!

There were quite a few characters on the lake, and Steve Knowles (whom I had met on the water and who had become a good friend) and I, used to amuse ourselves by coming up with nicknames for them all. One was the "Bubble Float Fella" a chap who seemed incapable of human communication and whose sole angling method was to fish a piece of Chum on an old fashioned bubble float, summer and winter! I never saw him catch a fish, which was probably because he never put out any free offerings! Just a bubble float and one piece of Chum which probably lasted him for months. Another chap who had a problem with technique was the "Butty Fella". He used a slice of Mothers Pride which he folded in half, pushed a huge hook through and cast out! After weeks of failure, and watching everyone pull fish out on boilies we had to re-christen him. He evolved into the "Green Boilie Fella". Out would come a huge, orange-sized, green boilie, which he presumably pushed the same big hook into and cast-out, freelined. For a couple of years he persisted with this method without success, then disappeared.

"The Nose" was a favourite of ours. This was an oldish chap with an absolutely huge and swollen nasal appendage. It totally dominated his entire face and he looked like that human character with the snozzle in the Pink Panther cartoons. The Nose was a very poor carp angler but quite personable. One morning, he was telling me about his pride and joy, a newly acquired appalling-looking buzzer. Half an hour later, there was a short buzz, followed by The Nose's only carp rod being dragged into the lake on

a run - his first and last ever. As the rod flew off into the centre of the lake, the pride and joy plopped off the rest into the margins, never to be seen again. I reeled in The Nose's rod half an hour later, and there was an eleven pound common on the end. He wanted a photograph of his carp despite the fact that I'd caught it on my rod. I had to take the photograph of The Nose with his common in the car park to get everything into the frame. Sadly, The Nose stopped coming and we heard that he had passed away. I still wonder today how they got the coffin lid down!

Another old boy was christened "Sweetcorn Joe". Now Joe, if that actually was his name, was a contemporary of BB's and would not in any way compromise traditional methods and float fished in the island margins with his cane rod, centre pin reel and catgut. Sweetcorn's status became legendary on the lake when he landed his one and only carp. This turned out to be a completely unknown and lake record common of 23lb which he beached in the channel. He'd forgotten his gaff. Unfortunately or fortunately for Joe, according to your point of view, his success didn't go down too well with the rest of the lads, and he sits there to this day, I'm told, unhelped and unchanged and is still referred to as 'that old lying so and so with the dodgy scales'.

Slightly more successful than the others I've mentioned was "The Gaffer". The Gaffer looked like Bill Maynard and even drove an old Rover like the character in the television series. He was very short-sighted and had to be helped tying his hooks on, otherwise the fish just dropped off with a hook in its chops, as did boilies unless you helped him with his hair stop. Despite his poor eyesight, he was always seeing thirty pounders swirling around on the top. He was quite a lucky angler, The Gaffer. At a club meeting, he took me to one side and said, "You've had incredible success on the water. Give me a bait, Paul, so I can too." Willing to oblige, but enjoying a wind-up, I wrote a bait recipe down on a piece of paper. It had 17 different ingredients in it. It would have required the chemical and stimulatory resources of the four continents of the world to put together. He bagged-up on it! The Gaffer evolved into the "Iron Lung" when, sadly, he developed severe chest and breathing problems. He had to be helped with his tackle and carried round a portable breathing machine with him. After the minor rigour of casting he had to don a facemask, start up his battery-powered machine that used to hiss, gurgle and spit, and breathe oxygen into his strained lungs. Job done, he'd have a fag! If he ever caught a fish the scene was nightmarish and a couple of times the kiss of life had to be administered. "Don't tell the missus," the Gaffer used to plead, amidst the coughs as he choked through his next fag. In keeping with modern times, The Gaffer gradually became re-christened "Darth Vader."

In September, I finally went to Crab and in my absence an incident on the lake akin in significance to the gunfight at the OK Corral took place. The previously silent Bubble Float Fella was caught hiding in the bushes on the island spying on Robbie and Bobbie, fishing opposite. When questioned, from afar, about what he was up to, Bubble Float shouted that he'd seen them fishing two rods, and he was going to report them to the Committee. He sped off on his bicycle, still clutching rod, reel and bubble float, with the rotund Bob in vain pursuit.

Loud rumblings in the committee rooms. All the carp anglers were told to attend an extraordinary meeting. Rumours of bannings and expulsions spread like wildfire. We were ushered sheepishly into the meeting room. There sat the entire Committee before us, stoney-faced. Even the aged President had been sobered up to attend and oversee the massacre. In came the previously uncommunicative Bubble Float Fella to give evidence. Since opening day, he announced, he had been keeping a dossier on the carp anglers. He had a list of people who had been using two rods. I asked if there were any witnesses or corroborative evidence to support the member's charges and if not, it was a case of one word against another and therefore couldn't be proven. The Chairman, always a democrat, told me to sit down and shut up. The names were read out. I came out of the bag first, then Steve, then Garrett. The next name took us all by surprise - Rod Hutchinson! "He's not a member!" I announced. Before the Chairman had the chance to tell me to sit down, Bubble Float said, "And Rod Hutchinson's dad, the old bastard." We looked at each other and it clicked, Bubble Float meant Robbie Hudson not Rod Hutchinson, whereupon Robbie Hudson's dad leapt to his feet to protest at being called an old bastard. He was told to sit down too. The next name was Pete Barker, which was greeted with numerous murmurs by the Committee who had had the pleasure of dealing with Pete before, courtesy of information supplied by Fat Ronnie Pendleton. Next name was: "The Milky Bar Kid over there," said Bubble Float, pointing to an unfortunate-looking youth in the corner, who then leapt to his feet and made for Bubble Float to stick one on him. We managed to restrain him, but it merely served to make Bubble Float read out the subsequent names with even more relish. Several more names were announced. The final name was Alan Woodall, who protested that he could not possibly have used two rods because he only owned one. At which point, the President reported that we were up to all the tricks and he'd seen people lend Woodall an extra rod so he, too, could break the rules. We found this quite surprising as the President hadn't been seen at the lake for years, presumably because there were no licensed premises to hand.

I asked where all this was leading. The Chairman informed the meeting that it had been decided not to ban us but to impose a strict one rod limit for the duration of the season, including the winter, and any member caught or reported to be using two would be expelled for life. I proposed moving it to the vote - after all, there were more of us in the room than them. The Chairman reported that according to the rules of the club this was not necessary as the Committee was empowered to deal with matters as they felt fit. I asked what rule he was quoting from, as I wasn't aware that a major rule change could be introduced without a majority vote at a special meeting or an AGM. The Chairman, told me that I'd said enough, he was fed-up with me and I was to sit down. Always the great democrat.

. . . .

I fished the lake for the whole of that winter with one rod. I continued to catch consistently despite the handicap because I focused everything on that rod and endeavoured to maximise efficiency. I learned a great deal that winter because I was forced to.

I had several technical advantages at my disposal I hadn't had the previous winter. Firstly, I had an established strong bait. I'd met a chap on a visit to Roman Lakes called Jeff Denny, and I'd seen him use PVA stringers - but they didn't have a name then. Jeff was the first person I ever saw using PVA. I'd got hold of some PVA tape which I adapted to present boilies on. I thought the new presentation on offer would be very effective and it proved to be the case. I couldn't use it though, if anyone was fishing close by, in case I lost the edge. It had also come out what Pete Barker had been up to. He was inserting polystyrene into his baits to make them pop-up - another southern tip-off. The fiddling about with the split shot just prior to casting was Pete pulling the shot down to the desired distance from the boilie. On reeling in, he'd pull the shot back up the hooklink to lie just below the bomb. I'd begun to suss it out on one particular day when I netted a fish for him and saw the split shot in its proper position. Pete's explanation of, "It's to frighten the fish when it bites on it," wasn't very plausible! I think in the end, Robbie found a hookbait in the water with the polystyrene inside it or possibly Bob pinched one of his baits, which by bitter experience, I knew he was prone to do. The pop-up presentation gave the hair rigged bait a new lease of life and it was to dominate my fishing on silt lakes for the next five years or so. Certainly, that winter, in a water where the detritus could affect hookbait efficiency at that time of the year, a pop-up was a deadly eye-opener.

Equally important, was the fishing approach. Throughout that winter, there wasn't an occasion when a bait wasn't in the water, even after I caught a fish. Unhooking, weighing and photographing a fish can take several minutes and when I only had one rod at my disposal I couldn't waste that time. There was no rule about not taking more than one rod to the water, so as I landed a fish it was retained safely in the landing net and an already baited hook was re-cast into position immediately. Then the formalities were dealt with. This is still part of my fishing today, when I think there is a need for it to be. Take Birch Grove for example. For the last few winters the carp have fed in very short spells, between long spells of inactivity. Perhaps an hour every day or every few days, even. It is very common to get two takes at the same time or close together and I've once had three takes on each rod in as little as 15 minutes. A spare baited rod and an extra landing net is part of my kit. At least one bait is always in the water no matter what happens.

I was always looking to be on the fish too. If I was in my usual pitch, I could normally rely on finding the fish in the already established cold water spots. But during a mild spell and at the start and end of the winter season, carp could be quite active and caught from a number of different spots. If you can fish two rods, of course you can put one on the normally safe bet spot in these situations and the other can be roving to pick out fish elsewhere. This wasn't possible. Sometimes also, I couldn't fish my normal pitch and fished an unfamiliar winter swim. Fortunately, when the fish were active in Halsnead they very often gave line bites. By dispensing with the clips and the cheese-wire lines, if the normal spots seemed a little slow, or I didn't know the swim too well, I resorted to what I call "fishing for liners". With the rod kept low I would fish far across and look out for liners. If I had a liner and no take seemed likely, I'd pick the lead up, pull it in a couple of yards, and await events. If the liners continued with no takes looking likely, I would repeat the process, then repeat again and so on. Once the liners stopped, I knew I was there or thereabouts. Incidentally, don't cast and re-cast the lead when doing this, as you are more likely to spook the fish, although pulling the lead across doesn't seem to as much. The problem with this method nowadays, is that on many lakes, fish no longer give you liners! However, if you are on a water where you still get them, try the method if you are struggling to find them.

By the end of the season, I'd caught every double figure carp in Halsnead, except one. Some I'd caught several times over. The one that eluded me was one of the small number of twenty pound commons and I went back from time to time to try and catch it over the next few years. Eventually, I did. I had a tremendous amount of fun, and caught a tremendous amount of carp - that season was the first one in which I caught over 100 doubles. I'd learned a great deal too. I learned that to be consistently successful you should aim to do things a little differently to everyone else. I learned how to maximise fishing time and to be very disciplined to succeed.

I'd learned too, that if you correctly applied a good food bait it would outfish anything else. For me, it demonstrated clearly the validity of Fred Wilton's HNV theory.

. . . .

A twist in the tail here. I was at a close season meeting of the recently formed Carp Society, headed very ably locally by Pete Barker. Geoff Kemp was one of the speakers and he highlighted the effectiveness of the new Green Zing flavour, sweetened in a milk protein. After the talk, two other Halsnead regulars were discussing this with Robbie and I. One said, "What he said about that bait was rubbish. We spent a fortune on it, put it all in Halsnead and completely blanked the first week. After that, we stopped using it."

Robbie, who by then, knew what bait I had been using turned to me and winked. We both broke into hysterical laughter!

Crab Mill Flash

Though I occasionally drop off for a moment or two at some time during the night, I find I sleep like a wild animal with one-half of my brain alert, a primitive sort of slumber and maybe not the most restful.
Towards dawn, when even the fish seem to cease from jumping, I am fully awake again. And the vapours drifting above the pool are very ghostly, assuming sometimes the shapes of ships and galleons, or strange outlandish giants which glide unaccountably across the far end of the water.
B.B. Dark Estuary 1953

When I think back to my time at Crab Mill, I remember sultry summer days and cold, mist-shrouded nights and dawns. I also have fond memories of the wonderful looking mirror carp which lived in that water and which fought like scaley-sided tigers.

Crab Mill was a deep, watery crease in the Cheshire countryside and at night and well into day, the mist was often so thick and clinging that it was impossible to distinguish water from land. Playing a carp in such conditions was a heart-pulsing and eerie experience, for although dawn may have brought light to the rest of the world, Crab Mill would still be invisible in its cloak of grey. You fought the ferocious tiger on the end of the line completely blind.

A long, watery crease in the land describes Crab Mill very well. It wasn't the classic carp pool. It looked more like a canal than a lake. Yet it had a strange beauty all of its own.

South Cheshire has been subject to many centuries of mine workings for rock salt - the ancient subterranean reminder that Cheshire was once covered by sea. Many of these old workings have collapsed, causing surface subsidence and waters in the area known as "flashes" of which Crab Mill is one of the most famous. The subsidence in the area meant that the lake was likely to vary slightly both in depth and width from season to season, and occasional pot-holes would appear on the bankside which were a potential hazard for the unsuspecting angler.

The water had always been popular in the North West but had also gained national recognition as a big fish venue in the 1970's due to the publicised catches of one Kevin Clifford, crowned by the then angling press as "The Carp King of the North", for his remarkable multiple catches on sweetcorn. To this day, there is still a pitch on the lake known as Clifford's. Kevin took the knowledge he had acquired at Crab onto Redmire Pool with him where his results were legendary. I first heard about the water when I read a chapter by Kevin in Frank Guttfield's book "The Big Fish Scene" where it was described as Bamcrill Flash, but didn't realise where it was and what it contained until a leading local light at the time, Kevin Dunne put me onto it. Kevin was the very enthusiastic organiser of the Carp Anglers' Association and he gave me the address to write off to in order to be placed on the waiting list. Fortuitously, my membership came through fairly quickly as the club had to expand its membership to acquire more waters.

Compared to Halsnead, Crab was a much more significant water. Not only because it contained a very good head of fish for those days - probably 15-20 twenties and a lot of doubles which averaged 18lb or so - but also because it had a lot of very experienced and successful anglers fishing it. It had the reputation of being a difficult water and also one on which a lot of new fishing methods and techniques had been and were being developed. Crab was a carp fishing cauldron of invention in those days.

One of the major advances which had been developed on Crab and spread out from there, was what I call the Cheshire method. Ironically, this approach had been pioneered by a Welshman on the water, Paul Roberts, and his small circle of friends. This involved the use of tiny mass baits - initially hemp - to create a feeding area, with another bait such as a peanut or boilie fished over it. Rod Hutchinson had been the first angler to develop the use of hemp as a bait successfully, but as far as I am aware Rod also used hemp as the hookbait. Paul took this one step further and employed a different bait over it, initially using casters as the hookbait - an established match fishing technique - but used for the first time in carp fishing. Paul used the hemp in small tightly baited beds and Crab lent itself very well to the technique, as it was primarily a margin-fishing water and the tiny baits could be easily catapulted out to the marginal shelf where the carp patrolled. It was quite amazing how close into the shallow margin the Crab fish would come and more often than not the bait had to be placed no more than 2-6 feet from the bank. Although once a weedy water, it had been bone-mealed by the club to cloud up the water to prevent the establishment of the weed. This policy had led to a weed-free main body of water but weed and scum could be found along the margins - this is what attracted the fish.

The aim of the method was to stimulate preoccupied feeding from carp whose natural food consisted of small items like bloodworm and snails, by presenting to them in abundance a tiny new food source which was easy to feed on and provided a very strong source of attraction, namely hemp oil. Hemp seems to be able to produce sustained interest from carp once they are really on it and they will stay in the swim until every last grain is eaten. It therefore follows that a steady application of the bait enables the angler to build up the swim and hold up carp moving into it for several days.

Others on the water had soon adopted the technique and, as always happens in carp fishing, experimented with different types of baits. One angler in particular, had been very impressed with the results of Paul and his friends and developed a similar approach with maggots. This was the very young Bernard Loftus an apprentice in those days of Peter Barker's. Bernard baited up with dead and decaying maggots, ponced off a local tackle dealer and he crammed as many live and better quality maggots as he could on a largish hook. Bernard too, was to have even greater success using this method, but his best results came when he suddenly had a lot of time on his hands and got an early tip-off about the hair and then pop-ups via Pete. Bernard was full-time on the water and, with the advantage of a full season on the hair and pop-ups when everyone else was still side-hooking, he did remarkably well including smashing the Cheshire record with a spawnbound fish of over 33lb from Crab. His success, like any success always does, attracted a bit of trouble for him from the bemused locals.

. . . .

When I arrived on the water it was the September of the Halsnead season. Bernard was still full-time on the water and still catching, but it was obvious that everyone was now on the hair and some on popped-up particles or boilies. The boilie/particle over hemp was still the main approach although others were using tares. Peanuts too, were much in evidence, and taking fish. Due to Bernard's general poverty, peanuts were more often than not his bait, although by the end of his long thirteen day sessions he ended up living on these himself and any bits of food he could scrounge off others, until he collected his giro. I was to often feed him over

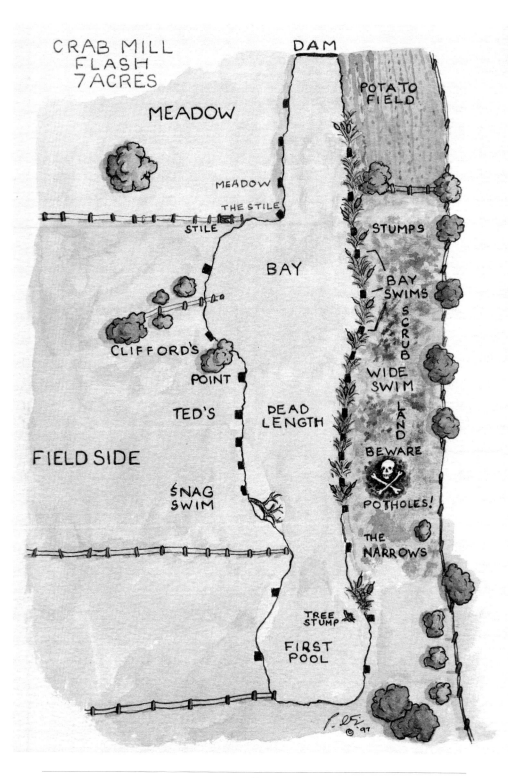

the next few years!

An interesting development had occurred just before my entry onto the Crab Mill stage. That particular summer had been very hot and the Crab carp were very much in evidence, cruising around on the surface when Robbie and Bobbie turned up for their very first session. With so much activity on the surface, they instinctively set up floater rods and started feeding Chum Mixers. They set up anchored mixer rigs, which because of the deep water required long tails. In fact, they were so long that they had to stand on their bedchairs to gain sufficient clearance to cast them out! No doubt amused at this performance, Bernard wandered around to see what they were up to. On seeing what they were doing, Bernard told them that they were completely wasting their time as they "don't take floaters on here." As he began to walk away, shaking his head, Robbie's clutch screamed out and his first Crab fish of 17lb was duly netted. Suffice to say, Bernard ran back to his swim to set-up a floater rod and was soon begging for some Chum Mixer! From that point on, Crab became a water where it was quite possible to catch carp on the surface.

This is an important lesson and I've experienced things like this myself many times. Anglers who spend a lot of time on one water become stereotyped. Waters where anglers pretty much do what the rest do, can be exploited by the angler who doesn't listen to what is supposed to or not supposed to work, and just gets on with the job and fishes the water as it appears it should be fished on the basis of experience. On every water there is what I call "conventional wisdom". When I go onto any water, I listen to this but generally have done what I thought needed to be done. This has often led to exceptional success. Conversely, when I have taken conventional wisdom on board and fished the water how I was told it should be fished according to it, I have struggled or not achieved anything more than the average. When I have worked things out for myself and done my own thing, I have always had success above the average.

The Selman luck ran true to form on Crab and I caught from the off and good fish too. First trip produced fish of 15, 17, 14, 18 and 21 pounds, and on my second trip I caught fish of 13, 18 and the biggest in the lake at that time - 'Arfur - (so-called because he had only half a tail, which was over the next few years to grow back) at 25lb 2oz. This was a very big fish for Cheshire at this point in time, as there were only a handful of fish over 24lb in the whole county. These immediate results were not all that spectacular though. The hair rig was at the height of its effectiveness and one became very blasé

Crab Mill Flash - a watery crease in the Cheshire landscape.

about just how easy it had become to catch carp. It was possible to catch as many carp in a couple of days as it was possible to catch in a season in the 1970's. I went in on a good bait too - the Halsnead Green Zing bait - and fished the boilie over hemp method which was still deadly. It was the rig, though, that was the key.

Initially, I fished running leads with the line tight and clipped up solid in rod clips, which was the most common method at the time. The rod clip achieved the same effect as a fixed lead. However, on getting a run this caused problems. The silt at Crab was thicker than any other water I'd previously fished and I soon found on getting a run that the lead - only 1.75 ounces - would stay fixed in the silt with the carp taking line through the lead swivel. This meant the carp had to be played back to the lead, the weight of the fish would then release the lead from the silt and the carp could be played normally. A couple of fish were lost as they were pulled back to the lead, presumably because there was too little pressure being applied which allowed the hook to pop out. To prevent this, the lead was fixed by means of a back-stop and this stopped the problem. The takes were incredibly fast, particularly as the line was still fished very tight in clips. The Crab fish in my first season were still not line-shy and didn't spook on tight lines and line bites were still common.

Crab was the first water I'd fished where the significance of bloodworm really occurred to me. It was the first water on which I was able to observe at close range bloodworm beds which were very visible in the clear margins. It was quite fascinating watching the bloodworm. They resembled bluish-red blisters on the bottom and the masses of tiny worms would stick out part of their bodies and perceptively sway - just like coral. This movement must attract cyprinids. If you lightly touched the bed, all of the worms would instantaneously shoot back into their holes as a defence mechanism and then re-appear a few seconds later. Their retreat wouldn't pose a problem to a hungry carp. Many used to remark about the mass of bloodworm in Crab and ponder why a carp would ever need to pick up a bait given the availability of so much easy natural food to browse upon. The answer is instinctive greed and nutrititional recognition. Bloodworms consist mainly of water and protein but a carp would have to consume a large amount of bloodworms to provide the same food value as just a couple of boilies.

Superb scattered scaled fish of 22lb.

The behaviour of the Crab Mill carp was interesting and pretty consistent for the three seasons I was to fish it. It was never really predominantly a night water - one caught one or two in the night but primarily it was a day water. This was interesting because it was quite a pressured water and one would have thought that the carp would feed in the night when it was quieter. From dawn to early morning was favourite, but one had a chance at any time of the day. The fish tended to move on a fresh wind and it was often worth moving onto fish. However, I found that in a 24 hour period fish would always visit particular swims at different times and in swims like The Point, The Stumps, The Stile, Clifford's (which Kevin Clifford told me he'd never fished!), The Snag Swim and The Wide Swim, one was never too far away from fish. Staying put or moving on, was an issue on Crab just like it is on other waters. I decided to generally stay put and choose a swim I knew would give me the opportunity to be on fish for a significant period of the time in the two nights and three days I usually had at my disposal. If there were few signs of fish when I set-up in the swim, this didn't worry me for I knew some of the fish would visit it each day. Funnily enough, some of my best multiple catches came when no fish were showing in the swim. The carp generally showed in the Main Bay - the widest stretch of lake - they would roll, head and shoulder and crash continuously. This used to attract anglers into the bay but very rarely would they catch on bottom baits although they could be taken on floaters although few anglers had the courage to use them. Those who fished the Main Bay with bottom baits generally struggled to catch anything. These very active carp were not feeding fish and those that were caught from the Main Bay weren't those showing at the surface. I found the most successful tactic was to ignore the Main Bay itself and fish the entrances to it - the swims known as The Stile, Wide Swim, The Point and The Stumps - where one could intercept fish leaving or entering the Main Bay. A few times I caught fish I'd seen leaping in the Main Bay a day or so earlier as they presumably left it to feed. On any lake, it is important to find out if areas where the carp show, roll, head and shoulder or leap are feeding areas or not. Contrary to the advice often given in "how to do it" books by other writers I have often found that they are not.

The only swim in the Main Bay I had any sort of success from was the swim known as Clifford's and the success came from quite close in next to underwater snags. There were all sorts of hazardous snags lying in front of this swim and wherever there are snags there are carp. Underwater features are a safe bet on any silt lake and should be sought out and exploited. My favourite snaggy area at Crab Mill though, lay at the end of the Dead Length and I had some big multiple catches from here. In this particular swim a long dead tree had collapsed into the edge creating a natural feature which carp could always be found around. I started fishing this from the rush-lined side of the lake casting across to it, but the degree of success I was having led others to plonk themselves right on top of it, which forced me to fish it from the other side with the bivvy and rods well up the bank and the rig thrown out by hand all of a yard into the margin. I had some huge multiple catches from here - one memorable two-dayer led to 18 doubles to 23lb 6oz! It was a case of finding a feature in a pretty featureless environment to find carp.

....

Mass Baits

By the second season of my membership, I was concentrating all my summer and autumn fishing on Crab and fishing Halsnead in the winter, when no fishing was allowed beyond dusk on Crab. In the second summer for the first couple of months, things were still pretty easy and the boilie over hemp method was still taking fish early on, although it was proving less effective and others were starting to secretly use other types of mass baits.

When using hemp or any other mass bait on any water you need to consider a number of questions. In summary, these are:

What mass bait should I use?

Where should I put down the bed of mass bait?

What should the size and appearance of that bed be?

How much bait should be used and how often should the bed be topped up?

Should hookbait samples be added to the feeding area?

How can the bait be introduced?

I'll look at each issue in turn

What bait to use?

In terms of which bait to use you need to consider the degree of exposure the particular bait has had. The normal starting point on most waters is hemp. Hemp has a very long productive life but if saturation occurs as happened on Crab then it starts to lose its effectiveness. If everyone is piling it in you'll still catch the odd fish but you won't get the totally pre-occupied feeding situation which you can achieve in its early days of use or can still achieve if use is only occasional and not heavy. I think I was probably one of the first to use hemp at Shillamill Lakes (top lake) in Cornwall and I caned it. The following season I went down and couldn't achieve the same result on it again - others had been using it. On Crab, everyone was ladling it in and I eventually found because of this that using a small amount of hemp in comparison was more effective. Around 1985, I started drying out the hemp and fishing it with boilies with the complete rig in a PVA bag. I had managed to obtain some PVA sheets and these were scrunched up to form a bag. Old hat now, but then I didn't see anyone else doing it. I caught fish using hemp again but nothing like the amount of fish when they were really on it. Tares are a good follow-on to hemp - but are not as good, and I did quite well on them on Crab and elsewhere. They have a tendency to fill the carp up and therefore need to be used more sparingly. After the hemp started to slow on Crab, the next mass bait to take the water by storm was groats.The small yellowish oat groats had been stumbled upon by Jeff Denny who thought they might just achieve what the hemp had once done. When Jeff first used groats on Crab he was staggered by what happened. The fish were so preoccupied on the baits that his indicators were never still but unfortunately for Jeff, he experienced several bite-offs from the carp's throat teeth. He was using worms impaled on the bend of the hook over the top of the groats. He resorted to using an anti-bite off T-bar rig which sorted

JEFF DENNY'S ANTI BITE-OFF RIG

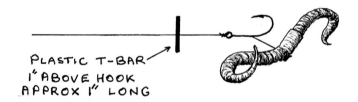

PLASTIC T-BAR
1" ABOVE HOOK
APPROX 1" LONG

the problem out and he started to land fish. The worms were soon got rid of as Jeff found that any bait worked fished over groats. Eventually, we all wised-up to what he was up to and switched over to the groats. Their success was phenomenal and it spread out from Crab. Groats are a very flexible and effective mass bait. They don't require cooking like other mass baits and can be prepared using lake water and allowed to soak for a few hours. They can be coloured by adding powdered or liquid edible dye to the water and they accept flavours readily by the same process. I soon grasped the potential of flavouring them by adding condensed milk straight from the can. The cloud and olfactory effect this created was incredibly attractive to the Crab carp. We were later to mix groats in with tiger nuts and this combination was deadly. The groats absorb the juices of the tigers readily to enhance their pulling power. The biggest advantage was that groats didn't seem to fill the fish up and when they were on them they had to work to pick out every grain - the preoccupation we'd seen with the hemp was achieved again.

Where any of these mass baits haven't been over-exploited they can be an absolutely killing method - as they were for me on my first forays down to the big bad southern waters as you will see. Over the years, I've tried all manner of mass baits and here's my list of them in the order in which they have been most effective.

Hemp
Oat Groats (with or without added tiger nuts)
Tares/Mini Maples
Mini Boilies
Maggots (scalded - not a pleasant process!)
Red Dari Seeds
Chopped peanuts
Chopped dried sweetcorn/maize

Where should the bed of bait be put down?

The mass bait feeding area should be created where you think carp will normally feed on a patrol route. That could be the nearside margin, a far margin or in the case of a gravel pit a known productive bar. The bed needs to be placed in natural feeding areas. On Crab, we were allowed to fish three rods and generally I fished the boilie over mass bait on two rods and a boilie or particle with free offerings of the same type on the third. One of the mass bait rods would be fished in the nearside margin, the other on the far margin unless there was someone fishing opposite or near, in which case the other would be fished in the nearside margin too but in the opposite direction to the other bait. The third rod - often the middle rod - would be fished in the centre of the lake. The margins and the centre seemed to be the most productive patrol routes.

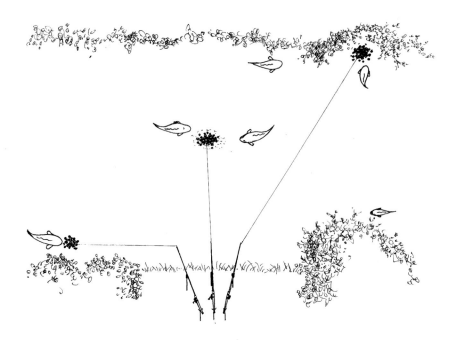

What should the size and appearance of the bed be?

I have always had most success with small tight beds of bait - by this I mean creating a feeding area of up to four square feet per hookbait. I've also tended to fish the hookbait in or around the centre of that area. I've rarely fished a line of bait such as which that can be created with a throwing stick with baits placed along it, because I couldn't see any advantage to the method on the lakes I've fished. The method lends itself to a situation where

LINE OF MASS BAIT

THIS SITUATION CAN BE
ACHIEVED WITH A
THROWING STICK

carp are moving past in a shoal at different distances from the bank. At Crab the fish tended to use the margins and the centre primarily. The angler must consider which sort of bed suits his water. As results on any mass bait begin to tail off, I have found very small beds of bait still work such as those that can be introduced by a PVA bag, which can re-vitalise the bait for a time as it presents a safe feeding area situation to a wary fish. Another way of re-vitalising the method is to embark on a heavy baiting programme all over the lake with the "blown" mass bait. The crucial thing here, though, is not to use it in a fishing situation to re-establish fish confidence in it. Unfortunately today, unless you have your own lake or are in a very small syndicate where the members co-operate, someone throwing in lots of mass baits or particles all over the place is a signal on the crowded waters for others to jump on the bandwagon and fish over the pre-baited mass bait which defeats the object of the exercise.

How much bait should be used and how often should it be topped up?

How much bait to use depends on a number of factors. Length of session is critical, as is the degree of exposure of a particular bait to a water and how strongly the fish are on it. If you only have a short session at your disposal such as an evening or a morning, it is simply counterproductive to put down a heavy feeding area. By the time the fish have cleared up the bait you may have left the water. A pound or so of bait, representing half a dozen pouches of bait initially per hookbait and then a pouch or two top-up between fish, I've found perfectly adequate for an evening session.

If the session is over a few days, then it is necessary to consider heavy baiting, bearing in mind that it can still take up to three days or longer for the mass bait feeding area to begin working, although results can also be immediate. It is critical to secure a swim that a number of fish could potentially feed in strongly over the course of a session. On Crab, when fishing my standard two night/three day session, I would bait up with about four pounds(dry weight) of hemp or two pounds (dry weight) of tares per night, and then top-up after a fish, or if I felt more should be out there in order to catch a fish. Four pounds of hemp per night or two pounds of tares (split 50/50 per hookbait) would be my average with a lot more in heavy feeding situations. You can only learn by trial and error, with the overall aim being to hold fish in the swim and achieve what we used to call the "cauldron effect" - when the water would be simply boiling with preoccupied carp. Nuisance fish are a problem on many waters but they haven't been for me where I have used this method. In circumstances where they are, it may be necessary to increase these quantities.

On many of the northern lakes that have seen the heavy use of mass bait feeding areas for over a decade, it is now very difficult on the pressured lakes to make the heavy baiting method work consistently, unless you can come up with a mass bait that hasn't been over-exploited or not used. In this situation, light baiting or using a small amount in a PVA bag with a few chopped and whole baits is likely to still produce fish. I've found a couple of situations where mass baits have been used but not really heavily - and by employing the old "fill it in" approach I've done well. One point to consider, is that many waters have seen very little bait other than boilies over the past few years and in that situation the mass bait approach could once again be highly effective. Most of the southern gravel pits haven't been exploited by mass baits and can be taken apart by them by someone having the courage to stick at it when surrounded by anglers solely using boilies.

I've always topped the feeding area up after a fish both at night and during the day. When the fish are feeding on mass baits, they seem to become oblivious to everything around them. A number of times when fishing with a large bait dropper, I've had a take within seconds of it hitting the water right above the feeding fish. Fish seem less prone to spooking when they are feeding on mass baits compared to any other type of bait.

Should hookbait samples be added to the feeding area?
With anything other than a very small feeding area, it pays to add some free baits to the bed of mass bait to get the carp searching for the other boilies amongst the seeds. Nowadays, I prefer to fish with just a single hookbait over a small or PVA bag presented bed when fishing short sessions, as I think this maximises the chances of the hookbait being picked up. I've tended always to fish a pop-up bait over mass baits, regardless of whether I've used a boilie or a particle such as a peanut. An illustration will explain why. One day, Peter Hanley came down to Crab and set-up just down from me. He proceeded to put out a large quantity of what looked to be peanuts dyed red. He cast out a rig baited with a single bait identical to the mass of free offerings. Within five minutes, he had a run and landed a good fish. A float angler fishing next to me remarked, "Did you see that? How did he catch a carp so quickly after putting all that bait out?" The answer was simply that he was using a pop-up that stood out significantly over the other baits - quite

possibly the first bait that carp had picked up. I've seen quite a few anglers do well on mass bait/boilie cocktails - mixing hemp, groats, tigers and boilies together. This seems to be quite a common method used by those I've seen using electric boats. Whilst I haven't used the cocktail approach myself, I've seen enough evidence to suggest it's worth trying should my preferred approach let me down. The variety of combinations is endless here, of course, so there is much room for experimentation.

How can the bait be introduced?

A catapult is the best way to introduce the bait and depending on the size of the mass bait used, between immediate margin and two rod lengths out can be achieved. A throwing stick can also be used but it won't reach the distance a catapult can. However, if you desire a straight line of baits running out from the margin for a few feet the throwing stick is ideal, although it takes practice to get it right. Beyond a couple of rod lengths (or a rod length if using a small bait such as hemp) it is necessary to use a dropper of one sort or another. Of the commercial ones on sale I've used the Gardner Bait Rocket which will put baits out to about thirty yards, but beyond this it is pretty limited. The best droppers I have seen have been home-made affairs - large plastic tubes with a round nose. I have seen these put out a long way with a stout rod. On some waters, boats are allowed or lilo's to take bait out - I personally see no problem with this provided the angler casts his bait out, rather than introducing it by the same method. I disapprove of remote controlled boats, because in my view unless the angler actually casts out his bait any fish caught don't count.

I've used PVA bags since the Crab days and this is a highly effective way of creating a small bed of mass bait around the boilie. One drawback with the method, is that baits have to be totally dried out which causes a degree of loss of effectiveness as it is the liquid attractors that create the pull. Some oil will leak out as the seeds soak in water and I've caught sufficient fish on the method to convince me that there is still enough attractor about to pull fish down onto the bed. The big advantage is that you know your hookbait is bang on the bed and of course, you can fish at long range. The development of PVA webbing and bags with different dissolving times have been a recent welcome development. If you haven't tried the PVA bags yet then do so, as they can add an extra dimension to your fishing. Dare to be different - most will be filling up their bags with boilies. In this situation, fishing a single bait with a quantity of small dried out mass baits can score by simply presenting to a fish a different scenario and a method it won't have seen for some time - if ever.

Particle Bait Development on Crab

Because on Crab one was allowed to fish three rods, I tended to fish two rods using the main method I was employing at the time, and with the third experiment a bit, usually with a particle. Peanuts were a staggering success on Crab and I caught many fish on that third rod whilst using them and sometimes their success would lead me to fish them on more than one rod. I tended to soak my peanuts for 24 hours without cooking them so that they remained very hard. I would not use peanuts today, for unlike the early '80's the potential harm they can cause to fish is well established today. Having said that, there was no evidence whatsoever that the Crab fish were harmed in any way by their mass use. Crab is a very rich water and there were many different types of baits and boilies going into the water to counterbalance any potential dietary deficiencies peanuts can cause. I am certain that fish lost weight and some died on the very hungry Cheshire waters through overuse and people cutting corners by using low grade nuts sold as bird nuts which contain toxins. Carp anglers today should simply not use them.

The peanuts started to slow down and indeed, on many waters, (but not Crab) it became virtually impossible to catch anything but nuisance fish on peanuts - this was certainly the case at Halsnead. As they slowed, people started to look for alternatives. Initially, I went down the bean route trying haricots and borlotti beans. Haricots I found not very effective and borlotti beans from the tin were too soft and prone to coming off. I had a spell on chick peas and these caught immediately but I struggled to catch any big fish on them. A new nut was needed and I looked at walnuts, brazils and hazelnuts. Hazelnuts I was particularly interested in because they seemed ideal for fishing over silt due to their buoyancy. In fact, a soaked hazelnut made a perfect pop-up. The hazels were very difficult to prepare and took a great deal of cooking to make them sink. I'd put a pound or so in the pan, cook them for a long period then test them. It might have taken as many as three cookings to get them to sink. However, they gave off a marvellous aroma and I was utterly convinced that they would do the job. They were a very expensive bait and it cost me no small amount of money to buy sufficient to bait up and fish with for a few weeks. They were a qualified failure. They caught me a few fish - but not big ones - and they were certainly not worth the effort and cost. The failure of the hazel nuts pushed me into thinking on a different track altogether towards looking at my boilies to see if I could make them better than anyone else's. Another contributory factor was that around the time I was using the hazels a sort of "rig panic" set in for a time on Crab which I'll look at below. The solution to the nut problem lay in tiger nuts. Why didn't I use them? Well, Rod Hutchinson published a book in 1983 and in the Carp Strikes Back he said that tigers were not in the same league as peanuts. At that time, Rod was God and whatever he said had to be true and this put me off looking into them. That seems silly now, but that is the influence the big names can have on lesser mortals. As someone who has somewhat reluctantly acquired a name myself I would hate to think that anyone would accept everything I say as gospel and reject an idea just because I do. My experience is all I am relaying to you, on the waters I have fished. That experience may not correlate to your experience on your waters. Think for yourself to be successful. I realised this truth from day one following my match fishing experience, but I still fell into the occasional trap of following other carp anglers despite the fact that I knew I shouldn't have!

My eyes were soon opened in terms of the tigers when two of the best particle anglers in the known universe descended on Crab and began to take it apart. Their names are more widely known in the north. They are called Andy Cooper and Jim Schofield and they deserve to be better known for they are two very fine and successful anglers. Their approach was very different from others using particles on Crab or anywhere I've seen since. They had made particle fishing into an art form, and in many ways they fish like Chris Yates but use modern baits and tackle.

Andy and Jim would probably say that most anglers when fishing with particles tend to over-bait. Their technique was to use the bait sparingly and with precision. They blow out more than the five grains of corn that Yatesey seems to use all the time, but no more than a pouchful - which has the uncanny knack of landing in the right spot. Then out goes the hookbait in the middle. This could be contrasted at the time on Crab with anglers fishing over buckets of particles! It reminded me very much of my roach fishing days with maggots and casters. If you fired out a couple of pouches of bait, roach would fly in from everywhere with the water flashing with small roach. I'd catch one but it would be a small one. I'd catch the bigger roach when I chucked out just a few maggots or casters, and there would be less of that frantic flashing. Andy and Jim did their own thing and did exactly the opposite to what everyone else was doing in terms of bait application. Their light, pin-point baiting approach maximises efficiency in terms of the free offerings/hookbait ratio when fishing for already feeding fish in front of them. They were not interested in sitting in a swim, baiting heavily and waiting for the fish. It was hit and run. Catch a couple of fish from a swim and when the carp move on, move with them. Pure carp fishing.

On a crowded lake, this wasn't possible. Fortunately for them, they fished midweek when it was possible to move swims easily and, like me, they left Crab when even midweek it became a veritable "bivvy city". I learned a lot from watching them. In the process of them taking photos for me and me taking photos for them, I got to know them very well and eventually they began to let me into one or two things. It was difficult to tell from observation what bait they were using as they were secretive and crafty with it. If anyone was near, no recasting or reeling in was done. The baits were very discreetly removed from the tub and the swim and margins scoured for signs of any grains of bait that might have slipped out of the pult accidentally before moving to a new swim or leaving. I was catching well too, using a completely different approach and our dual success brought us together. They let me in on the fact that they were using tigers - ahead of anyone else - but I was busy pursuing my own thing at the time so had no intention of using them. The tigers were noted for future reference. The condition of their tigers was quite interesting. The inside of their bait bucket looked like a honeycomb with tigers jelled together and clearly in various stages of fermentation. They really were growlers! They'd break a piece off the tacky mess and use that. I've caught a few fish on tigers that could only be described as ancient. I like mine to be somewhat mature. Others though, are very fussy. Alan Young, for example, will tell you that he will only use very fresh tigers that have just been cooked. No doubt, Youngie would shake his head at the state of the tigers Andy and Jim used. Confidence is the key factor here - use baits you are comfortable with and have caught on.

The rigs Andy and Jim were using were interesting too. They were using very long dacron hooklinks of around two feet with the tigers popped up with cork inserts on quite long hairs, with quite light leads.

This could be contrasted with the rig mainly in use at the time, which was 6 - 9 inches long, short hair, and heavy fixed leads. Their rig did interest me and it made sense to be different again. They also used cotton hairs. Initially, this was because they fished the Thorneycroft Hall lakes where it was possible to catch many fish and in the days of nylon hairs they had started to use cotton to stop the hairs being continually broken on landing a fish. But they also noticed that cotton gave a more active movement to the popped-up bait than continuing the dacron hooklink as the hair or when using nylon line. I switched over to cotton on the third rod and the difference was noticeable. There was a problem with cotton though. It tended to twist after several casts and the hair might completely disappear as it coiled up into itself. This didn't seem to drastically affect the efficiency of the rig as the bait would invariably be tight to the hook.

Jim and Andy's particle rig.

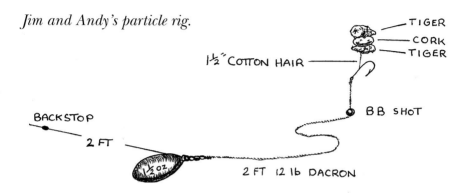

The Great Crab Mill Rig Panic

Initially, on Crab, everyone was using the standard anti-eject hair, which differed from the original hair rig presentation in that the hair was mounted mid-shank instead of at the bend. Baits were generally popped-up from 1"- 4". Running leads had been replaced by fixed or semi-fixed leads fished with tight lines from the monkey climbers or in rod clips. In the early days of this rig, catches were spectacular and many waters once regarded as very hard seemed very easy. But all good things come to an end. Things started to slow down dramatically in the second season I fished Crab. Takes slowed down and the fish were clearly avoiding tight lines. They were also avoiding swims where they had been hammered. The well known Stumps Swim was an example of the latter. A prolific swim in previous seasons, it died completely and fish seemed to swim through it very quickly without settling to feed. Unfortunately, it was Robbie's favourite swim and he kept going in there despite us all going on at him to avoid it. He had a terrible season with blank after blank.

One rig development which still produces a result anywhere in the right conditions emerged out of serendipity. Robbie's dad had picked me up en route to the lake with Robbie and cousin in tow and I went into the Wide Swim. I cast out three popped-up baits with a few free offerings around them. I didn't really like fishing that side of the lake and was contemplating moving. Robbie came down for a chat and a coffee.

Whilst chatting, my memory went into gear.

" I don't know whether I've put any shot on the hooklink to hold the bait down," I said to Robbie.

"You're a wally," said Robbie, "you'd better reel in and check."

"I will in a bit. I'm thinking of moving anyway," I replied.

"Wally," said Robbie, walking away.

As he walked away, one of the buzzers screamed off and I duly landed an 18 pounder on a bait fished about a foot off the bottom! Robbie christened the rig the Wally Wafter rig and we used it with great effect on a number of waters and fished the baits at all sorts of different depths off the bottom. We even resorted to standing on bedchairs to cast out with the really long rigs! It works particularly well during hot weather conditions when the fish are cruising well off the bottom and in waters which are quite deep. We had a lot of fish on it at Birch Grove in the mid-'80's and it still catches the odd fish there today. In the south, this rig is often referred to as the Zig rig - heaven knows why. I think our name for it - the Wally Wafter is much nicer. It is not a prolific rig but it is one that can be pulled from the drawer in scratching conditions. It works straight up from the lead but it does benefit in terms of a good hookhold if you still add a largish split shot a couple of inches up the hooklink from the lead. This helps to prick the fish, as it eliminates the complete free movement of the hook-length from the lead.

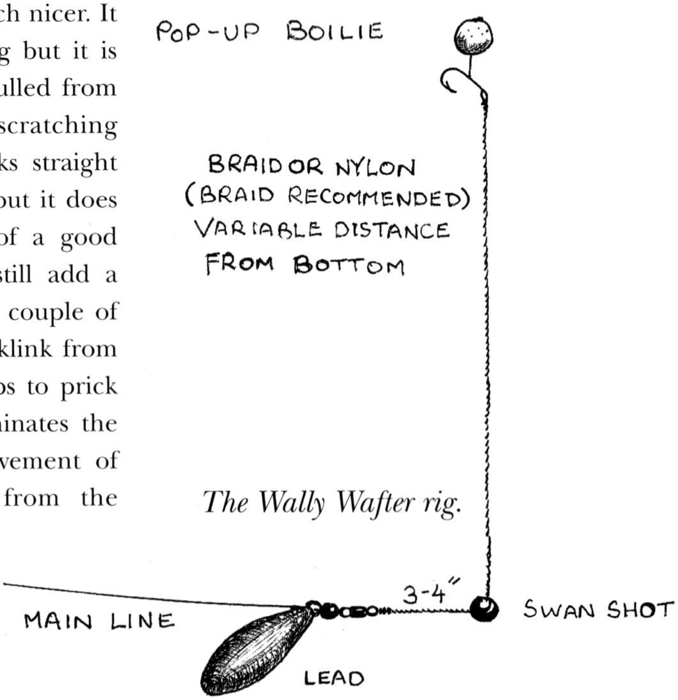

POP-UP BOILIE

BRAID OR NYLON (BRAID RECOMMENDED) VARIABLE DISTANCE FROM BOTTOM

The Wally Wafter rig.

MAIN LINE
3-4" SWAN SHOT
LEAD

As I said earlier, the carp were definitely avoiding swims with tight lines in them. The solution initially, was to fish fixed leads and a slack line with the line in rod clips to avoid false buzzer bleeps. This was an improvement but still posed problems due to the weedy margins. The slack line would fall into the weedy scum which would cling to the nylon. On getting a take this would remain on the line and there was the risk of clogging up in the rod rings. A couple of times whilst playing fish, I had to put the rod down to unclog weed from the line to allow it to be retrieved at all. A solution had to be found. It seemed to me that a method had to be found to fish a tight line from the rod tip whilst still keeping the line on the bottom. I scratched the old brain cells and remembered a method I'd been shown by a well known bream angler fishing the open circuit in my match fishing days. I was having a problem with the marginal current when fishing a river when ledgering in the slower middle. The current was forcing the line downstream pulling it off-line from the rod to the lead when I wanted a direct line. This chap showed me a way of combating this by sliding a nylon loop with some swan shot on it down the line to keep it direct to the lead. I thought this might solve the problem. I made up some nylon loops with three swan shot on and slid them down over the marginal scum and weed. This gave me the tight line to the bottom I wanted and a sunken line. After a few weeks of use, I swapped the swan shots for a small lead whipped to a curtain ring with a slit in it which made it easy to remove when playing fish - the swan shot link was somewhat fiddly to deal with when playing fish. I christened it the Back Lead and tried to keep it quite but on Crab this was just impossible. Eventually, I wrote the first ever description of it in an article of the same name in an old CAA magazine. Within months, commercially made ones were available and still are, although I still prefer to use my own.

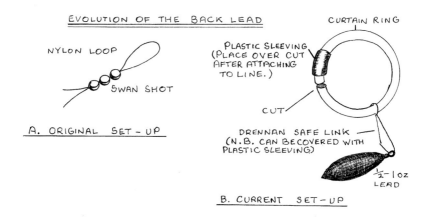

EVOLUTION OF THE BACK LEAD

NYLON LOOP

SWAN SHOT

A. ORIGINAL SET-UP

CURTAIN RING

PLASTIC SLEEVING
(PLACE OVER CUT
AFTER ATTACHING
TO LINE.)

CUT

DRENNAN SAFE LINK
(N.B. CAN BE COVERED WITH
PLASTIC SLEEVING)

½-1 OZ
LEAD

B. CURRENT SET-UP

The Back Lead was certainly significant and it solved the problem of the fish avoiding tight lines - for a time. It didn't solve the problem though, with the slow down at the hook and bait end. The Crab carp were clearly sussing things out and had learned to eject the baits more effectively. Whilst it was possible to have the occasional big hit and multiple catch when they really fed, it was getting hard to consistently catch fish between the red letter days. We'd gone from an average of several fish a day to one fish a day if you were lucky, particularly at weekends - in a year.

As a response, anglers started to experiment with all sorts of weird and wonderful rigs in a bid to revive the halcyon days. There were all sorts of whispers about wonder rigs. A really silly spell of rig panic hit the water and I'm afraid I fell for it too for a time.

We were all basically looking at altering the different angles at which the bait could be presented to the hook, and the relationship between bait and hook. By this time, chemically sharpened hooks were out and most of us had switched to Kamasans or Drennan Super Specialists - the Au Lion D'Ors were confined to the tackle box. A number tried out the "D" rig which had filtered north and the Revolving Hair with the stiffened hooklink above the hook. I tried out a number of different rig arrangements and concentrated on two which I did feel at the time produced one or two fish I might not have caught. One of these was Clive Diedrich's and Malcolm Winkworth's Spring Rig which was clearly effective but could only really be used in snag free conditions and there weren't many swims on Crab that were snag free. The second rig arrangement involved placing the hair just under the barb. I initially used a short hair and I used 2lb b.s. nylon that would break as the hook took hold as I thought the bait might impede hook penetration. This worked but I eventually moved on to using a thicker hair of 6lb b.s. which provided a spring-like effect on the bait. When using this, I used a longer hair of about two inches. Again, I caught fish. The problem was though, that I still wasn't catching the amount of fish that I and everyone else had been

THE `D´ RIG

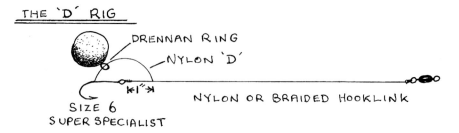

DRENNAN RING

NYLON `D´

SIZE 6
SUPER SPECIALIST

NYLON OR BRAIDED HOOKLINK

REVOLVING HAIR RIG

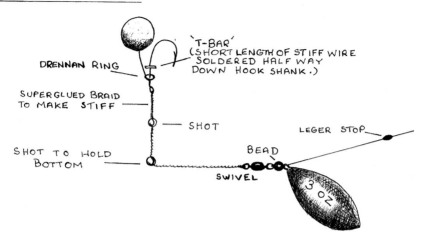

DRENNAN RING

'T-BAR'
(SHORT LENGTH OF STIFF WIRE
SOLDERED HALF WAY
DOWN HOOK SHANK.)

SUPERGLUED BRAID
TO MAKE STIFF

SHOT

LEGER STOP

SHOT TO HOLD
BOTTOM

BEAD

SWIVEL

3 OZ

catching when the original hair was at its height. The hair was such a revolutionary leap forward - all we were really doing was tinkering and messing about to try to achieve a possible minor improvement. It was difficult to evaluate whether or not the fish I did catch were really because of the new rig variation. I might have caught them on the standard anti-eject hair anyway. It was a frustrating time and I toyed with all sorts of ideas including multiple hooklengths and hooks, welding two hooks together side by side but offset slightly from each other and self hooking rigs working on

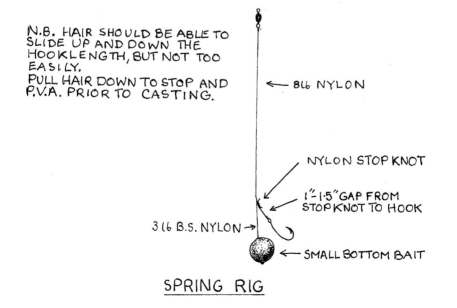

N.B. HAIR SHOULD BE ABLE TO
SLIDE UP AND DOWN THE
HOOKLENGTH, BUT NOT TOO
EASILY.
PULL HAIR DOWN TO STOP AND
P.V.A. PRIOR TO CASTING.

← 8lb NYLON

NYLON STOP KNOT

1"-1.5" GAP FROM
STOP KNOT TO HOOK

3 lb B.S. NYLON →

← SMALL BOTTOM BAIT

SPRING RIG

spring systems! These were tied up at home but never tried out for ethical reasons. Others had fewer qualms. One quite well known angler today, was caught casting out a pop-up on a treble hook and given a warning that if he was ever seen using it again his health would suffer. I was amazed to see another angler fishing Clifford's - the snaggiest swim on the lake - with the much-whispered about elastic rig. No, don't go looking for a description of this rig within these pages, for you won't find one. It is irresponsible in the extreme to use such a rig. Don't believe me? Well, ask Roger Smith about the marathon fight he experienced when using the elastic rig on Savay - with a tench!

My conclusion as that particular season drew to a close was that the rig panic had been just that and it had pointed to the reality that none of the rigs used were very much better than the standard one and, in fact, some were probably not as good in certain situations.

....

The Final Season

Before my last season on the water, I thought a great deal about matters. I'd come through the rig panic and decided for the new season I would revert to the standard anti-eject rig but look at what others were doing in terms of length and type of hooklength, size of lead, whether it was fixed, running, or running up against a stop and so on. Whatever was most in use I decided to do the opposite and buck the trend. I expected most to be still on short nylon or dacron hooklinks with a heavy fixed lead, with one of the new rig arrangements such as the D rig. My prediction about what rigs others were using proved to be right.

I became interested in trying out alternatives for the hooklink - in the hope of finding a particular material that the carp had not come across before and which would feel different to anything else they were picking up. I'd played around with dental floss and wool hooklinks in the 1970's and decided that this was a dead end. My thinking went along the path of presenting to the fish something much finer than conventional mono or braid but which still remained sufficiently strong to handle a big hard fighting fish. The first rig I came up with involved using several strands of 2lb nylon as a multiple strand rig. This worked well and I also tried several strands of cotton which worked less well. The success of the multi-strand rig made me look for an even better material and through a chance conversation in a local tackle shop with a professional rod builder I stumbled across multi-stranded Kevlar fibre. This was incredibly strong and offered superb presentation - because it offered something totally different to the standard. It caught from the off, and I used it with great success that season but had to be very secretive about the whole thing which I didn't particularly like.

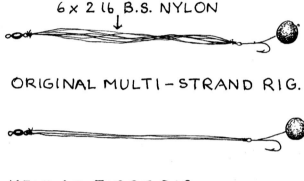

6 x 2 lb B.S. NYLON

ORIGINAL MULTI-STRAND RIG.

KEVLAR FIBRE RIG.

Herein lies a tale. A season or so later, I was asked to do a slide show on rigs for the local CAA branch in Wilmslow. As part of that talk, I decided to reveal the multi-strand Kevlar rig and I invited the rod builder to come along to show some of it off. The show went down very well and the venue was packed. The following week I went to a BCSG meeting and the then RO, Jim Hindle, said that a mutual friend of his had been very impressed with my talk and particularly, the multi-strand rig I'd developed on Crab. The mutual friend was going to look into it and maybe if he could obtain some good material he would market it. Ten years on, that mutual friend is one of the biggest hooklength material suppliers in the world! I still remind him today that he still owes me 10% of his earnings for giving him the idea in the first place!

In terms of bait, I decided to forget about the quest for a new particle and decided to concentrate on my boilie. I knew already that my bait was probably better than most fishing the lake in terms of its attractors and nutritional quality. Many were still using semolina/soya based carbohydrate baits but quite a few were going back to milks. Fishmeals and birdfoods were rarely used at this time. The most common fishmeal bait was the proprietary baits such as Seafood Blend sold by Rod Hutchinson, which although it was a good bait was quite expensive and so people didn't seem to put much of it in. I was sure this couldn't compete anyway with the milks which people were baiting up with. I'd been busy reading articles by a number of leading bait writers at the time such as Dr. Keith Sykes, Tim Paisley, and others. I re-read everything Fred Wilton had ever written, and old articles by Duncan Kay. I'd also been delving into the various papers produced by the Japanese professors. The material produced by Keith Sykes I found particularly interesting and I discussed a number of matters with him. I felt that I had to look at making my bait better than anyone else's. If I could do this, I felt this would overcome the rig problem completely and give me an edge. My basic aim was to improve on the milk protein bait I was using. To put together a bait based on high quality food grade milks, a lipid (fat) source, vitamin and minerals with a high biological value. The bait also utilised enzymes and amino-acids.

4oz Acid Casein (90 mesh)

2oz Rennet Casein (USA Spec. 80 mesh)

2oz Lactalbumin

2oz Casilan (Calcium Caseinate)

2oz Egg Albumin

2oz Bengers

1.5oz Davina Protein food

0.5oz Carpvit (from Geoff Kemp)

5ml Sesame Seed Oil

5ml Olive Oil

5ml Cotswold Computer Flavour

1 teaspoon Cotswold Milk B Enhancer

Glycine, Lysine, Cystine, Phenylalanine, Methionine 0.25gm of each per 1lb

Boiled for 50 seconds

Some of the powdered ingredients I'd used before but some were new to me. The rennet casein was a particularly interesting ingredient in that it was produced differently to acid casein which was precipitated by hydrochloric acid. This meant that some trace minerals remained in the ingredient. Lactalbumin is an ingredient I particularly like and use it in quantity in my milks today as it has a terrific amino acid profile. The problem with lactalbumin is that it has quite a short shelf life and, as it is produced abroad, it is vital to obtain it from a reputable supplier to ensure it is still fresh. When you get it, roll up all your baits quickly for the season and freeze them. The egg albumin was primarily included to help keep boiling time to a minimum to reduce the chances of the ingredients being de-natured and to provide a hard-skinned bait. Bengers was an ingredient I'd heard a lot of whispers about. Used in a variety of situations in human diets it contains the enzymes trypsin and amylase. The other whispered of enzyme was bromelain, and whilst I had access to the pure form of this through college I was uncertain of levels so opted again for a good source of bromelain that was used in human diets. That was the Davina Protein food drink - which is no longer available, either. Both enzyme ingredients were obtained from health food shops and used on the recommendation of a friend into body-building. Dr Keith had a protein-splitting enzyme ingredient for sale (which I suspect was trypsin/bromelain) but I decided to opt for these proven ingredients which also contained a number of other interesting ingredients. Enzymes are controversial - but I honestly don't see why. The benefits are scientifically proven as much as anything else and, used correctly, they can theoretically improve the biological value of the bait for carp. There is much confusion about nutrition and protein levels. Nutrition is not about the x percentage of protein or whatever which is eaten by the carp but is what is used by the host system - its digestibility. I feel that the presence of relevant enzymes in a milk protein bait can help the carp's system break down the complex ingredients these baits contain. Unlike humans, carp have no stomach and nutrients have to be utilised by enzymes found in the gut. The presence of active enzymes breaking up the protein chains makes for a more convertible food which therefore benefits the carp. In order for the enzymes to begin to do this it is necessary to leave the paste bait to stand for some time, unless you do that you are wasting your time. Generally, I left the paste bait for one hour before rolling. I also think that in reacting with the baits ingredients there is a significant release of free amino acids which adds to the attractiveness of the overall baits itself. In my experiments with baits containing enzymes I did not intend to fish with, I experienced some "Quatermass" effects. Other experimenters with enzymes may know what I am talking about!

Some writers have discussed at great length about ph and enzymes in terms of achieving a certain ph in the bait or some of its ingredients in order to get the most out of them. I tended to ignore all this as although you can measure ph in a bait in the kitchen once you throw it into a lake there are so many variables that I think you can forget about it. Trypsin and bromelain are the two key ingredients and, like a lot of things in baits, if they don't work in specific instances they are not going to do any harm and you won't lose anything by their inclusion. All I know is that their inclusion increased my catches and produced bigger fish too and I didn't bother with all that ph stuff.

Although Bengers and Davina are no longer available there are still products in the health food shops containing the same (and improved) ingredients - you'll identify the proprietary compounds by the futuristic brand names on the packet. Better advice still, is to contact Nutrabaits. They purchased the last remaining supply of Bengers and the recipe. They can offer you a Bengers alternative made to order. Trypsin beef pancreas and pineapple bromelain is available from them. The Addit Digest ingredient they sell is excellent, and instructions are clear and unambiguous. All baits using enzymes should be used fresh from frozen for maximum effect. In the early to mid '80's, we believed that the life-span of the bait was 24 hours fresh from frozen. In a recent discussion with Bill Cottam, he felt that this was the life-span for winter use but felt summer active life was considerably shorter.

Do enzymes still have a role in carp baits today, well over a decade since I used them? I don't think the enzyme baits we used then do. Things have moved on considerably with the development of new ingredients, meals, liquid foods and extracts. A lot of the earlier theorising about milk proteins and enzymes have been contradicted to a degree. In the early to mid '80's, I believed a milk protein bait would outfish anything in the summer. I don't think they can hold a candle to the quality fishmeal and birdfood combinations used today. Milks are now just a part of the bait. However, I believe similarly derived ingredients have a very significant present and future role, via the use of pre-digested ingredients such as pre-digested milk proteins and fishmeal etc.

The smell factor in the bait revolved around a flavour which Keith recommended called Computer. It was a weird-looking flavour but had one of those smells that one knows is going to attract. I considered this the unique label for the bait that I was looking for. The other ingredient was a powdered attractor called Milk B which provided a nice background taste and improved overall palatability.

Sesame seed oil and olive oil were added as a source of fats which clearly are a part of any nutritional bait. It is important not to use too much sesame seed oil as it can mask the smell of the flavour, hence the olive oil. Bear in mind, though, that at higher levels sesame seed oil can be a devastating attractor in its own right. In fact, the idea for using bulk fish oils in the mid to late '80's in fishmeal baits came from the prior success of individuals such as Ian Brown of Kent who used bulk sesame oil in his baits. I think Wilton hadn't considered the role of fats beyond eggs in his mixes. Keith Sykes thought lipid sources were necessary in a nutritional bait and in that respect he was perhaps one of the influences - along with Ian Brown - on the bait revolution of the late 1980's initiated by Geoff Bowers of what became Premier Baits fame.

The last ingredients are perhaps the most controversial of all - but I don't see why as they are the essence of all natural life. I'd used amino acids by using the proprietary baits of Duncan Kay in the late 1970's, particularly his Red and Yellow Slyme. Duncan clearly established that amino acids were effective in practical carp fishing. I caught many fish on his baits in paste form. His base mixes though, were pretty poor in terms of nutritional content and I began developing my own baits with similar amino acid combinations but on more nutritional bases with success. These were in soft paste baits. When the hair rig/rock-hard carbohydrate baits came to dominate the early 1980's amino acids were forgotten. I felt on Crab Mill that I should look at them again. I felt that providing boiling time could be reduced to a minimum, they still had a role in boiled baits. In Carp Fever, Kevin Maddocks, felt that they had no role in boiled baits at all. But it seemed to me that providing the boilie had a relatively uncooked soft centre, the amino acids here would not be destroyed and would leech out of the bait as it began to soften, creating a strong source of attraction. I still use amino acids in my baits today. This particular amino combination I had used in the late 1970's with demonstrable success.

I had no doubts about this bait whatsoever. In practice, the theory was mostly borne out, for I was to have my most successful season on Crab. I caught all the biggest fish in the lake except one. I had a string of good twenties on the bait and most of my doubles were better than average fish.

There were several factors that could have distorted that result. One is that it was my third season on the water so I was fishing it with more experience than before. Accepted. I also complicated matters, by occasionally fishing that bait over hemp when everyone else had given up on it. I shouldn't have done this. These two factors taken together would have been sufficient to discredit the bait as the decisive factor would it not have been for the fact that another member fishing the water, using a virtually identical bait was having similar results, initially without my knowledge. That member was good friend Ken Dallow who had clearly also been reading and talking to Keith Sykes! Ken had really struggled on the water until he had gone onto that almost identical bait totally unaware that I was also using it. Again, he had a string of good twenties, which suggests more than coincidence. I can say that ten years later, Ken Dallow was still catching big fish from Crab on that very same bait!

As a result of that season's catches, my other results locally and my catches in the Midlands in the 1970's, I was accepted into membership of the British Carp Study Group which was then much more difficult to get into than it is today.

One final point about Crab Mill needs to be said. There was quite a social scene on the lake and every evening would see the local pub *The Rookery* full of carp anglers with me often leading the charge. I'm not ashamed of that in any way and see no reason to be. On every water I've ever fished I've always left the water for a couple of hours a day to go to the pub, to shop or enjoy a meal. I am a firm believer in giving the swim a rest for at least a part of the day. On Crab, this going to the pub used to upset those who insisted on sitting in a bivvy staring at the bobbins all the time. Not because we were rowdy coming back - because we never were and one would have to strain the ear to hear any noise. They complained because the pub anglers caught more fish - a lot more fish.

Before going to the pub and the local Chinese take-away, I'd bait up my spots. But my lines wouldn't be in the water for a few hours so the fish could get their heads down without fear. Whilst in the pub, we anglers together would talk fishing - what we'd seen and where, what we were doing. You learn a lot in the pub. I've made life long friends from those social get-togethers. The break away from the lake refreshes and charges you up. On Darenth, where there wasn't time to go to the pub I'd reel the rods in for most of the unproductive day and socialise. When you've left the swim alone you're ready for it again instead of stagnating. Don't get me wrong here, I'm not advocating people getting steaming drunk with the stereotypical Clone Valley pub/club/Indian scene. Far from it. But there is nothing wrong with a gentle drink, a nice cooked meal, a time of relaxation and most importantly, taking the pressure off that swim you are in. I don't think leaving the water for a couple of hours a day has cost me a fish anywhere. It has caught me many more. Also, there is more to life than doing solitary confinement in a bivvy.

. . . .

Right: A pretty upper double on a deserted Crab. Caught from the Snag which can be seen in the background.
Below: 24 pounder on boilie over hemp.

There were some amazing characters on Crab Mill - too many to recall them all - but three in particular I still remember with great fondness today.

The first was Bernard Loftus who was more or less resident on the water. He's never been an oil painting our Bernard, but at this time he looked more like an alien from outer space than a human being. He was incredibly skinny with translucent skin and tousled hair. He had huge, red, saucer-sized eyes that popped out of his cranium due to lack of sleep. He was doing so much fishing that if he ever went home he slept on his bedchair because he couldn't sleep in a normal bed! For most of the time he seemed very disorientated and was prone to strange behaviour. For example, one very hot afternoon he woke me up from my siesta in an excited state, "I've caught thirteen," he said, "come and see them!" I hurried down clutching my camera in the excited anticipation of an incredible Billingsgate multiple catch shot. As I arrived in the swim I looked for the mass of sacks in the water but couldn't see any. "It's no good looking down there," said Bernard popping his head out of his bivvy (which was so smelly it growled at you). "They are in here." A bewildering notion swamped my mind that Bernard was keeping thirteen big carp in his bivvy. Had he gone insane?

On entering the bivvy, with breath held, Bernard thrust an open and virtually empty can of Ambrosia creamed rice into my face. It was a can he'd scrounged off me the previous day. There, swimming and buzzing around in the cream residue at the bottom of the tin - were thirteen wasps...

Barney was another favourite. He drove an old Robin Reliant which was always breaking down and expelled more oil per journey than the Torrey Canyon. Consequently, Barney was often covered in oil and to make matters worse, sweated profusely. He also smoked a pipe which added to the overall olfactory effect. Despite these afflictions and the fact that he was also wide-eyed and deranged looking, Barney thought he was still irresistible to the ladies and he took a liking to Wendy in particular. He would often carry my tackle when Wendy arrived to take me home so he could chat her up. Unfortunately, Barney had a speech impediment and Wendy couldn't understand a word he said, so all his chat-up lines fell on stony ground. With Barney, "F's" came out as "B's" and "G's" somehow came out as "M's". Every other word he ever uttered was an anglo-saxon four letter one. His pronunciation was often a problem for him. For example, when we were fishing with the groats, we told Barney what they were and the sort of places he could get them from. For several weeks, pet shop owners and grain dealers in Manchester were confronted with an incomprehensible, foul-mouthed, oily, smelly, pipe-smoking scruff seeking out "moats."

Barney was a one fish a season man - his biggest fish ever being a 24 pounder caught on a small green potato which Bernard had discarded from his Irish stew. One of the old school was Barney and he lived in a tiny canvas bivvy usually half-way along the Dead Length. The bivvy was so small that you could see the outline of his shoulders on the canvas when he was sat on his bedchair. Barney was a soft paste man when everyone was on boilies or particles, and used tiny leads on link ledgers when everyone else was on heavy bolt rigs. One morning, I was playing my fourth or fifth fish of the session and Barney lumbered down to grill me. "Are you on that buckin' hairy rig?" he asked. I told him I was and, after landing the fish, I showed him exactly what to do and I also gave him a single boilie to try out. Half an hour later he landed his first and only fish of the season - a 17 pounder. I fully expected him to be on the cadge for another bait but he never reappeared. When I called at his bivvy to collect him for the pub, I asked what he thought about the rig and bait. "I'm not using that buckin' rig again," he exclaimed, "it's buckin' unethical!"

Barney made all of his own tackle but he wasn't much of a craftsman. For example, his home-made buzzers used to sound for some length of time at the slightest twitch but on a full-blooded run would remain silent. We often observed his bobbins flying up and down whilst he slept on none the wiser. He made his own floats, which either sunk or sat out of the water so high that it would have taken a Great White shark to pull one under. One opening morning, I landed the largest carp in the lake but discovered I'd forgotten my weigh sling. I nipped down to Barney to borrow his. When I told him what I'd caught he said, "Buckin' 'ell you'll need my big one." When we got back to the fish, I noticed that the weigh cords on the weigh sling looked rather long. I ended up on Barney's shoulders whilst he stood on my bedchair so we could get sufficient height to lift the fish off the ground!

My final memory of Barney is a fond one. I was on what proved to be my final ever session, fishing next to the snag at the end of the Dead Length. Barney came down and was walking the opposite bank. As he drew level, he looked across to me - billowing pipe in mouth - and raised his hand in greeting. He moved forward a pace, still looking across and waving. In a flash, he was gone, as he plummeted down one of the yawning Crab Mill pot holes. All I can remember is a cloud of smoke and a loud strangled cry of "Buckinnnn 'eeeeelllllllll!!!"

The Square-Headed Fella, as Robbie christened him, lived in an even smaller bivvy than Barney's on Clifford's. He was a tiny little chap with no neck and a head Picasso would have admired, hence his name. He wasn't very popular, for he had adopted a unique approach to try to catch a Crab Mill carp. This entailed living for months at a time on Clifford's with the rods permanently cast out in the hope that a brain-dead fish would eventually succumb to the ploy. This meant of course, that no-one else could fish Clifford's. We all did if we wanted to though, by simply casting into it, for the remarkable thing about the Square-Headed Fella was that he never, ever, emerged from his bivvy until just before dark when he would re-cast his three rods and then retire until the following evening. We used to spend hours speculating about just what he did whilst he was in the bivvy because it was so small and there was barely room for him to turn around in it.

One morning, I was in The Stile and young Gary, fishing The Point, came around to me. Excitedly, he announced, "I'm sure I've just seen the Square Headed Fella leave the lake. I've checked in Clifford's and he's left his rods out."

"Teach him a lesson," I said, "pull all his line off the reels so he will think he's had a run on every rod when he gets back. He still hasn't had a fish all season, so he'll be gutted."

Gary scampered around to Clifford's and started to pull yard after yard of line off each reel in turn. I could hear the faint noise of the buzzer as he did so. As he was just about to start on the third reel, the bivvy door flew open and there stood the Square-Headed Fella, resplendent in silk pajamas. "What do you think you are doing?" he enquired of a somewhat red-faced Gary....

One day, a brain-dead twenty one pounder took pity on Square-Head and sucked in his peanut. Within minutes, the bivvy was down and out of Clifford's, after five weeks residency. As he went past, I asked when he was coming back and for how long. "I'm not coming back here ever again. I came here to catch a twenty and now I've caught one. This is one of the hardest lakes in England and I reckon if you can catch one from here you can catch one from anywhere. I've caught one. I'm now going to write a book about carp fishing..."

I still look out for the Square-Headed Fella's book on carp fishing. I still haven't come across it. I suppose he couldn't interest a publisher in a book with a photo of just one carp in it, despite the saving on reproduction costs. Sad, that.

"What do you think you are doing?"

After three good seasons on Crab, I felt the need to move on. The water had begun to get very crowded and on Fridays a bivvy in every swim had become the norm. Even though I loved the place it was time to pull up stumps. Although one or two carp I still wanted to catch were being stubborn, I was still basically catching the same fish over and over again. I'd learned a great deal on the water. I'd made mistakes too. The major one being that my sessions on the water - two nights on average - hadn't really been long enough to give the fish a real seeing to. Bernard, for example, had been fishing thirteen day sessions and it was often ten days or so before he really started to catch in numbers from a swim. I could have competed time-wise with that for at least two months. But then it might have cost me my wife, my job, my house, my other interests ..... there is more to life than carp.

I started to look elsewhere to fish.

Fate took a hand. I often observed a chap (who always fished on the opposite side) watching me whenever I played and landed a fish. He would stare across with hands on hips, shaking his head, for he was singularly unsuccessful on the water and the Crab carp punished him on a regular basis. He was a cheesy-faced character, sporting large glasses and short dark hair. He looked a bit like Roy Orbison and a character appearing regularly in a TV advertisement at the time for "R Whites Lemonade". He was no "secret lemonade drinker" though, and through the weekend revelries at *The Rookery*

My first twenty from Crab Mill.

I gradually came to know him quite well. His name was Brian Garner and he was a regular angler at a certain big fish water in Shropshire that I had acquired a ticket for but hadn't yet fished seriously. He suggested I start fishing it with him. Despite the fact that I suspected he just wanted to bleed me dry of all of the secrets that I led him to believe I had up my sleeve (I didn't have any actually - although he wasn't to know that), I readily agreed.

So began a friendship with the extraordinary Brian Garner and a love affair with Hawk Lake that was to last for several years.....

The big fish called Ringo - what a starr!

First capture of Arfur' at 25lb 2oz. A big fish for Cheshire then.

Hawk Lake

"Oh fair enough are sky and plain
But I know fairer far:
Those are as beautiful again
That in the water are."
A Shropshire Lad, A E Houseman 1897.

Whispers of a water in Shropshire containing lots of good fish including many big commons, were often cause for hushed conversation in the public bar of *The Rookery*. Halsnead regulars, Peter Barker and Peter Dumbill were fishing this water which was known as Hawk Lake, but the crafty old boys clammed-up whenever I mentioned the place to them. Robbie and Bobbie had found out a bit about the water and decided to go down on an exploratory winter day trip. Bob had a stroke of luck, when he landed a superb personal best common of 24lb and lost another within an hour of casting out into the water!

I was fishing Halsnead and, when the boys returned, they tried to convince me Bob had caught his fish from Halsnead. As soon as I saw the photograph of the fish I knew it was from Hawk. I really fancied a go at it after seeing Bob's lovely common. Alan Young who was a Hawk member, owed me a favour, and he successfully sponsored me for membership. I still couldn't drive, so I would have to rely on others to get there as it was a good fifty miles from home.

The summer was spent on Crab as usual, fishing with Robbie and things were going well for me but not for him. I was catching - and catching well - but he was really struggling with blank after blank piling up. He was getting very depressed and every fish I caught seemed to put him lower

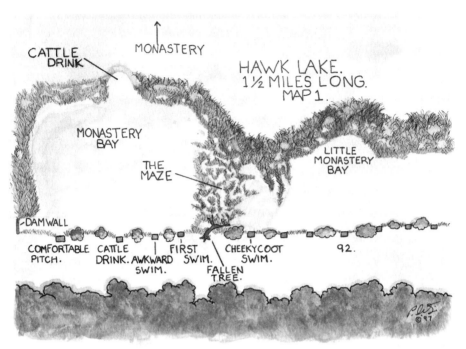

CATTLE DRINK

MONASTERY

HAWK LAKE.
1½ MILES LONG.
MAP 1.

MONASTERY BAY

THE MAZE

LITTLE MONASTERY BAY

DAMWALL

COMFORTABLE PITCH.   CATTLE DRINK. AWKWARD SWIM.   FIRST SWIM.   CHEEKYCOOT SWIM.   92.

FALLEN TREE.

down. He needed to get off the water to recharge the old batteries and I suggested I ask Wendy to run us down to Hawk for my first look at the water.

We set up next to each other in what is known as the Second Bay. It was mid-August and hot. First morning, I had four runs in an hour, landing two and losing two, with the best fish an upper double figure common. I'll never forget the look of despair on Robbie's face when that buzzer of mine roared off yet again. There was a song by Rod Stewart in the charts at the time called, "Some Guys Have All The Luck" and it seemed to be on the radio an awful lot. As I played the first fish it was lilting across the airways again. Robbie put down the landing net, grabbed hold of the radio and threatened to throw it into the water. I pleaded with him to put it down. I never switched on the radio again that season when he was in hearing range! Worse was to come. On the last night, he had a minor drop-back - his first action of the season virtually - and, by the time he had got to the rod, the fish had kited through one of my lines. I thought I'd had a take too, struck and played what I thought was a fish. The inevitable tug of war developed. We sussed out what had happened. The fish was close into the bank in front of me and we were separated by a huge tree. I suggested I land it and if Robbie's rig was in its mouth it was his fish. I got the fish in and it was a small common with Robbie's rig in it.

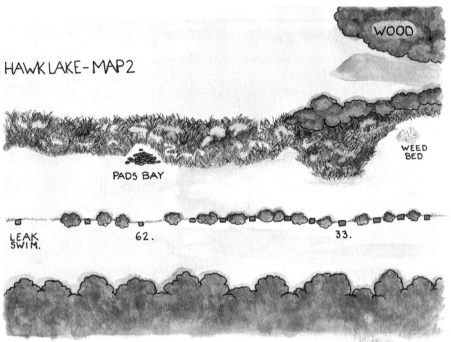

HAWK LAKE- MAP2

WOOD

WEED BED

PADS BAY

LEAK SWIM.

62.

33.

"What is it?" asked Robbie.

"It's only a small common. But it is your fish," I replied. I got the hook out and, whilst I was trying to clear all the mess away it started flapping and flipped back into the water.

"It's jumped back in, Robbie," I said apologetically.

Robbie got it into his mind that I'd actually landed a big fish, but because it had his rig in its mouth, I'd let it go so he couldn't count it. I tried to convince him of the truth, but he sulked back to his bivvy. I caught another fish in the morning which did nothing to lift the gloom. He was blowing out - and he knew it. He fished a couple of times after that, but he'd lost interest. The success of the early hair rig days could not be repeated and he wasn't prepared to fish without guaranteed success. That was the last season that Robbie carp fished and I have never seen him since to this day. A great pity, because he was a good angler and a valued friend.

I'd not really had a good look at Hawkstone on that first trip as I'd only fished at the one end. I'd caught though, so when Brian suggested I fish the lake in the winter with him and Hawk bailiff, Bob Tapken, I was both enthusiastic and confident because I'd had fish from the water. That confidence was to receive a severe kicking over the winter months on my weekend trips! On my first trip in November with Bobbie, I had an eighteen

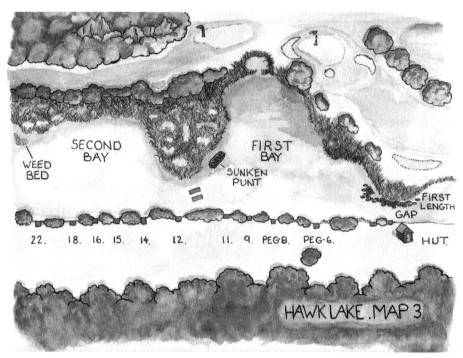

pound leather from the First Bay. I didn't catch a carp from the water for the rest of the winter, and only ended up with a respectable tally of winter carp by retreating onto Halsnead a couple of times a week.

I made a number of mistakes. Looking back, that was all part of an important learning curve and so I benefitted from those mistakes at least.

First up, I'd gone onto a difficult water I knew virtually nothing about for a harsh winter. I will never do anything like that again, and would strongly advise anyone not to either. Secondly, I didn't realise how competitive - not to say cut-throat - my two companions were, particularly Brian. Brian just had to catch fish and didn't like it if anyone else caught, let alone had the chance of catching. Other than that he was excellent company! Brian has a very sharp competitive edge to his personality which he would be the first to admit to. Brian and Bob took delight in stitching me up and then winding me up! They were concentrating on the First Bay and it was obvious that the fish were stacked-up in there that first winter. They could always get to the water before me. I'd do everything I could to wangle time off from college on Fridays only to find them fully installed in the two going swims, sporting huge grins! I'd get in as near as I could but I wasn't on the fish. What I should have done was to ignore the pair of them, let them get on with their games, had a good look round and done my own thing. But I didn't know the water and was slightly intimidated by it because of its size. Despite being stitched-up and having my leg regularly pulled, I still enjoyed their excellent company on the bank. Bait was my final mistake. I used my Crab Mill bait without really establishing it. I wasn't putting it in and it hadn't been pre-baited. I didn't know what bait Brian was on - the old so and so wouldn't tell me - but he'd obviously been establishing it for some time. I didn't know whether Bob was on the same bait as Brian, but I doubted it. Bob only really fished Hawk, so it was natural to assume his bait had been going in for some time. That first winter was a disaster, but I swore that I wouldn't let that water beat me. I would have the last laugh on Messrs Garner and Tapken too...

. . . .

I decided to concentrate on Hawk the following season for my summer vacation and weekends, with short evening sessions on Grey Mist or Halsnead. Steve Knowles had also got a Hawk card and was keen to have a go too. Steve was a much more laid-back fishing companion than Brian. He liked catching, but he had none of the Garner paranoia which emerged when others had the cheek to catch what he saw as his fish.

We'd decided to all club together - Steve Knowles, Brian, Bob, Steve Allcott (who was by now fishing Savay) and myself and buy bait ingredients in bulk, in an attempt to get together to dominate the water. We were all to a greater or lesser extent milk protein buffs and this was therefore the natural bait choice. Brian had discovered a source of rennet casein via a company in Devon, and we had good, reliable sources for all of the other ingredients. Bob had contact with a company producing a particular product called Lactein and we looked into that.

The base mix we agreed on was as follows:

4 oz USA Spec. Rennet Casein (80 mesh)

2 oz Lactein '75 (percentage protein)

1 oz Soya Isolate

1 oz Lactalbumen

1 oz Calcium Caseinate

1 oz Egg Albumen

This was a very effective base mix with high quality ingredients. The egg albumen was used to reduce boiling time to a minimum and was obtained from a company making wedding cakes by Brian. Lactein is no longer available, but was a very good ingredient, although we found at the end of the season that the Lactein 75 did not have quite as high a biological value (ie. that which the carp's system can utilise and use) as a product called Lactein 50 produced by the same company, despite its higher protein content. Bob got some stick for that - after the event - as if it really was that significant!

The attractor combination was one which came out of one of the alcohol assisted discussions in *The Rookery* via Paul Roberts, who had told us about the obvious effectiveness of an attractor developed by Tim Paisley. This consisted of garlic oil and a Richworth Blue Cheese flavour. Liver Extract had also been effective when used with garlic, but we opted for Blue Cheese. There were no sources of concentrated garlic oil at that time but we were told that Tim had used Hofels Garlic Perles (capsules) as the source of garlic. The capsules were pierced with a pin and squeezed into a flavour bottle. The attractor combination was:

5 ml Hofels Garlic Perles (Original type: not the non-aromatic type!)

3 ml Richworth Blue Cheese

1 ml Rod Hutchinson Emulsifier

This particular bait was to produce many fish for all of us and the garlic/Blue Cheese combination was certainly a killer smell. We all agreed to stick to the same bait, but I doubted if anyone did strictly. I added amino acids - glycine, methionine, arginine, cystine, lysine and phenylanine at 0.25 gm each. I was also adding a bulk liquid food source - Minamino - which I'd become very interested in. I was also still messing around with enzymes and added these, although Brian sussed this out when he saw some of my baits basically dissolving in front of his eyes following a cock-up. He told me off, so I dropped the enzymes but kept the aminos in the base mix.

Looking back, ten years on, I'd make the following observations about that bait. The base mix is a very good winter base mix but there are much better alternatives now for summer use. A good fishmeal would destroy it. Back then though, it was better than anything else in use on that water. The garlic/Blue Cheese smell is a first class attractor and will still be effective on any water today. I haven't used it in a fishmeal or birdfood, so I don't know how effective it is in those sorts of baits. In cold water and milk protein it is very effective. I think we probably used the Blue Cheese at too high a level for a long term bait - 1-2ml would have been more appropriate. Garlic Perles are still the most effective source of garlic to use in any bait in my view, as garlic is one of those essential oils which is easily over-dosed in its pure state. The garlic in the perles is on a soya oil carrier at low level and at 5ml seemed just right. We thought the emulsifier - which basically allows water to mix with oil and thus improve attraction - was very necessary, but on reflection I don't think it was important.

Rigs were pop-ups fished on dacron hooklengths and popped up 1-3 inches on the new Drennan Super Specialist chemically sharpened hooks. Because of the soft silt, we thought the pop-up would be absolutely vital. I found out by the late winter that this wasn't all that important after all.

That summer was exceptionally hot and the fishing was very difficult. I caught odd fish from the off, but it was hard going with the fish just not interested in feeding for long periods due to the heat. They cruised around invitingly with their backs out of the water. Due to the quiet fishing many members gave up and went elsewhere, and most of the time we had this beautiful water to ourselves. We walked its picturesque banks, watched its carp, fished, lived, without seeing another soul for days. It was like our own private water. Initially, we concentrated our efforts on the First and Second Bay, but we soon realised there was more to life than that and that there was a great long water to explore. We grew to love the wild far end of the lake - The Monastery Bay, The Maze, The Pads and we became more interested in this end too, when we realised that a lot of fish spent more time at this end of the lake. Many anglers didn't fish in this area because of the horrendous walk. Luckily, we introduced ourselves to a farmer whose farmhouse was across a field up at this end. He liked the look of us and gave us permission to park on his land. This cut the walking down considerably and meant we had direct access to our favourite section of the lake. Ironically, the first good fish came to my rods in the Second Bay and I started to catch steadily whilst Steve struggled. I think the reason for that was that I was more patient than Steve and would sit in a swim and wait for fish to come into it, whereas Steve was up and down stalking and I think fishing for moving fish which were not really feeding. Steve was first and foremost a floater angler too, a much better one than me - but the Hawk carp were not interested, (not yet, anyway) in floaters. But my catches were hardly spectacular - it was hard fishing.

Still, I was learning. Because it was quiet and hot there was a lot of fish movement and a lot of my time was spent watching carp at quite close range. I began to understand what was going on with the fish. That knowledge has helped me on many other waters since. Fish that crashed right out, perhaps several times in short succession, were not feeding fish - they had already fed. The crashing is because they have fed and are clearing their gill rakers

Snapshot of some of the ingredients in use in the late 80's.

of silt. Sometimes, when argillus is rife they crash to try to shed these parasites on the skin. Some fish seem to crash a great deal and a lot more than other fish which suggested to me that these particular fish seemed to just enjoy it! The fish were often mooching around on Hawk and it became clear what sort of movement indicated feeding mode. If a carp swam past at some speed in a straight determined manner, it was not going to feed in the swim one was fishing. It was off to feed elsewhere, or to follow instincts about where it should be. Often, these were single fish or just a couple of fish. Sometimes, they seemed to be looking for other fish to join. I often saw carp "roughing each other up" by ramming their snouts into the bellies of other fish, presumably to try to induce spawning behaviour.

If the carp was idling along, browsing and varying its depth in the water - stopping and starting - it was a potential feeder and could be caught. Certain swims on Hawk used to have more movers than browsers in them and were not as good as swims where browsers predominated.

The far bank at Hawk could not be fished and was fringed with rushes. Throughout the summer months, the fish rarely strayed in the narrower parts of the lake more than about two feet away from them. This was the case even when the lake was very quiet and the fish were unaware of any anglers being present. Having the close reassurance of several yards of water-filled rushes to retreat into was a priority for the carp, who seemed very nervous in certain areas. The areas where the carp seemed much happier to move around in open water were the wide bays which, ironically, were the most heavily fished - so you would expect them to hug the rushes even more enthusiastically. However, the rigs in the bays were more often than not being fished on the rushline - so the area the carp felt safest in was in the un-fished open water. Looking at my catches, in the narrower areas my carp were caught generally tight to the rushline, in the bays, they were caught two-thirds of the way across in open water. Looking back, I wasted a lot of time that first summer by fishing tight to the rushline in the bays and struggling, when it would have been more profitable to fish the open water where they were much more likely to pick up a bait and feed. This was a case again, of listening too much to others, instead of trying things out for myself. The experienced anglers on the water were all telling me I had to be within inches of the rushline on Hawk or I wouldn't catch. That proved to be absolute nonsense, but I struggled as a result of listening to that advice until a session in early September. The reality was to dawn on me when I had my first big multiple catch in what were almost hurricane-type conditions.

On Hawk, the wind was the key factor in terms of fish movement and feeding. A lot of carp would move on a fresh, warm wind and completely vacate areas of the lake. Any type of wind was welcome in the summer, although, typically, south westerlies blowing down towards our preferred Monastery Bay were favourite. Any wind was helpful though, with the water being generally shallow - averaging three to four feet - any wind got the water oxygenated and the fish on the move. Still, calm conditions were less productive summer or winter. My first big hit on the water took place in some of the most horrendous wind conditions I can ever remember fishing in. I set-up in the First Bay in calm conditions and within the next 24 hours, a storm blasted across Shropshire which uprooted trees and bivvies in its wake. My original game plan had been to fish the far rushline as usual, but when the big wind hit this proved impossible and I resorted to fishing two-bait stringers as far as I could cast - which just happened to be three quarters across. Serendipity. In between hanging onto the brolly pole which eventually snapped, I had five takes in as many hours, landing a brace of twenties and three doubles. I thought this was a freak occurrence due to the weather at first, so on my next trip I still fished a rod on the rushline and a rod on the three quarter across mark. The two fish I caught on the next trip came from open water. I was now convinced that fishing open water in a situation where most were fishing the rushline would be the most productive approach. This was confirmed when summer turned to winter. Steve and I intended to fish right through and fish the lake very seriously, as we still had it virtually to ourselves, but realised that situation would not last forever. We started off fishing the three-quarters across line and I continued to catch fish, whilst Steve still struggled. He'd had one fish from the water in total, despite his efforts. One particularly calm, mildish day, we both noticed very tiny bubbles rising to the surface in short bursts of three or four in several different places. The bubbles were very small, and at first, we thought they were probably natural gas emissions. However, when we

Hawk Lake, magnificent, beautiful and wild.

watched the bubbling through binoculars we were able to detect slight movement. The bubbling was appearing at the surface at the half-way to just under half-way mark. These had to be carp feeding. We repositioned our rigs to the half-way mark and I caught fish fairly quickly and went on to enjoy success on that line throughout the winter. That winter, we concentrated on the wide bays at either end of the lake because that was where we thought concentrations of fairly sluggish fish would be. The water was slightly deeper, and because the areas were more open would be most affected by warm wind and sunshine. It seemed to me that if you offered a carp a stretch of water thirty yards wide or a stretch of water eighty yards wide, they would choose the latter in the winter. Choosing to concentrate on the bays at either end proved to be the right decision. We kept the bait going into these areas when packing up to keep the fish actively feeding - a lesson I'd learned from Brian - and we'd generally fish a midweek overnighter and weekends. I had some superb catches - particularly on the overnighters - with some good multiple catches in horrendous conditions, although Steve continued to struggle. This mystified us, with the only factor we could think of being that I had first choice of swim by agreement, being the driver and having to go considerably out of the way to pick Steve up. But having said that, Steve was on an identical bait just a few yards away. His rigs were much better than mine - I tended just to throw things together - and he was much better organised than me. I had no organisation whatsoever. It didn't seem plausible that the fish were so localised that there were no carp in front of Steve. It seemed to be just pure luck on my part. Not for the first time - and it wouldn't be the last!

We'd both put a snide third rod out after dark - after all we were often the only anglers fishing a forty acre water in a remote spot - and I tended to fish this rod in a very lazy fashion. I'd chuck it out anywhere and just stick a bottom bait and stringer on it because I couldn't be bothered testing a third pop-up rig out in the dark. Interestingly, this started to produce just as many fish as the pop-up rods and I began to think that we had been overestimating the need to keep the hookbait above the silt.

By mid-March, I'd caught a lot of Hawk fish. I'd caught eleven twenties - a good total for that time and that water. That was a lot more than anyone else. I'd caught those fish by adapting my tactics largely as the result of accidental occurrences, although undoubtedly establishing a good quality bait had helped considerably. It had started to come together and I think I could have really gone on to do some real damage the following season, if I hadn't decided to concentrate on the southern pits. Steve eventually got amongst the fish on our final two trips of the winter, which included a memorable final week session when we caught a number of fish after spending hours smashing up the ice which threatened to ruin a glorious close. Satisfying as well, was that Brian and Bob, went a little bit quieter too.......te, he!

....

I continued to fish Hawk on and off for the next couple of seasons, but not with any great intensity. I was still successful though, and still learned a great deal on my occasional summer visits and more frequent winter visits to the water. I seemed to catch fewer fish than others, but had the knack of catching a high proportion of twenties - although I never caught one of the handful of fish into the upper twenties the water then contained. The water became more widely known over that period of time and a lot more carp anglers started to fish the water which made the fishing more problematic.

The carp still moved on a warm wind but the fish also moved when pressured by anglers, although it took me some time to really realise this. On a south westerley, a good number of fish would end up in The Monastery and The Maze. You'd catch one or two over a period of a day or so, but the fish would move back down the lake after a few had been picked off. Anyone

Fishing on, despite the odds.

fishing the Little Monastery Bay further down would catch as the fish moved past. If you were fishing the Monastery you tried to work out how many fish were still left as you picked a couple off. Interestingly, the fish seemed to tolerate more pressure lower down the lake, particularly in the First and Second Bays. It seemed possible to draw a line across the water in the centre around peg 60, and regard either side of this mark as two different lakes in terms of fish behaviour and movement.

It was possible to catch fish at Hawk at any time of the night or day, but most of my multiple catches came at night. Day carp and night carp are two very different animals. I think fish that feed at night are easier to catch than fish that feed during the day, because they are much more tolerant of unnatural activity such as bait and leads landing in the water, carp being hooked near them and so on. It seemed that at night, fish would move past and clear up any baits in front of them including the hookbait. If you didn't top the swim up with bait no more takes were forthcoming as the fish moved on past to the next food source. Provided you kept bait going in you could have several runs before the carp moved on past. In the day, it was more difficult to do this as the fish seemed much more conscious of bait going in and would melt away at the first signs of unnatural activity.

Technically speaking, nothing developed rig-wise over this period, although I had another of those pleasant accidents. People started to experience problems when using back-leads. The fashion was for heavy leads and on picking up a hookbait, the carp would move parallel to the water for a good way before giving any indication at the buzzer end when using back-leads. As a solution, many resorted to fishing with rod tips virtually touching bottom to enable the line to be sunk but also to ensure direct indication to the buzzer. I'd also adopted this approach which worked satisfactorily. However, on one session I fished a swim with a wooden platform out in front which made it difficult to position the rods with the tip sunk. I opted for back-leads again, but decided to try lighter leads of 1.5oz, which I thought would increase the number of full blooded runs as opposed to drop-backs. This was another stroke of fortune, as I found I was getting more runs and deeper hookholds as the fish had become used to feeling for resistance from the heavy leads others were using. Light-leading proved another vital edge, in a situation where everyone was fishing virtually identically with big leads.

Around this time, Steve and I became pre-occupied with trying to find areas of the bottom that were different from the norm - areas of light silt deposits or hard spots. We felt if we could find areas of difference we could

First Hawk carp. "Some guys have all the luck."

present baits more cleanly. There were two well-known areas of hard bottom in the lake - a small area at the far side of the First Bay underneath a tree and a largish hard patch in a swim in one of the narrow stretches. These had been discovered and produced many, many fish. In truth, though, they had been hammered and had ceased to be so productive. We reasoned though, that if we could find harder patches or lighter silt deposits elsewhere we could reap the benefits before they got fished out. We spent an awful lot of time plumbing and casting leads, and we did find particular areas in most swims where the silt was thinner and found a couple of small harder bottomed areas of clay. We caught fish off these areas - but they were one rod spots - and we caught almost as many carp on the other rod in the softer silt. So, whilst I would argue that it is always better to fish in areas of light silt deposits or hard-bottomed areas surrounded by soft silt because hookbait presentation is made more efficient, do not follow this advice all the time. It is far better to pin-point areas where the carp actually feed, and these spots can very often be very silty areas which should not be ignored. Generally on Hawk, I put my rigs in the spots where I had caught fish from before in a particular swim. Either they got picked up or they didn't, but usually the same old silty spots produced time after time on Hawk - probably because most of the carp were always moving and they tended to follow pretty predictable routes when they did. I also think another reason for my silty spots staying productive was that most swims were more or less featureless on the bottom, and so every angler approached each swim differently. Consequently, no particular spots took a continuous hammering. The carp had definitely become nervous about picking baits up off the two hard spots I mentioned earlier. They were so well known that anyone fishing either swim naturally put a bait there. I remember one of the Patshull lads, Jason, caught some good fish off the hard spot in the narrows, including the biggest mirror in the lake. But it died on him and he experienced blank after blank on the spot after that initial success, due to the carp always finding a rig on it.

Abandoning the slavish adherence to the advice to fish the rushline opened our eyes to just how close to the near bank some of the carp patrolled and fed. For example in one of the smaller bays, the Little Monastery Bay, we found one very productive spot - summer and winter - was so close in to the near bank that it could be reached with an under-arm flick of the rod. As I said earlier, it was only in the very narrow stretches that fish tended to hug the rushline.

What we did definitely establish was that particular types of silt - dark, sour silt - should be avoided. There was one particular area in the Monastery Bay where some inflow of dubious looking origin entered the water. Baits and leads cast in the vicinity of this inflow came back black and foul-smelling and we could never get a take from that area. Similarly, there were one or two small bays on the rushline that were perpetually in the shade due to overhanging trees. The silt here was dark and contained a lot of flotsam and jetsam. Again, this was best avoided as baits fished here were just not taken and the carp seemed to skirt around these little dark bays.

The two significant developments over this two year period related to baits.

The first development was single-handedly pioneered by Steve Knowles. As I said earlier, Steve was a floater fanatic, and was determined to turn the resistant Hawk carp into floater feeders. One trip, I dropped him off on the way to Rodney Meadow and he'd brought with him a mass of mixers. He was determined to get them onto these in the hot conditions which then prevailed.

I was sceptical, but on my return found that he had indeed caught some fish on the surface. Others seeing his success had jumped on the bandwagon and were pouring floaters into the lake. It was a lesson in determination and showed that if you believed and persisted in a particular method it would pay off eventually. I've tried to copy Steve's approach on non-floater waters - like the Tip Lake and the Mangrove - without success, because I don't have the self-belief in floaters or the patience in the method that Steve has. I have no doubt that he would catch some carp off the surface on either of those two waters, given the chance to apply himself.

The second development was the conquering of Hawkstone by the ready-made boilie, specifically, the Richworth Tutti Fruitti boilie. The influx of anglers on the water had also coincided with the popularity of this particular ready-made bait and it was being tipped into the water by the barrow-load. They were taking fish with great regularity as few other types of boilies were going into the water. Our little baiting team had drifted apart and gone on to other waters. It seemed silly to me to try to fish against such a quantity of bait going into the water. My baits were nutritionally better, but the amount I could possibly introduce compared to the daily avalanche of Tutti's going into the water was negligible, given the limited time I had to fish at my disposal. It seemed sensible to jump on the bandwagon whilst it lasted. So I bought a load of Tutti Fruitti's as did Steve. We caught on them straight away and some good fish too. I publicised a couple of fish I caught on them in the angling press and got a bit of stick for it in *Carpworld* because a self-confessed "bait-buff" had resorted to such an approach. I couldn't see a problem, as it was simply carp "taking advantage of the most available food source" to quote Wilton. I knew the success of these sorts of baits wouldn't last - they were not nutritional enough for that - but I was simply cashing in. Others were effectively baiting up for me and with my knowledge of the water I was going to catch anyway. I could have tried to disguise

Two-Tone at 24lb plus. Winter capture from the Monastery Bay.

what I was using like others did. Paul Ainsworth, a very successful Hawk regular, used to put his Tutti's into an anonymous plastic bag and referred to them as "Shrewsbury Specials" firmly tongue in cheek!

As the cold water came, we customised our Tutti's to increase their pulling power. They were the perfect attractor bait. Our method was to put the frozen Tutti's into a large polythene bag which already contained a couple of mls of our booster attractor. One of our favourites was Nutrabaits Cajouser attractor, closely followed by Premier's Mungo Juice. We'd give the bag a good shake to ensure full dispersal of the liquid attractor which would then be sucked into the baits as they thawed. A primitive version of bait soaks, I suppose. Pop-ups we'd make by baking a thawed Tutti in an oven at Gas Mark 4, then removing the baits before they developed brown patches. On talking to my good friend Bob Baker a couple of years later, he confirmed to me that he had also had most success on his baits when adding "custom" smells. They were tremendously successful for us, those baits, although we both knew that they wouldn't last forever. That is the problem with baits that rely on pure attraction. Once the carp have eaten a number of attractor baits they learn that they don't gain much from them and you have to change the attractors to fool them back on to the base ingredients again. You're not fishing with food, you're fishing with a smell that mimics food. I've seen it on Rodney, Harefield, Halsnead and Grey Mist. You have to be sure about a range of different attractor combinations to have confidence fishing like that. If I went onto Hawk with those customised Tutti's today I'm sure I could still catch one or two carp on them. But I'm equally sure that if I wanted to take it apart I'd have to use a nutritional fishmeal or combination nutritional bait. That's the difference stated boldly.

By the late 1980's the quality fishmeals had begun to dominate the water. Almost a decade later, they still do.

Hawk was the only water I've fished where I really felt it was a better winter water than a summer one. The water contained a big head of fish but it was not easy and the winter fishing was difficult. However, in the winter the fish definitely shoaled up in certain areas of the water in great numbers and providing you could find them you could catch them. Carp were always in numbers in the First Bay, the middle of the Second Bay around peg 16 and in The Monastery. I concentrated on these areas and always caught consistently. There may have been other areas holding fish, but when I fished the water there wasn't the angling pressure to force me to try elsewhere. If you got a take, it was never an isolated feeder and you caught

One of the good twenties caught in the hurricane session. The five fish I caught in as many hours told me I'd been doing it all wrong.

several within the space of a few hours. It was still hard though, because although you were on fish you had to wait for them to feed, which didn't happen every day. I'd often think after experiencing nothing for a day or two days that the fish had moved. But they had not. They were still there but not yet feeding. The secret was being there when they did - and this is still the secret of winter fishing today. I fish Birch Grove in winter today and it is the same there. I'm on fish, but just waiting for them to switch on and feed. Others I know think they have done something wrong, or their bait or rig is useless when they struggle to catch. This is rarely the case in the winter.

Just wait and they will come. Keep putting that bait in and importantly, keep going - that is what I learned from winter fishing at Hawkstone.

....

I have wonderful memories of Hawk, but I also remember witnessing the most appalling example of bad carp angling there I have ever seen. One very cold winter, a local chap started fishing the water for the first time. He was quite an experienced angler - I'd heard of his success on other waters in the area. First trip, he set-up in the First Bay, put two rigs on the rushline and proceeded to spod-up with pound after pound of tiger nuts. This was followed by our chap catapulting several hundred boilies out. I gazed on in amusement, but said nothing.

I walked round to the golf course opposite early afternoon, to put a few baits out before packing up. As I walked past and level with his pitch, I could clearly see both of his rigs on the bottom in a foot of clear water, with resplendent yellow boilies popped-up. There were no signs of tiger nuts or free boilies, so they must have been dropping short. As I was packing-up, he caught a coot on both rods which didn't surprise me. For the next five weekends, our hero went through exactly the same ritual - spodding out thousands of tigers, rigs to the rushline, firing out boilies etc, despite the fact that he saw me fishing half-way across with just stringers and catching fish. All he caught were coots, and plenty of them, for there were thousands of these resident in his swim looking for all those free baits. I just couldn't work out what was going through his mind or what his tactics were intending to produce. Peter Scott would have had a coronary if he'd been exposed to the sight of all of those coots being hooked and played! His swim was a mass of feathers. I began to wonder if he was actually fishing for coots...

One weekend, our hero turned up only to find his beloved swim taken. Some lunatic had interpreted all the coots being present in the swim as a sure sign that carp were there too. I saw the chap set-up next to Bob Tapken in the Second Bay. I knew what would happen next, as our chap got out the bucket of tigers and proceeded to fill up the first load into his spod. As the first salvo hit the water, Tapper's head shot out of the bivvy. The coots in the First Bay screamed out and fought with each other for pole position as they scampered across the surface to enjoy the feast being served up for them in the Second Bay. On the second load, Tapper stood up and gave chappie the

Big common known as Arthur. One of the Tutti Fruitti captures.

old Clint Eastwood scowl. As the third scud blasted the surface, it was hands on hips, with great nervous agitation clear. As the fourth scud was in flight, Tapper ran up the bank screaming, "I want to see your ticket, I want to see your ticket!" As chappie was about to fill up his baitdropper again, Tapper had grabbed him by the throat. Much shouting and bawling followed, but I did hear our friend crying out loudly in his defence, "but I haven't had chance to put out any of my boilies yet!"

A veil is best drawn over the proceedings which followed. Two middle-aged, overweight men, bawling at each other and rolling around the bank arguing over something as insignificant in the world as carp fishing was not a pretty sight....

It also turned out Bob couldn't ban him or confiscate his ticket either - because he didn't have one!

Halsnead Park in winter. Inset: Cold, soggy common and angler at Halsnead.

A pretty Crab Mill upper double caught from the Snag Swim which can be seen in the background.

Arfur' - third capture. Caught on Opening Day at Crab Mill.

A superb Crab 20 plus linear and an old Terry Eustace bivvy!

What I went to Halsnead for - my first twenty pound common.

Superb, hard-fighting twenty-two pounds plus common. Winter again.

Chunky winter twenty from the First Bay at Hawk Lake.

An upper double taken in a blizzard at Hawk Lake.

Opening Day set-up in the Second Bay at Hawk Lake.

Returning a Church Pool twenty to the clear depths

A 25lb common on a boilie - one of the few nights the eels went to sleep.

The Black Common. A lovely 22lb fish caught in very cold conditions.

The fish known as The Corpse, caught at Church Pool on the Garlic/Blue Cheese HNV.

The Road Bank at Church Pool, taken during the first year of the syndicate when the water was particularly weedy.

A brace of commons caught at Rodney Meadow during the commons only session.

A long, mean fighting machine caught on floater at Church Pool.

A classically-proportioned Church Pool twenty plus.

One-Eyed Jack from Rodney Meadow at 24lb plus.

The Pet. My second capture of this beast at 31lb 4oz.

Part-time exhibitionist, John Buckley, freeing a fish from the surface of a Rodney Meadow bar.

A superb twenty from The Corner at Rodney Meadow.

The Church Pool

"Cultivate your luck. Prop it up with omens and sign of good purport. Watch for magpies on your path. Form the habit of avoiding old women who squint. Throw salt over your left shoulder. Touch wood with the forefinger of your right hand whenever you are not doing anything else. Be on friendly terms with a black cat. Turn your money under the new moon. Walk around ladders. Don't start on a Friday. Stir the materials for Christmas pudding and wish. Perform all other rites as you know or hear of. These things are important in carp fishing".
H.T. Sheringham Coarse Fishing 1912.

All habitual carp anglers will one day fish a water that will be a bogey water. The Church Pool at Patshull I consider to have been mine. I did catch a few good fish from the lake and others have said to me that they consider I did as well as most on the water. I am not inclined to agree. My usual luck deserted me for once. One of the other reasons I regard it as my bogey water was that when I did catch a fish - with the exception of those I caught off the surface when floater fishing - I never quite knew why I had caught it. Knowing why is important if you want to apply experience gained to future waters.

The water had been a rather expensive day-ticket water for several years and noted for its head of superb-looking common carp into the big twenties, that had been stocked into it from the nearby Great Lake. It was a classic-looking carp water with its mature wooded banks, beds of Norfolk reeds and pads dotted the margins of the gin-clear water. In the first couple of seasons, it had provided quite easy fishing and lots of people caught lots of big twenty pound commons. But as always happens, the fish wised-up in the end, and the day-ticket fishing became very difficult with most fish falling in the last hour of fishing before darkness - a sure sign the carp had matured. Then the decision was taken to operate a syndicate on the water which would mean night fishing would be allowed. Visions of bagging-up with loads of big commons were too much for the little group of carp anglers I was fishing with at the time and we all joined on inception. Brian, Tapper and myself joined the syndicate, whilst Steve Allcott being a local lad was granted privileged membership of the club which controlled the water.

What a rush of blood to the head that decision to join the syndicate was!

The notion that the fish would be throwing themselves on the bank after dark, proved to be a folly as although night time did prove to be the best time to catch, the fishing was slow, not least because the huge head of eels that populated the water devoured boilies with relish.

I made a preliminary visit in July - with the other lads concentrating their efforts elsewhere - and was rewarded with a 14lb mirror off the top in the sweltering morning heat. After dark, the eels murdered me. The Optonic would bleep once or twice within seconds of the boilie touching bottom and on retrieval the baits would be gone. I don't like eels. To be honest, I despise them with a vengeance and would cheerfully wipe them all off the face of the earth if I could. It amazes me that people actually set out to fish for the horrible perishers. Something deeply Freudian there perhaps. There was certainly something deeply Freudian going on at the bottom of the Church Pool which must have resembled a Medusa-like writhing mass, that insisted on eating my very expensive and carefully hand-rolled boilies.

On reporting back to the lads on the big adventure, it was decided to leave the water alone until October when hopefully Anguilla Anguilla had gone night, night, in the cooler water. Brian in particular, was very supportive of this course of action. He is very frightened of eels and his face was a mask of horror as I recounted the tale. I added the odd embellishment of monster eels peering up at me from the dark whilst I tried to extract the hook, just for effect.

On a cold October morning, Garner and I set forth. There were one or two locals on the water who greeted us in a fairly friendly manner. I was prepared for this but Brian wasn't. I think he expected to be met with the open aggressive hostility with which he generally greets others who dare to come to fish his waters! They don't talk English properly in this area of the country but I was already experienced at translating the Black Country dialect, having spent some of my student years downing copious amounts of Bank's beer in the area.

"Youm be best drippin' in wez Baz beein fishin on t'agin bawrel. Aagh. Baz 'e yad a twentee. Mus' bee sum daaan there coss e's a ussless bugger e' is. Uum."

Brian scratched his head, somewhat bemused at the local's advice, but I understood the pidgin English perfectly and I pointed to the Barrel's Swim, so-called because two large buoys were sited on the surface in the pitch. I went in on the right, Brian on the left.

After an hour, I noticed a strong smell of garlic in the swim. This worried me in case I had somehow absent-mindedly overdone the smell level in the baits. Close inspection of the grass surrounding the bivvy revealed that whoever Baz was, he had kindly left behind in his wake a considerable amount of boilies. One consolation was that at least they hadn't been dumped in the swim. Or had they? I spent the next two nights in a state of sleepless paranoia, for I had inadvertantly gone into Baz's swim when I actually thought I'd tucked Brian up by putting him in it. One possible consolation was that at least Baz and I were using the same smell! Brian thought it all very amusing...

On the final morning - after a protracted fight - he landed the most magnificent common either of us had seen. It was a mid-twenty with massive shoulders. It was later christened Tyson. I blanked.

The local had Brian bemused again, with the comment he made as he put the superb fish back, "Youm mus' be disappointed with 'im. E's ownlee the average size o' fisssh for the water. Aaagh. Uuum.."

. . . .

That fish encouraged us. We decided as a group to fish the water that winter but not too heavily as we were still intending to fish Hawk. We fished alternate weekends. We all went in on the Garlic/Blue Cheese milk protein bait, thinking that few of the locals were using good nutritional baits. Ready-mades seemed to be the most common bait going into the water. Rig-wise we would see how it went. Standard pop-up or bottom bait rigs would be used, depending on which the fish seemed to prefer. We'd bait sparingly when fishing - using stringers at most - but bait up when leaving to keep the fish looking for bait and to get it established.

In truth, that winter was a good one for myself and Brian on the lake, but not so good for Bob who blanked save for one small fish. Steve only fished a couple of times - without success - for he was starting to get afflicted with the Colne Valley wanderlust and we didn't see much of him. The Church Pool was quite heavily fished throughout that winter but we did quite well. I tended to concentrate on the Boards side of the lake; as by the time I could get to the water on a Friday evening all of the bank swims would be taken. Brian who could manage to get there early Friday or even Thursdays, usually fished on The Meadow towards the dam end of the lake, which was on the

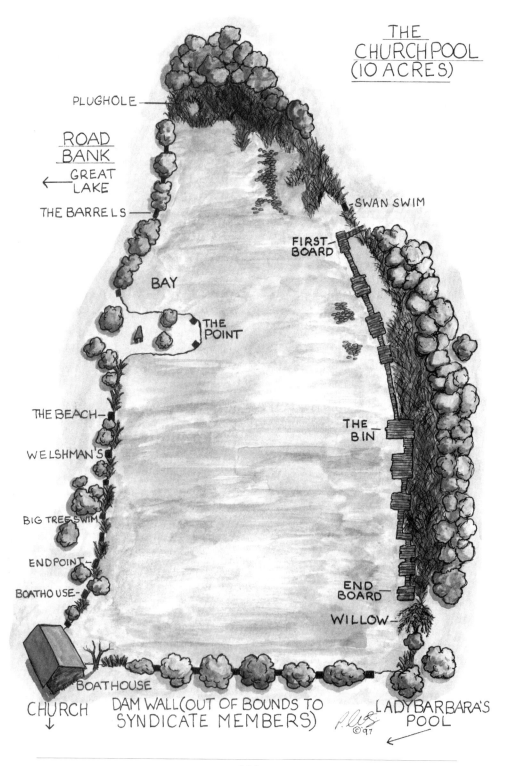

THE
CHURCH POOL
(10 ACRES)

PLUGHOLE —

ROAD
BANK
← GREAT
LAKE

THE BARRELS —

— SWAN SWIM

FIRST-
BOARD

BAY

THE
POINT

THE BEACH —

THE
BIN

WELSHMAN'S

BIG TREE SWIM

ENDPOINT —

BOATHOUSE —

END
BOARD

WILLOW —

BOATHOUSE

CHURCH
↓

DAM WALL (OUT OF BOUNDS TO
SYNDICATE MEMBERS)

LADY BARBARA'S
POOL
←

end of south-westerlies which dominated that particular winter.

Most of my fish were basically the result of flukey casts out in the dark with stringers and bottom baits which landed somewhere in the water, mainly from the swim on the Boards side known as The Corpse.

Therein lies a tale. The swim was named after a former regular day ticket angler who was given the unfortunate nickname of The Corpse. According to legend, this was because he had a ghostly, pallid complexion, stared out with empty, piercing eyes at the water and refused to reply to or even acknowledge others who tried to speak to him. His nose constantly dribbled. So the story goes, he was fishing this particular swim one day and he caught a 19lb common. Ordinarily, that would have pleased most people but not The Corpse, for on that particular session everyone around him was catching twenties. Because the fish was a mere 19 pounder he was seen to curse and wail and then kick the fish back into the water! The fish, though obviously damaged, was seen to swim off. The Corpse was banned from the water, although a lot of people wanted to kick him in it.

Coincidentally, my best fish from the Church Pool that winter was that very same common, which was christened The Corpse and I caught it ironically, from The Corpse swim. It had one eye missing and had a pronounced lump on one side, presumably where it had been given the Dr Martin's treatment. It hadn't been seen since it had been so disgracefully treated two years earlier. When I caught it, it was a mid-twenty. This illustrated the richness of the water in that such a damaged fish could continue to grow and flourish. I'm told it is now a thirty. I caught a few other fish that particular winter, including several twenties. Although I was using a good bait and rig, I never really understood why I caught those fish for I never identified any feeding patterns or definite hotspots. I might just as well have cast out blindfolded.

Brian did even better and, importantly, he knew why, for he had found a number of fish and the means to catch them and he enjoyed consistent success that winter with some big fish in the upper-twenties range. The Dam Wall was out of bounds to mere syndicate members and could only be fished by club members who paid just a fraction of the fees paid by syndicate members. Most of the club members were floatmen and there were just one or two carp anglers who seemed to go into hibernation during the winter and hang up the rods. On the Boards side there was quite a long reed-lined stretch between the End Board and the Dam Wall which was a favoured spot. It could only normally be reached from the Dam Wall or from the End

Board. It seemed to be a constant fish-holding area. In a winter dominated by mild south westerlies, it was always likely to be the area to try. Put an expert extreme range caster like Brian Garner on the Meadow swims by the dam - in the End Point or the swim on the right of the Big Tree pitch - and it could be reached from that area too, providing no one was fishing the Dam Wall which, fortunately for Brian, was a rare event. Brian was never an angler to waste an opportunity when one was presented to him and he seized it and fished very well. He fished single pop-ups just off the rushline at around 120-140 yards depending on the swim fished.

Some anglers seem to have reservations about fishing single baits in winter. I have no such reservations, for whilst I often prefer to fish a stringer in winter, I have no problem confidence-wise in using a single bait at ranges where the stringer becomes unrealistic, or when I think fishing a single bait will give me a better chance of a fish than a stringer. I'm talking about a single pop-up bait here rather than a single bottom bait. The latter I do have little confidence in. Having confidence in a single pop-up bait was something Brian Garner taught me by his example. On the extreme range waters such as Redesmere and Harefield, I've never seen any angler capable of casting stringers 140 yards in a strong cross wind - despite claims I've seen in articles - and a single bait on fish is always going to be better than a hookbait and free baits where there aren't any carp. Fishing the far bank paid off for Brian, but such a tactic couldn't be employed today, as the Dam Wall at the Church Pool

Looking across from The Point to the End Board.

is heavily carp fished all year round.

In order to keep the fish active in the area and looking for baits, he baited up along the reed-line before leaving. Keeping a constant supply of bait going into a swim holding fish is vital in winter. If food isn't being introduced regularly, the carp are more likely to go into complete shutdown in cold water. The classic example was the very heavily stocked Birch Grove of the early 1980's. This small water contained at least 400 doubles then and in a typical day's summer fishing it was easy to catch a dozen or so fish. In the autumn, the water closed for duck shooting and only opened up again towards the back-end of the winter. Regular summer anglers used to pile down there when it re-opened expecting to catch but they were always disappointed. With no bait going in for several weeks in the late autumn and winter the fish had slowed down completely. It took a fair bit of bait to go into the water again for the carp to get into feeding mode and eventually a few would get caught in the final days of the season.

Bait must continue to go in then, to keep the carp active. Whilst carp aren't in the torpid, semi-hibernating state they will feed regularly each day in the winter in brief spells. I think too, carp feed with much less caution than in the summer months where they feed for longer periods and are presented with a greater variety of food sources. Carp test baits out much more often in summer than in winter. In the winter, they seem to activate into feeding mode and wolf any bait near them down in a determined "I'm having that" manner. Some of my best multiple catches have come in winter in these short feeding spells, when they seem to throw caution to the winds.

For this reason, I always use two landing nets in the winter and keep a ready-baited spare rod on standby. You might ask why - although if you remember my Halsnead one-rod winter you'll remember why. In cold water, carp are grouped in tight shoals and tend to feed all at the same time. I've lost count of the number of times I've had a brace of fish in a feeding spell lasting 10 minutes or less. It can be days before the next short feeding spell in a typical winter. By the time you've hooked, played, landed, weighed, photographed and returned a fish you are talking about 15 - 20 minutes by which time the feeding spell might have finished. When I get a run, I play and land the fish and it is then retained in one of the landing nets. The spare baited rod is cast out to the same spot that produced the take, the spare landing net is placed at the ready and only then is the landed fish dealt with. This way I maximise productive fishing time. I've also found on some waters - a winter Capesthorne was a good example - that the carp will only pick-up baits that have been in the water for a certain period of time. At Capesthorne this was about an hour. Getting the hookbait out as quickly again as possible in the winter is vitally important.

That first year of the syndicate (1986, if memory serves), was the only season when our little band put in anything like a serious campaign on the Church Pool. As friends, we began to drift apart. Steve was already fishing Savay, and by the following season I'd begun fishing in the south. Brian and Bob started to drift elsewhere but remained members for another year until they settled on the Mangrove. I stayed a member of the syndicate for the next three years or so, but my fishing on the water was limited and followed a pretty predictable pattern. I'd fish the opening weekend of the season. It was a pleasant place to open up on with the lads always organising some sort of social event and a few fish were always caught in the first week, mainly off the surface. I always caught at least one fish off the surface on the opening weekend when the fish had forgotten their usual caution. After that, I would only fish the lake for two or three weekends in the winter.

The syndicate fee was quite high to justify this limited fishing approach I suppose, but I always hoped that something would happen in terms of the eel problem. If the eels disappeared I then felt I would really do well on the water. The club brought in a professional eel trapper to try to sort them out but his nettings were abandoned due to the depth of the water - twelve to fifteen feet on average. When the eels were brought to the surface they died which meant they lost their commercial value. One freezing winter's night, one of the club members beckoned me into the boathouse which was built on brick stilts over the water. He had something to show me. It was a large boathouse with a lot of lake water underneath it. He lifted up a floorboard and shone a torch into the clear dark depths. The torchlight revealed what looked initially like millions of long grey candles rising up from the bottom. What I was actually seeing was thousands of eels lying vertically in suspended animation. The sight of those tiny, ghostly eyes reflected in the torch beam made the hairs on the back of my neck creep. A sinister thought crossed my mind..... With a bundle of dynamite I could blow up the boathouse and take them all out in one fell swoop! In the end, I decided this would be a rash course of action no matter how satisfying the end result. It was a fairly liberal-minded club, but I suspected that blowing up an ancient boathouse and probably half of Pattingham would inevitably lead to at least a year's ban!

The only thing I ever learned at Patshull, served to confirm what I already knew to some extent. It was a winter lesson. In my last winter on the water, John Freeman, a regular on the water (he had actually put the fish into the lake from the Great Lake) had an incredible run of winter success with numerous fish when everyone else was struggling. This was unusual, for although John tended to fish every day on the water in the summer and autumn living local as he did, he had never previously fished in the winter for carp, preferring to fish elsewhere for pike. I studied what he did with great interest. First of all, he selected an area he knew held carp in the winter but which it was difficult to reach with a degree of accuracy from any adjoining swim. This was on the Boards side of the lake and in front of a long walk-way which had platform swims some way away from it. It could be reached by a longish cast from the opposite Road Bank but not with pin-point accuracy. This area he baited every single day with his usual ready-made Tutti Fruitti boilies to keep the carp interested. He fished only days - never at night - for it was difficult to set-up comfortably or safely on a narrow walkway. He'd blow a few baits out on arrival and cast out a single hookbait. Invariably, he'd catch at least one fish - in a water where the average fish was over twenty pounds in the winter. I was fishing very infrequently, but kept track of his progress via the telephone. One weekend I was on the water and witnessed him catch a couple of twenties. He was up to something else and knowing I fished the water too rarely to be a threat, he showed me what he was up to. He was using normal Tutti Fruitti bottom baits but with a pair of scissors was trimming away the middle of the bait to expose the soft centre. He called it his "apple core" rig for that is what it eventually looked like. I asked him what he thought the advantages of this were. John felt that with baiting up each day prior to fishing, his free baits would have started to break down when eaten by the fish. Thus a bait that already appeared to be breaking up would be regarded as much safer than a normal round and solid bait and would be more readily taken. Secondly, an

THE APPLE CORE RIG

exposed inner would release a higher concentration of attractors - pulling the fish down onto the hookbait.

I felt at the time and still do, that the latter factor was the most important and the cut-up bait would have a similar effect as a soaked bait. It seemed to me that the second factor John cited contradicted the first in that any bait that has started to break down would lose most of its flavour. Thus, the apple-cored fresh bait would have had a much higher smell factor and so not be considered as safe as the surrounding baits - if it is at all possible for a carp to be that clever. I don't think a carp can be and I don't think a carp cares to discriminate between baits according to their physical appearance. John would have had to use hookbaits that had been soaked in a jar of cold water for the same length of time as his free offerings to convince me of his first argument. (Room for experiment here, chaps?). I do think carp prefer to pick-up baits when the attractor level is right - which explains why carp persistently pick-up baits in certain waters after they have been out in the water for a certain period of time.

I think John would have caught just as many fish on conventional Tutti Fruitti boilies. The key factors for me were:

a. *Keeping a regular trickle of bait going into a good, winter swim holding carp.*

b. *No one else fishing the area to pressurise the fish or introduce other baits.*

c. *Being able to fish that baited swim every day.*

d. *Being a good and attentive carp angler.*

....

The summer fishing I always considered more difficult than the winter fishing. The eels restricted both night and day fishing to baits that they had difficulty with. Tiger nuts and other hard nuts such as brazils and walnuts, were the most resistant bait and invariably, these were fished over hemp or another mass bait. It became a tired method on the water through overuse and it was noticeable when wading, that clouds of rotting hemp and nuts would rise to the surface, blackened by the silt. The amount of rod hours per fish was silly, simply because the method was so stereotypical. Fish were caught still, but on observation this tended to be due to where the bait was fished. If it was fished in open water and in the main body of the lake, people tended to struggle. If it was fished in areas normally considered safe by the carp they could be caught more easily. This led to Church Pool anglers adopting a particular method of fishing which I did not agree with, and this was one of the main reasons I rarely fished it in the summer save for the opening. Members often used chest waders to bait up the margins on the pool. It was possible to do this, because there were no accumulations of soft, deep silt which made walking on the bottom easy. Chest waders made it easy to put out tight beds of hemp or whatever and ensure the hookbait was spot on. That was fair enough, in my mind. On the Boards side of the lake there were two extensive beds of reeds on either side of the walkway, and on the Road Bank there was a large bed of reeds dotted here and there with pads in the corner. During the day, carp invariably liked to lie up in these three areas. Some members then simply walked into the reeds and hand-placed a hookbait in this normally safe area because, of course, it was not possible to cast into reed beds. It was then necessary to just walk back to the swim, peeling line from the spool. When a take occurred, it was rare to get a full run because the fish was in a dense reed bed, but some indication would be apparent. The angler would then simply wade back into the reedbed complete with landing net and scoop up the weeded-up fish. No matter how I looked at it, this did not seem to be carp fishing, and I for one, would not resort to this method just to catch a fish. Many of the bottom caught fish were caught in this manner.

I remember one particular opening weekend I had a group of three carp feeding on floaters on the Road Bank in open water in front of a bed of pads. They were growing in confidence and I was certain that one would take the hookbait. They were all big fish. Suddenly, I saw rippling waves emerging from the Norfolk reeds behind the pads. Initially, I thought it might be a big fish emerging from the reeds attracted by the feeding activity of the fish which was getting stronger. Two minutes later, an angler emerged from the reeds who had been fishing the far bank and had seen the fish I'd got feeding through the binoculars! He was in chest waders, floater rod in hand and now, standing two yards behind my fish against the pads in four foot of water, he prepared to cast out his float. In a flash, my fish were gone. I looked across at him and shook my head. He carried on fishing for two minutes for fish that were no longer there and then retreated back into the rushes. On another occasion, an angler caught a 24 pound common in the rushes off the End

My best mirror from the water.

Board, went in for it, scooped it up, weighed it, photographed it, returned it. Half an hour later, the same fish was caught by another member in the rushes off the Road Bank, who went in for it, scooped it up, weighed it, photographed it, returned it. When I remarked to him about the situation he couldn't see any problem. That poor fish had been man-handled out of reeds and dragged through the water onto a wooden platform and weighed and photographed. It had then swam right down to the other end of the lake to lie up to overcome the trauma, only for it to be subjected to it again. To me, fish must be allowed to have safe areas where anglers can't get to them where they can relax and not feel stressed. This is in the anglers' interest too, for whilst there are safe areas the carp isn't stressed all the time and it is more likely to feed on our baits when it leaves that safe area to feed. Carp are never completely resident in safe areas even though they may spend a lot of time in them. Most carp after capture like to lie up somewhere to recuperate and these areas are generally snaggy areas or reedbeds like those on the Church Pool. Such fish deserve to be left alone. For those reasons, I have never fished - on any water - very snaggy areas or areas I could not cast a bait to with rod and line. Unfortunately, others don't have the same ethical standards and this was the case at Patshull and it has been the case elsewhere. The worst case I remember, was on the Tip Lake at Darenth where I saw an angler - quite a well known one - perched on a tree directly above a mass of fallen trees and snags in the area known as Shithouse Bay. A known thirty was lying up after recently being captured and the guy was trying to tempt it by dropping baits on its nose. On seeing what he was up to, I asked him how he intended to land the fish without harming it since he couldn't lift a thirty straight out of the water like a two ounce roach!

His reply was, "I'll cross that bridge when I come to it."

The sad thing about that little episode was that the tree-perched angler was a bailiff on the complex!

I could not live with this method on Patshull which did account for many of the bottom caught summer fish, and when I then saw sad characters who weren't too keen to pull on chest waders getting remote control boats out, I thought it best to leave well alone until the winter. I still see bait adverts featuring grinning anglers posing with Church Pool fish caught by such methods, and I often think if only people knew how such fish had been caught, perhaps they wouldn't be so impressed with the effectiveness of the advertised baits!

On my opening session visits, I still tried boilies, mostly without success. Nine times out of ten, as soon as it started to go dark, I would get the odd bleep on the indicator, reel in and find the bait gone. One opening night, I fished with very large rock-hard boilies - around 30mm - to see if they could survive the eel onslaught. What happened was that they were just whittled down until large enough to slide down the old snake's throat. That took several hours to happen, but whilst the eels were active on the bait the carp couldn't get a look in. I'm not sure, but I think if eels are feeding on the baits carp are put off eating them, whereas if other nuisance fish are, like roach and bream, they are not. My French friends tell me that carp are definitely put off by Poisson Chat hanging around the baits and I suspect it's the same with eels. Eels are strange creatures though, and they don't seem to feed every night. You do get odd nights when for some reason they just don't feed. I experienced a couple of nights when for some unknown reason the eels were inactive. On both occasions I caught carp - which convinced me that if

A twenty three pound opening day common. Caught on mixer.

the eels ever migrated like they are supposed to or were got rid of, the water would soon become a bait water which would suit my normal fishing approach.

The other aspect to the eel problem was that quality food baits were not going in and this was limiting the growth potential of the carp. The carp had shot up from doubles to twenties very quickly but going on from there looked a problem, particularly in view of the lack of water management in relation to the fish biomass per acre. There was a huge head of largely unfished for roach and tench, with most of them of specimen size, and whilst the water was rich, it couldn't sustain an ever-increasing fish population forever. With proper management - removal of most of the roach and tench, a big effort on the eel front and so on - the water was definitely capable of producing monster fish. Unfortunately, this looked like never happening and it was one of the other reasons why I eventually left the water, besides the high cost and the lack of desire to fish it regularly.

A year after leaving, I received a telephone call from a friend who had recently joined the water. He was deliriously happy after catching Billy the big mirror and numerous other good fish. I was delighted for the fellow and congratulated him on his success. I asked him what he had caught them on. I was shocked when he said he had caught them on boilies - particularly as it was the height of summer. He'd caught one or two eels - that was all. Throughout that summer and autumn, the regulars fished confidently with boilies and caught stacks of good fish - in many cases after seasons of struggle. The eels, it seemed, had either died, migrated or whatever eels do when they vanish. I felt as sick as the proverbial parrot - for surely I would have made my mark on the water that season if I hadn't left.

Told you it was my bogey water!

Postscript: After a couple of seasons of pure heaven for anglers on the Church Pool, I am now told that the eels are back. Tee hee!

A Church Pool winter mirror. No doubt an original fish, looking ancient as it did.

Humpy again at 25lb plus.

Rodney Meadow

"If you want to do something enough, you do it."
Roger Smith

In 1986, I scraped through my driving test at the first time of asking. I became a motorist - although the three cars I was to write-off fairly quickly would probably not agree with that description if they could but speak. In fishing terms, it meant that I was no longer reliant on friends or the long-suffering Wendy to ferry me about and I could travel further afield.

I really wanted to catch a thirty pounder.

Catching a thirty locally wasn't a realistic prospect. There was only one thirty in the whole of Cheshire and Lancashire - the Redesmere female common - and the club that controlled the water didn't seem to want me as a member. There were a handful of thirties in Shropshire (there was even a forty) - one of which lived in the Church Pool which I could fish. But I had no real luck on the place and felt somehow destined not to catch that particular fish.

The angling weeklies were full of slimey, grinning Cockneys, with armfuls of huge carp. There seemed to be shedfuls of thirties down there. "Go South young man," said the prophet. It was time for me to get in on the act. There was another aspect to my thinking. I might have been one of the established bees-knees locally, but could I really cut it in the big, bad south against the local boys with all the cards up their sleeves? I wasn't learning much where I was fishing and the challenge of the southern gravel pits was appealing, as of course, were the shedfuls of thirties.

I made enquiries and bought a few tickets. The first was a season ticket

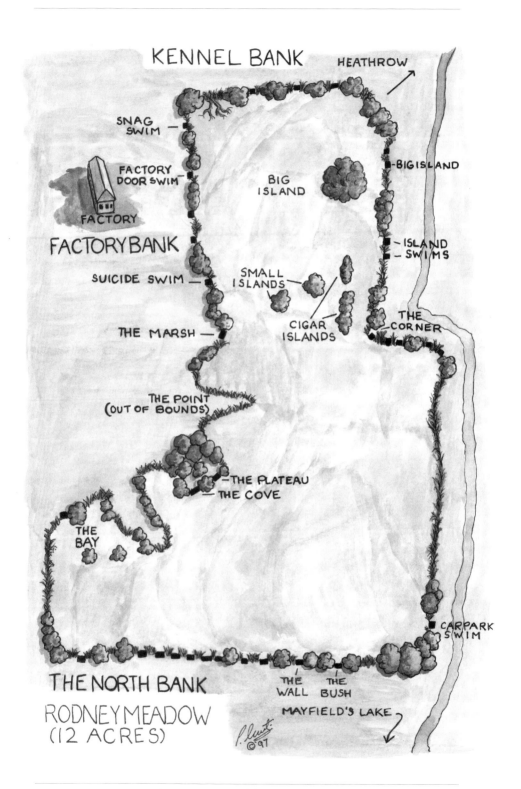

for Savay. I put my name down for the night syndicate but didn't particularly relish the prospect of trying to sleep overnight in a battered old Ford Fiesta. I purchased a ticket for Longfield. This was a fifteen quid, straight in, no questions asked job. It seemed strange to me to be able to buy such a cheap ticket for such a tiny little water containing at least one forty pounder and loads of big thirties. Did Leisure Sport know something I didn't? I also obtained a joint Harefield/Rodney Meadow ticket for the princely sum of £55 from William Boyers. Harefield I'd heard of, Rodney I hadn't. I had become an instant southern big fish man.

My southern career was somewhat delayed by a few little automobile mishaps and it was to be early August before I could embark on an exploratory three day trip. I hadn't seen any of the waters. It was a case of having a look and dropping in a swim if I fancied it. The basic aim was to get a feel for the new scene - a fish would be an undreamt of bonus.

Longfield was my first port of call. It was a lovely-looking water and one I was keen to fish. One or two quite famous anglers were fishing, as were a couple of the not so famous. The first angler I spoke to was very nice and friendly. There had been nothing out for a couple of weeks and the only two swims producing regularly were occupied more or less permanently by the aforementioned names. There was a lot of weed in the available swims - a new phenomenon for me - and I felt a little bit intimidated by it. Thrashing the water to a foam with the lead to find a clear spot wouldn't go down too well with the regulars I reckoned, so I decided not to fish the water to avoid being exposed as a complete gravel pit novice.

Harefield was the next stop, as I had no idea of how to get to Rodney Meadow even though it was quite close to Longfield. The Fiesta chugged into what used to be the Caravan Bay. The first two guys I bumped into appeared to be duck shooting! Their mean-looking fishing rods were almost angled vertically from the ground and supported thick nylon lines sticking out 15 foot above the water. A real culture shock.

Although mostly incomprehensible, they suggested that the lake was fishing so badly that I'd be better off fishing Rodney which was "fishing its 'ed orf, mate." It was back to the Fiesta and off to find Rodney. A good two hours later - after exploring the back streets of Uxbridge, Hillingdon and eventually, West Drayton, I found myself at the somewhat imposing entrance to the Rodney Meadow complex.

Half an hour later, after struggling with the rusty padlock, I found myself at the side of a beautiful carp lake. Well, it would have been a beautiful carp lake if it were not for the fact that there seemed to be a bivvy every few yards around the lake. I had never seen such pressure!

The water had been stocked with fish from Willow Pool (which I had put my name down for) which had boosted the already good stock of big fish significantly. Three thirties and ten big twenties had been introduced and as always happens with new fish when introduced into a strange water, they were getting caught. There were big twenties and thirties flying out everywhere, which was the reason it was so busy.

I had a good walk around and was beginning to think that I'd have to go back to that awful-looking Harefield, when I came across a swim that was hidden away in some bushes and which covered quite a lot of water which no one was fishing. That would do - at least I could hide myself away for a couple of days to avoid embarrassing myself. This was a swim I later discovered was called The Plateau. I set-up and got the plumbing rod out. Ten minutes of plumbing revealed no features whatsoever, just silt, silt and more silt. I'd come all this way to learn to fish gravel pits and ended up in the siltiest swim on the lake! Still, at least I was very familiar with what was in front of me!

I remember thinking as I sat on the chair after getting the baits out, that this smallish water contained more big fish than could be found in the whole county of Cheshire - and it was just a middling big fish water for the South East!

The first night was uneventful for me and I heard no other buzzers sounding. Around 9am, I found that I was attached to a fish after a screaming run. It seemed like a miracle! This turned out to be a long, lean Rodney double which fought like an animal all the way to the net. It wasn't the prettiest fish, in fact, it looked more like a long lizard than a carp but it was my first Southern carp. I now knew I could catch down here. I took the lizard round to the next swim to get it photographed. The two lads fishing it were a little puzzled by my accent and quite surprised I'd actually caught a fish from what they thought to be a no-hope swim. I spent half an hour or so talking - and, of course, clocking everything they were up to. They were regulars on the lake but clearly had not been carp fishing for many years. They were basically "instants", just add water and hey presto!

I was shocked when I saw the rigs they were using, for they would have struggled to get a pick-up in Cheshire on such crude set-ups. They were using short six-inch nylon hooklinks, a very short hair, and a heavyish fixed lead. Hooks were quite large - probably a size four. Impaled on the hair was a ready made Richworth Tutti Fruitti boilie which were in widespread use in the south by then. Incredibly, they were catching well. One chap, who later became a very good friend, Steve Newman, announced that he'd caught a thirty and now was trying to catch his first twenty! He'd caught his thirty on a Honey Yucatan and now was trying out a Tutti Fruitti!·

I had a good look at what people were up to around the water and quite simply was amazed.

Most I saw were using the same crude rigs and ready-mades. The one exception was the full-timer on the lake who seemed to be in a coma in his bivvy for most of the time. He was using tigers because he couldn't afford boilies and didn't like reeling in once he'd cast out. A tiger lasted forever on the bottom (until a carp ate it), which meant little hassle and none of that reeling in every day to re-cast nonsense. Incredible! The full-timer went by the name of Peter the Sleeper, not surprisingly.

Funnily enough, seeing those crude rigs and shop-bought baits put me in mental turmoil. Perhaps I was doing it wrong? Perhaps I was over-complicating things? I slunk back to my hidey-hole in the bushes and was troubled by what I had seen all the following night.

The following morning, again at around 9am, I found myself attached to the largest fish I had ever hooked up until that day. I played that fish for a good twenty minutes and had several close looks at it. It had to be a thirty. In the end, I lost it due to a freak accident. As I was trying to get it towards the net, it suddenly shot-off and somehow when back-winding frantically in response, my main line got caught around the reel handle of the Cardinal 55. I was in a state of absolute panic - I couldn't reel in or give line. I pressured the fish to see if I could get it in on the long line and I got it so close to the net but then it powered off again. Not being able to give line it snapped the nylon with a loud crack! I stood, shaking and somewhat bewildered at what had occurred. After a few seconds, I noticed line peeling off the other rod which had been sunk on the bottom. Thinking I had another run, I picked up the rod and started to play the fish in. It dawned on me as the fish neared the net that this wasn't a different fish but the same big one - it had picked up and got tangled around the other line as trailers often do. I'd been given another chance - but I knew in my heart I would not succeed. This was confirmed when the rig on the second rod emerged with the other line clearly wrapped around the hooklink and hook. Agonisingly, I could see the first line running out over the rig into the lake, in slow motion almost. In an instant, everything went slack and the fish was gone....

Several anglers saw the action from various parts of the lake and within minutes, the swims either side of me were taken. I was boxed in and couldn't cast out very far because I had lines going across right in front of me. Time to go.

On my final trip to the car, Peter the Sleeper's buzzer sounded - his first run for almost two weeks. Obviously, a carp had finally got irritated with his tiger nuts. I arrived in his swim to see the biggest fish in the lake at that time being landed. This was the original big fish of the lake - Big Rod - and he weighed a colossal 34lb. I couldn't believe the size of that fish. It made a huge impression on me. It was like a whale compared to anything I had caught. I had a chat with Peter about his fish and fishing. I have to say he was a very nice chap and very friendly - as was everyone.

I'd had my first taste of southern carp fishing... and I liked it. The realisation that I could catch down there and most of the anglers were maybe not as experienced as me, sunk in as I journeyed home. I'd almost caught a certain thirty on my very first trip. I had to get back down there. But that awful, awful, pressure meant that it would be almost a year before I could face going down to Rodney Meadow again.

. . . .

Sunset in Suicide.

In the close season of the following year, I received a letter from John Stent informing me that in view of the exeessive pressure on the lake, a syndicate was being formed of just 60 members and would I be interested? The fee was quite high but I felt I had to have a crack at it. I paid my money and decided that all of my summer vacation would be spent fishing Rodney Meadow in pursuit of my first thirty pounder.

That close season I thought about fishing the lake a great deal - in short, I did my homework.

The thinking processes I went through in approaching Rodney Meadow I have since applied everywhere else I have fished with success. Let me outline my method which has served me in such good stead.

The first step was to find out as much about the water as I could from others. I knew no one on the lake at all, but I fired hundreds of questions at John Stent and his head bailiff. I listened to what they said, took note of some information which I thought important, but stored general tactical advice for future reference only. I was going to fish the lake my way. Sounds corny, but true.

Secondly, I got hold of a map of the lake. It wasn't a particularly detailed map but it gave me some clues. Maps have been done of every big carp lake in this country by anglers and they can be very useful - but only as a guide, they should not be relied on too heavily. They can't tell you how the fish behave or where they feed.

Looking back on all the lakes I've fished, on all of them I've adopted what I call "the favoured swims approach." I basically select three or four swims on which to concentrate. I think on every lake I've fished there are very good swims, there are good swims and there are poor swims. I'm interested in those very good ones. The swims I concentrate on have to meet the following strict criteria:

1. *They are known feeding areas and have produced carp in the past and/or feeding carp can be observed there regularly.*
2. *They allow a number of different fishing options and features in terms of presenting a bait and free samples to the fish.*
3. *They command a significant amount of water and cannot normally be intruded into by other anglers or other anglers' lines.*
4. *They allow me to fish with maximum efficiency, ie presenting bait accurately, with a high percentage of landing fish to hooking ratio etc.*
5. *Ideally, they should be away from "social banks" or other anglers, if this is possible.*

I will fish other swims when I have to if my favoured swims are occupied but I am always looking to get into one of them if they become free. I'm not happy fishing where I "can get in" or fishing in a line of anglers without a distinct advantage over them I would rather go home than have to fish in a "going through the motions" situation which is so common on the circuit waters. Once I have identified the swims I am interested in, I will then learn as much about them as I can by plumbing and leading about.

On Rodney, the swim that had the major appeal for me was the one known as The Corner. It was a swim to me that seemed head and shoulders above the others. There were so many fishing options. It was possible to fish the main body of the lake as well as the water running behind a cigar island to the right of the pitch which led into a large arm of water to the right of the pitch. There was also the option of fishing the water between the bank and the cigar island. I didn't know if the Rodney carp followed the wind, but in this swim it wouldn't matter. Whatever the wind direction, I would always be on the carp moving from left or right in the main lake or left or right into or out of the arm.

The cigar island was potentially a hazard when playing fish, as it was likely the fish would run behind it. This possibility had obviously been

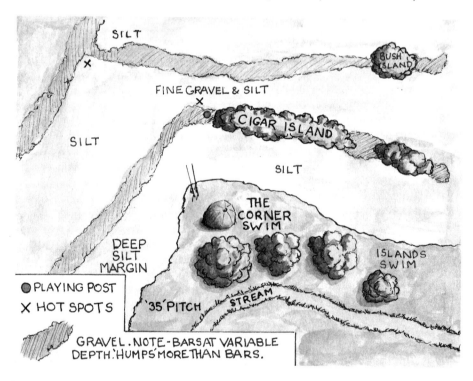

experienced, as one of the bailiffs had driven a scaffold pole into the top of the bar right up against the island which had a plastic roller fitted to it. This enabled the angler to keep the line against the roller if a fish ran around the back of the island and play it safely back to the post. Ingenious! This was my first choice swim. My second choice swim was opposite and was called The Marsh. This was next to the swim known as The Point which had been occupied by Steve Newman and his friend on my first visit. This had been closed down due to swim-hogging, as anyone fishing The Point could monopolise a huge amount of water. To me, The Marsh didn't offer as many options as The Corner but it was significantly better than the rest. The third choice swim was down the arm and was known as the Big Island swim. The island in front of this swim would obviously be an attractive feature for the carp but the map also revealed some other interesting features, including a couple of small bars topped by lily pads and some interesting margins with overhanging trees. The fourth choice swim was The Island Pitch between the Big Island and The Corner - but this was very much the fourth choice. Of course, if these swims were taken, I'd opt for the best-looking prospect from whatever was left.

After swim choice, the next issues to consider were rigs, bait and tactics.

Choice of rig was easy. I suspected that most would continue to use bottom baits, perhaps a few would opt for pop-ups - but on short hooklengths. Most would be using nylon, but dacron was getting a lot of coverage in the few angling publications at the time and so a few would no doubt be using this - I'd been using it for ten years already! The guess that most would be using short hooklengths was borne out by subsequent observations as the season wore on.

RODNEY MEADOW RIG

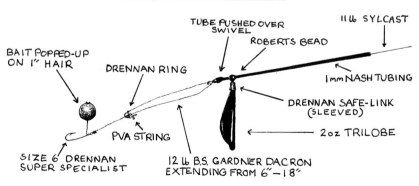

TUBE PUSHED OVER SWIVEL
ROBERTS BEAD
11 lb SYLCAST
BAIT POPPED-UP ON 1" HAIR
DRENNAN RING
1mm NASH TUBING
DRENNAN SAFE-LINK (SLEEVED)
PVA STRING
2oz TRILOBE
SIZE 6 DRENNAN SUPER SPECIALIST
12 lb B.S. GARDNER DACRON EXTENDING FROM 6"-18"

It seemed to me that employing a long hooklink rather than the short ones the fish were used to encountering would give me an edge. The problem was that it wouldn't take long for someone watching me to see that I was using a long hooklink. The solution was to use a sliding rig utilising a Drennan ring. Securing the ring with PVA just above the hook gave the appearance of using a short rig. After casting out, the lead could be pulled into position at the back of the bar and once the PVA melted, a hooklink of twice the starting length would result. In the past, I'd had success using hooklinks up to 24" in length but, beyond this, I'd encountered problems with some aborted takes on my local Grey Mist experimental sessions. I used 2oz Trilobe leads, as I thought this shape lead would help me grip the sides of the bars more easily. On reflection, this was just about the most irrelevant feature of the overall rig and any standard lead would have been equally effective - my preference is for Zipp-shaped leads both over gravel and silt nowadays. Two other aspects to the rig were important. I figured that if most were using either pop-ups or straight bottom baits, then a slightly different presentation was called for. I opted for hookbaits that required just the weight of the hook to hold then down. Using the same sized squares of polystyrene each time to the same sized bait achieved just what I wanted. The final aspect related to the hook. I was anxious that the straight pointed Drennan Super Specialist (size 6) that I'd become fond of using, might get easily damaged or blunted on the gravel. This I solved by placing a block of PVA over the hookpoint and barb. This was made by knotting PVA string several times. This worked a treat and ensured the hook was always needle sharp.

Bait was a much more difficult thinking exercise. Although most were using ready-mades, I doubted whether many would be piling them in. On my first trip, I noticed that most just fired out a handful of baits around the hookbait. Overall, there wasn't much bait going in. I felt that a better quality, more nutritional bait with a proven attractor would be a better proposition than joining in with the crowd. The milk protein and Blue Cheese/garlic bait I had so much confidence in was the perfect choice. I was certain the fish hadn't seen much quality bait and they would not have been caught on that attractor combination before. There was a big problem to overcome though. Rodney Meadow was 186 miles from my doorstep and I had no access to a local freezer to keep fresh baits in. I was very confident in using fresh from frozen baits in order to get the best out of them. I had no confidence in rolling milk protein baits on the bank, or using baits that had been thawed for 24hrs or more. I went to the expense of purchasing half a dozen large glass flasks, a large coolbox and a large number of icepacks. After experimentation, I found I could keep baits frozen with this combination for about three days. Each flask could take just over a pound of 15mm boilies and a dozen or so hookbaits.The plan was to use one flask of bait a day, having planned to fish from Sunday through to Thursday mornings for the eight weeks of my summer vacation.

I was still not happy using this limited amount of bait. I was fishing with potentially a lot of fish in front of me if I could get my two most favoured swims. They would be moving past regularly and I wasn't confident that this amount of bait would hold them for any amount of time. I felt certain that a mass bait could hold them and was confident that no one else had probably used this method successfully on the lake before. It seemed totally boilie-orientated, although I had seen one or two using peanuts. I thought hemp might have been used, so chose to employ groats liberally sprinkled with tiger nuts.

The groats merely needed to be mixed with lake water and I took ready-prepared tigers with me, with others being boiled on the bank as and when they were needed. The groats/tiger nuts combination used as a feeding area with boilies over the top had been developed on the Cheshire and Shropshire meres with tremendous success. Would it work on a gravel pit? I was certain it would.

. . . .

My first trip was a little traumatic. I had a blow-out on the M1, couldn't get my wheel nuts undone to change the wheel and had to ring for a mechanic. It never occurred to me to give the jack arm a good sharp kick with the boot, which the young mechanic very successfully employed to loosen the cursed wheelnuts. He looked at me most strangely and shook his head!

It was about midnight when I got to the lake. Having forgotten my torch, I set up half-way down the convenient North Bank as best I could. I tied a lead to the end of the line on my marker rod and cast it out as far as I could in the blackness. I pulled the lead back and found three bars, one at about 80 yards, one at about 60 yards and one at about 20-30 yards, with silty gullies. No weed. The second bar seemed favourite and out went two stringers which were pulled quickly into the back of it. I must have fallen asleep, for the next thing I was aware of was a screaming buzzer. It was light when I bent into the fish and an eventful fight followed. I was quite surprised to even get a take in such fortunate circumstances and even more so when I played an obviously big, yellowy-looking fish up and down the deep margin. After ten minutes of taut nerves it was in the net and hauled onto some grass at the back of the swim. (Interesting that, in as recent a time as 1987 I had never seen an unhooking mat - I never saw one used at Rodney despite the hard gravel banks. It hadn't occurred to anyone to put a little bit of foam under the fish!) It was a lovely looking high-backed fish just under 25lb. My first southern twenty!

The action had been observed by the handful of others fishing the lake and surprisingly, the guy fishing my fancied Corner Swim moved right next to me into the well-known Wall Swim. I quickly packed up and went right round to The Corner. He looked at me as if I was quite mad!

The rest of the session went quite well. I spent most of the rest of the first

day plumbing and record-ing features in the pitch, and felt I had made sense of it particularly as I had action. I caught a further five fish from The Corner with the best around 19lb and I lost a couple too. The groats/tigers feeding area started working fairly quickly although I no doubt raised eyebrows when spodding. A few members came round for a chat periodically and what amazed me was their friendly welcome. The attitude was so relaxed and all of them were only too willing to offer advice and tell me more about the water. I'd never quite

First southern twenty. The impressive "Humpy." encountered this before on my northern waters - especially when I was catching.

I'd found a couple of productive spots. I concentrated· the particle feeding area in a gulley about 5 yards past the Cigar Island on what felt like fine gravel flanked by two coarse gravel bars. I saw it as a gravel table ideal for eating carp food off! This was clearly a gulley carp moved through regularly in numbers. It was only about 20 yards out. I had five takes in that spot, landing three. The two I lost were largely my fault because I allowed the fish to move too far before I pulled the line around the playing post and pressurised them. Using the post took some getting used to, but once I'd established the best way to utilise it I had few problems. The other spot was straight out in front in a gap I had found between two gravel mounds. This was quite a tight area which had to be located with the marker float unlike the cigar island spot which could be located easily by sight. The second spot was about 50 yards out. It was an area that I thought would intercept fish moving along the adjoining gravel bars. The bottom here was smooth silt, but the cast was tricky, as the bar sides were covered in weed and it was necessary to drop the rig right on the marker float.

I greatly enjoyed the whole new experience. I'd spent my fishing life up to that point on silty, largely featureless lakes, and the sudden bang on the

Rodney Meadow when the water was lowered prior to the netting. Here is The Corner looking across to The Marsh. The water level is about eight feet down. The Playing Post can be seen as well as my hotspot - the gulley between the island and the next bar.

rod, the delicate tap, tap, tap or lock up, proved very addictive. The rod wasn't just a casting and playing tool, it had became the main guide to the underwater world and an extension of the carp fishing brain. I saw the bars as corridors which the carp moved along, and I found the whole exercise of trying to work out what I had in front of me quite fascinating and much more interesting than fishing my local lakes.

The bars in Rodney were not uniform at all and seemed to follow a general pattern of extended humps. The incline of the humps contrasted between sheer and gentle and the water above the bars could also vary between inches and several feet in a matter of yards. The surface of the bars again varied. I found rocky gravel, smooth gravel and a horrible-looking blue-black clay which always seemed to have weed stems growing up from it. I thought it best to avoid this. The gulleys were dominated by silt as were the areas where no gravel humps were present.

Interestingly, the two spots I plumped for initially, proved to be the real hotspots in that swim all summer. I managed to get The Corner on my next three trips, by getting to the lake on early Sunday mornings before the weekend anglers moved out. This meant travelling overnight with little sleep but I've always found since I started travelling that to compete with local anglers you have got to put yourself out.

The success of the first session carried on into the next three. I was catching about half a dozen fish a day on average, these being mostly upper doubles with a smattering of good twenties. That thirty was proving elusive! The two spots produced again, with the Cigar Island attracting most attention over the groats/tigers feeding area. This was getting stronger and stronger and, on a couple of occasions, I had takes as a fully-laden spod crashed right on top of the hookbait. The carp were so preoccupied that they were indifferent to the surface disturbance and their mates being picked off. Despite my success, and the fact that many of the locals were struggling to catch, no one got wise and copied the method for some time even though I was perfectly open about what I was doing.

I had one memorable session in particular, when I caught nothing but common carp, and funnily enough, all of the other carp caught elsewhere from the lake that week were also commons. I caught 14 of them into the low twenties. Just why only commons chose to feed that particular week remains a mystery, although I've thought about it often since. However, as one who has been fortunate to fish many waters containing big commons, I have come to appreciate that they are almost a separate species of carp when compared to mirrors. They have different habits, feeding patterns and traits. The most difficult fish to catch in many lakes are the big commons.

The thirty pounder was still proving elusive but newly acquired friends like Gary Bolton, Steve Newman, Gary Verity, Albert Hayes and John Buckley kept reassuring me that it would come, particularly in view of the exceptional action I was having. It did come, although not from my beloved Corner for one Sunday one of the members beat me to it and, as The Marsh was also occupied, I set-up in The Big Island pitch. At dawn, I landed a small bream - this was quite customary at first light on a Rodney morning - and, five minutes later, experienced another drop-back bite which I took to be another slimey. The fight which immediately followed was completely unspectacular, reinforcing the notion that it was just another bream. The horrible little snotty somehow contrived to snag me on some tree roots in the margins, and I can remember putting the rod down on the ground to pull for a break by hand. I remember too, the force with which the line was ripped from my hand which led me to conclude that this was, in fact, a carp - and a big one too. Twenty minutes of struggle and high tension followed

which led to a considerable body of carp flesh being netted. This was a a big, grey, high-backed Italian fish known affectionately as The Pet - a well known thirty. I was ecstatic - my first thirty after all those years!

The Pet also forced me to reconsider the habit of my carp fishing lifetime up to that point in relation to publicity. I'd never before reported my captures to the angling press, but John Stent was very keen to get publicity for his waters and asked me to send off a photo of the fish with the story of the capture to the Angler's Mail. Not wishing to upset him, I reluctantly

The magnificent Pet - my first thirty.

agreed to do so. The feature appeared in the newspaper and, in all honesty, I quite liked to see my name in print and the cheque which arrived a fortnight later was most welcome given my fairly poor financial circumstances. Interestingly, the capture was given quite a large feature and The Pet described as "a huge carp." Nowadays, it might just get a small mention amongst the masses of upper thirties and forties which are now so commonplace!

I caught The Pet again a fortnight later, which was a little disappointing, in that my second thirty was also my first. The fish kept coming, so I was always ever-hopeful that one of the other thirties would succumb to my efforts. I was enjoying my fishing though, and looked forward to each trip with great anticipation. My succession of multiple captures might give the impression that Rodney Meadow was an easy water, but this was far from the truth. It was a difficult water. Many members struggled to catch and there were few others catching consistently. I was benefitting from the application of a new approach and method of fishing which had not been tried before, having mid-week time at my disposal and from being able to concentrate my efforts more often than not in the best swim on the lake. I was learning all the time, not only from my own efforts but also from the approaches of others. It was clear that there were some very good anglers fishing the water.

There were two very hardworking anglers on the water in the shape of Chris Ladds and Simon Lavin. They were a fishing partnership and this drew a little derision and innuendo from some of the other lads - but they certainly knew their stuff. On Rodney, Chris was known as Frogger and Simon as Mr Magoo. Funnily enough, by my Harefield days, Chris was known as Care Bear and Simon had become transformed into Frogger! At Rodney as at Harefield, it was Chris who caught the lion's share of the duo's fish and the biggest too, but they are both exceptional anglers. I learned a great deal from watching them and they were always very friendly and ready to acknowledge my success too, which embarrassed me a little. They always kept in touch with the water by visiting it every evening and gathering information from others. Sometimes they fished if they thought the conditions were right and a good swim was free. Often, they would stay late into the night just to watch the fish moving and rolling. They avoided popular banks like the North Bank and preferred the same swims as I did. They were very crafty too. When fishing overnight, they would cast out but would not bait-up until after dark so it was difficult to work out exactly which spots they were fishing to. They always fished with sunken rod-tips so it was difficult too, to work out where they were fishing to. They gave nothing away. They baited heavily with boilies only,, but it took me some time to find out what sort of baits they were using. They turned out to be Richworth neutrals, sprayed with flavours of their own choice. They were very quiet, buzzers were kept low to avoid attention and they just got down to business without fuss. They hadn't been carp fishing for long, but had been very successful big tench anglers which I have always considered to be more difficult to catch than carp.

John Pope wasn't quiet by any means - in fact he was downright noisy - but he was also an innovative if somewhat irritating angler at times. John liked his floater fishing and although the Rodney Meadow carp could respond to floaters quite well as the season progressed, the fish showed a definite aversion to taking Chum within catapult range of the bank. They would only take free offerings that had drifted on the wind some considerable distance from the bank. The best fish I caught off the surface was a 24 pounder and this was taken on a single mixer when I allowed the controller to drift over 80 yards out - fish were just not confident of taking surface baits closer in than that. "Popey" developed the technique of casting mixers in a bait dropper at range to create a confident surface feeding situation. Not only did this present mixers quickly at the catching range without relying on the wind, but when the mixers fell out of the spod they would be grouped in a tight little bed in numbers. This created an entirely

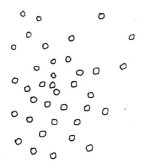

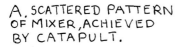
A. SCATTERED PATTERN OF MIXER, ACHIEVED BY CATAPULT.

B. TIGHT BAITING PATTERN OF MIXER, OBTAINED BY BAIT DROPPER AT LONGER RANGE.

different presentation situation as a catapult spreads the baits over a wider area. This new method inspired confidence in cagey carp, who didn't seem too bothered about spods landing near to them. Light line and a good controller enabled one to simply present a mixer in the middle of the tight bed. This method proved devastating and Popey and Steve Newman caught many fish as a result. I've since tried it on other waters, also with success. Unfortunately, the method has one main drawback. Because of the distances being fished, encroachment into other swims occupied by other anglers on a water the size of Rodney was a problem. A couple of members made complaints to the management that John had cast controllers and spods into their swims, and vociferous old Popey was relieved of his ticket. Mind you, he'd started to lose interest when his poor old dog had his ticket confiscated too, for growling at one of Rodney's notorious bailiffs!

Gary Verity was another very successful angler on the water. Gary favoured The Marsh swim where he had identified his own particular pick-up spots and he caught very well out of there when others struggled. When he couldn't get The Marsh, he'd often fish quiet, rarely fished areas - marginal trees and bushes being a favourite, where he'd buck the trend and fish the margin with pin-point baiting and a light lead set-up. Gary was very successful due to the fact that he always looked to do something different to the rest. A very good little angler who still catches huge fish from the Colne Valley waters today, quietly and without fuss.

John Buckley was the most unlikely consistent catcher of carp from the water. Buckley did everything wrong. His rigs were awful and his tackle was an absolute shambles. He'd arrive straight from the building site in his donkey jacket and wellies, throw up a bivvy which always threatened to blow over in the slightest of winds, jam some indicator needles any old way into the ground so that they generally collapsed on a run, cast out and planted his collection of rods on a pair of dodgy buzzers. Fond of a snide rod was our John, and it was fun to try and work out whereabouts he had hidden it. John very often arrived on the venue with no bait whatsoever and generally relied on boilies ponced off people on the bank. He'd use anything, provided it was free and has probably caught more thirties on other people's bait than anyone else in Britain. One night, he borrowed some baits off me and then had the temerity to complain to me in the morning before he went to work, that they were rubbish because all he'd caught on them was a four ounce perch! Despite all his shortcomings in the technical stakes and his somewhat crude personality, he was an exceptional catcher of Rodney Meadow carp.

The first Rodney summer passed far too quickly for me. I didn't want it to end. But end it did and the beginning of a new academic year meant that I would have to concentrate again on my local waters as Rodney was too far from home for weekend trips.

. . . .

For the second summer, I decided to take exactly the same approach as the first. The fish kept coming and coming as before. But this time the results were different, for I couldn't seem to get amongst the big fish at all. I was catching double after double and even single figure fish. This wasn't what I was after. After three or four trips, I came to the conclusion that perhaps the groats/tiger nut feeding area was blowing and the smaller fish I hadn't caught the previous season were the only carp now getting on it. To make matters worse and to confirm my suspicions, I was catching many more bream over the feeding area. I was greatly concerned about the situation, although friends told me the run of small fish would end soon. I wasn't convinced, and felt the solution lay in abandoning the mass baits altogether and upping the amount of boilies I was using drastically. At great expense, I purchased several more very large vacuum flasks to double my daily quota of garlic/blue cheese boilies and I also decided to bait initially on both of my proven spots with six pounds of boiled baits as soon as I arrived at the water.

I caught from the off, and I ended the first four day session on the new approach with seventeen fish but the best was still only 19lb. I knew it wasn't the bait, because Albert Hayes had gone onto the same bait and caught Nelson at 33lb first time out and was stacking up the twenties. It was just one of those things. I did lose a fish of considerable size through over-cautious playing. Lenny Lake was fishing the next swim to me and was ready to net the monster but I contrived to allow the hook to fall out in the margin. His sideways-look at me as the line went slack said it all.

I had to get away from the lake to re-charge the batteries and get off my mind the fact that I'd caught sixty odd fish but failed to catch a twenty. Some may think that was not a good attitude to have and they may be right, but I could have caught fish of that stamp five minutes from my house. I was paying a lot of money I couldn't really afford for a ticket, petrol and various sundries to catch big fish and I couldn't seem to get one at that moment in time.

Lenny sensed how I felt and suggested we both went off to Darenth the following week to get a break from the water. The Darenth ticket only cost about thirty quid then and Lenny and Popey suggested I should get one and that I'd like it down there. All of the Darenth waters were twenties waters with some big fish on top. The following week, I met Lenny in The Singles swim at Darenth Big Lake.

Whilst I was away, a certain mischief maker, who had influence with John Stent, saw fit to tell tales and cause trouble for me. When I got back from Darenth there was a message for me to ring John Stent. The outcome of the telephone conversation was that I was no longer to fish at Rodney Meadow. After I left, problems which had begun to arise concerning the management of the water which had contributed to my ban and those of others got worse.

From a fishing point of view, interesting things were happening. Albert who I'd let onto the bait was having tremendous success on the water when others were struggling. He caught many big fish on his shortish trips with some of the rarely caught big fish amongst them. In contrast, Chris and Simon's catches tailed off, presumably because their attractor baits couldn't fool the Rodney carp any more. They moved on to conquer Harefield. Proof positive again though, that a good HNV food bait with good attractors will last and last.

One of the big mysteries was the disappearance of the most sought after fish in the water, Big Rod. He'd been caught in the opening week of the first season of syndication at 35lb plus but hadn't been seen since. This original Rodney fish had disappeared for several seasons between captures before, but rumours that he had been caught at over 40lb and moved to a water further up the valley were rife. We knew one or two fish had been taken in recent times, so it seemed plausible Big Rod had gone too.

The problems I hinted at earlier, related to the bailiffing of the venue. John Stent's bailiffs were notorious and some members were annoyed that they were being asked to produce tickets when the bailiffs knew full well that they were members of a close-knit syndicate.

I was more concerned about the amount of bailiffs on the water occupying swims. I use the term bailiff very loosely, for most of them did very little. There were over a dozen waters on the Boyer scheme and any bailiff on any of them was entitled to fish any water anytime they liked. Unfortunately, most seemed to be gravitating towards Rodney. Sometimes there were more bailiffs fishing than members! Fair enough. But what wasn't fair enough was that they were leaving bivvies up in prime swims during the day when they went to work, fishing only at night - often for a week long stretch. Fee paying punters like myself often couldn't get into the prime swims. After I left, members also started to complain about the numbers of well-known anglers being given free fishing on Rodney. John liked to attract "faces" onto his waters, and anyone who was very well known was invited to fish Rodney Meadow for a session. Numerous big name anglers did so (all of them unsuccessfully I might add!) but this merely caused more friction with the guys who'd actually paid to fish the water. People who spoke out (like me) were threatened with bans. One or two bans followed. The complaints reached fever pitch. At the same time, certain anglers who had very recently started to fish Harefield were saying Harefield could do with more big fish in it. Here was the chance to shut the "Rodney complainers" up once and for all and up-grade the Harefield stock still further. The decision was taken to close Rodney Meadow and move most of the big fish to Harefield with the remainder boosting the Farlow's stock. A story was circulated to the media about the closure being necessary due to urgent work having to be done to one of the banks at Rodney. Everyone knew this was rubbish. Before the water could be drained to net the fish, Rodney members were told that if they caught a fish they had to contact a bailiff to ensure the fish was removed from the water and taken to Harefield or Farlow's. Rodney members who had paid a lot of money for their fishing, were expected to co-operate in removing the fish to Harefield which they had no guarantee they could fish in the future, with a good portion of the season remaining! Not surprisingly, some refused to do this and there was tremendous aggravation on the water for some weeks.

To me, looking in from the outside, the whole thing seemed ridiculous and it didn't make much business sense. The Rodney fish were growing well in the water and there were already plenty of big fish in Harefield and Farlow's was an action water already. Boyers had two top quality big carp waters in their portfolio and now they were only going to have one. Putting one's eggs into one basket is a risky business in relation to moving fish. For some of these fish it was their third or fourth move! I felt most sorry for those who had a genuine affection for Rodney. It was a lovely, medium-sized water and fishing a big windswept pit like Harefield or a very commercial fishery like Farlow's wasn't everyone's cup of tea. For some, Rodney was their only water - many of the Colne Valley waters like The Cons, Fisheries and Harrow were, and still are, difficult to get into, even for locals.

The netting of Rodney proved very interesting. All of the Rodney regulars thought the number of twenty plus fish in the water to be around thirty, including the four thirties and another couple of fish near to that mark. When electro-fished prior to closure around 42 different 20lb plus fish were caught and others evaded capture. Eleven different twenty pound commons were removed (we thought there were four), unknown thirty and twenty-eight pound mirror and other mystery fish.

A few weeks later, one of the bailiffs caught a 28lb common - which had been rumoured to have been last caught ten years previously. This fish was put into the adjoining Mayfield's lake. There was no sign of Big Rod - which seemed ominous - but several big fish evaded capture by retreating into snags.

The Rodney netting as well as the subsequent Longfield netting, shows that even on very pressured waters, not all the fish are known or get caught and there is always the possibility of a surprise. I believe that on the vast majority of the so-called "circuit waters", the same fish are caught several times each season - fish like Rodney's Nelson, the Tip Lake's Scar and Parrot etc. then there are some fish that slip up once or twice a season. There are other carp that get caught very occasionally, perhaps a few times in a

particular season but then they disappear for several seasons. There are other fish that may never or very rarely get caught, because they don't feed on bait or certain types of baits. I have caught individual fish on particles that I can't catch on boilies on a couple of waters, for example. The percentage of fish in each category will vary from water to water, and in the latter category there may be just one or two fish. Commons in particular, often dominate the rarely or never caught category. I am certain there is a very large common in Harefield - certainly over forty pounds that has probably never been caught. I saw this fish in the Goose Bay once, Bernard Loftus saw it when he fished there and I suspect Stuart

Playing a fish at the back of the Cigar Island with the help of a Carp Ladder (pat. pending). Gary Bolton looks on.

Gillham probably lost it in his record-breaking Harefield season.

The decision taken to close Rodney, made a lot of people move onto other waters outside of the previously excellent Boyer's scheme. For example, the Rodney Meadow Crew invasion of Darenth was underway. To the Tip Lake with me - much to the chagrin of the regulars - went Albert Hayes, Steve Newman, Gary Verity, Tony Olivo, John Buckley, Lenny Lake, Del Batty, Frank Williams and John Pope.

. . . .

The Rodney problems began in the second season of the syndicate's existence. The first year was a magical one for everybody and even today, people who fished it then have very happy memories. It was a fun place to fish, full of characters who more or less all got on well with each other. Friendships for life were made.

Southern carp anglers intrigued me for, they were very different from their northern counterparts. Due to the hearty bivvy breakfasts perhaps, they have a tendency to be large blokes, not to say, portly, and have a liking for tattoo's, jogging bottoms, T-shirts, mocassins and short cropped hair. Surprisingly, I found they were fond of calling each other "gal" which didn't quite equate to the appearance. To be called a "gal" in the north would be the equivalent of calling someone a "jessie" which would result in a thump from most or a kiss from Tony Baskeyfield! The southern carp man always seemed to have a lot of time and cash at his disposal. Occupationally, most on Rodney seemed to be taxi drivers or "did a bit of this or that" or "ducked and dived." All quite vague, but I always thought it diplomatic not to enquire further.

Albert Hayes became a dear friend. He was born and bred in the north, but had retired to Surrey. He considered it his moral duty to ensure that I, as a fellow northerner, had an edge over these southern gals. Albert liked fishing The Corner too, and funnily enough, Albert was nearly always fishing The Corner when I arrived at the water. By pure chance, he was always fishing The Dry Dock when I arrived at Darenth too!

Albert was a great talker, but not everyone's cup of tea, for talking to Albert was a form of psychological warfare. He enjoyed winding people up but sometimes he went too far, and those not aware of the game he liked to play could be reduced to tears, anger or frustration. The charming silver-haired gentleman who joined you for a cup of coffee and a chat really wanted to have a go at you and put you right about things.

As I set-up, Albert would sit for hours and hold forth on a multitude of controversial topics. Knowing my occupation, he was even more interested in seeking my views, even though he knew I knew what he was up to. The lazy youth of today was a favourite topic, how to deal with crime and criminals another, tackling declining moral standards with National Service and corporal punishment another. These were topics which I would refuse to be drawn on. The periodic head-nod would cover me throughout his monologue. Others would be drawn into his web. I remember that John Buckley blew his cool completely on one occasion, when he realised that Albert's derision of the lazy youth of today included him. "That's the trouble with the youth of today," complained Albert, as Buckley walked past my swim tackle-laden, "they don't want to work." Poor old Buckley had just done a full day's graft at the building site!

His carp fishing topics would follow similar themes. The modern carp angler's attitude to catching carp at all costs was an old chestnut. The cruelty of fishing was another favourite subject and philosophical considerations of whether we should really be fishing for carp or not would follow. He was fond of giving lectures on how to hygienically deal with calls of nature, disapproved strongly of carp anglers breaking wind or belching, and derided the general decline in standards of bankside dress and manners.

I'd not get drawn into an argument with Albert on these matters and he would always then attempt to throw in his ace-card - the subject of bait for carp fishing. He knew this would get me to rise but I always drew short of taking the hook he was casting out. I'd mutter a few general principles in reply, offer numerous head nods, but always remain sufficiently non-committal to deny him any satisfaction.

I knew his game you see, but others responded differently to the coaxing, leading to the heated argument and aggro which he loved to generate and thrive upon. His victims were many. He could get someone to pack-up and go home out of a swim we wanted to fish with remarkable ease.

Another characteristic of many southern carp men is exhibitionism. Naked displays of masculine prowess seem common on many southern waters. I presume we don't have this in the north due to the colder weather, which causes an individual's masculinity to shrink somewhat, rendering it too minor a feature to display with any pride. There were numerous examples of this on Rodney but chief stripper was Tony Olivo, otherwise known as Ollie. Ollie was very proud of what god had given him and it was a surprise to find him wearing any clothes at all, although, of course, he always wore the obligatory bait company T-shirt for big fish photos. Ollie has stripped his way from Rodney, to Darenth and then back to Harefield and no doubt Horton regulars are still being entertained by him today. It wasn't much of a culture shock when I then encountered Essex John and Essex Alan at Harefield, although the brazen nakedness still took a bit of getting used to in the remarkably Bohemian *Horse and Barge* and particularly when trying to concentrate on devouring an onion bhaji in the Indian.

John Buckley was prone to exhibitionism but was never a real devotee. For the handful of you who possibly don't know, John single-handedly dragged a 70 pounder from the depths of the North Arm at Cassien. After that, he became unbearable, for he had to constantly remind everyone of his achievement. In every conversation, he'd work it in somewhere. New faces were pounced upon and made to pay homage. "I've had a 70 pounder" was his major chat-up line in the pub disco and many young, naive maidens were to misinterpret this or just catch a whispered fragment. They went off with him on the strength of it, only to be greatly disappointed later. His high point came when he entered a huge blow-up of the monster in the Carp Society Conference Photographic Competition at Dunstable. The picture showed Buckley returning his leviathan to the Cassien depths. For full impact, Buckley spent the whole day standing right by the display wearing exactly the same clothes that he was wearing in the photograph, just in case anyone didn't notice that he was the great man.

One of the best ever wind ups was played on Buckley. One session, he caught Nelson at 35lb on a bait he scrounged off someone. He caught the great beast in the middle of the night. A couple of hours later whilst Buckley was asleep, Tony Long moved Nelson and the sack very carefully along the margins into the next swim, replacing the aforementioned sack with an empty one. In the morning, Buckley summoned everyone round with the cameras to witness another moment of glory. Picture the scene - an army of camera-wielding carp anglers gathered around the superstar who carefully untied his sack and began lifting it from the water. As the water drained out of the sack, so did the colour from Buckley's face, as the realisation dawned on him that the fish was gone and he'd called everyone around to witness a non-event. A hard man was Buckley, but his bottom lip quivered and tears welled up in his eyes. Longey tormented him a little bit longer by allowing him to pack up and head for the car. Just as he was about to get into the car to drive home blubbering and blarting, Longey shouted, "It's over here, John......"

An even more cruel, long-term wind-up was played on young Simon from Twickenham by Gary Bolton and myself. Simon often used to like fishing next to me when I fished The Corner. I didn't mind, for he was good company and he'd set-up in the nearby Thirty-Five Pitch. Gary and I found out that Simon had a morbid fear of rats - he lived in terror of them. There were one or two rats on Rodney, they used to navigate the little stream behind the water, but they were not really a nuisance. Gary always enjoyed a wind-up and we hatched a little scheme. Gary always called in after work to see what had happened on the water and he'd come and chat on The Corner for a fair bit. Weil's Disease had been in the news and the prospect of encountering disease carrying rats used to play on Simon's mind. Gary would heighten the fear, by tales of anglers he knew who were lying in hospital stricken with the disease even as he spoke. I'd chip in by saying I had heard rats in my bivvy and had encountered one sitting on the bottom of the bedchair etc. Simon's face used to go green during the re-counting of such tales. He took to hanging all of his cooking and eating implements on the spokes of his brolly to avoid rat contamination.

Gary would circulate around the lake and come back to The Corner just after dark, to work on Simon a little more. "So and so, on the North Bank had to fight off a rat with a bankstick last night," he'd say, "as big as a dog it was" and so on. Whilst this was going on, I'd rig up a length of fishing line to come out from under my bivvy to the back of the swim, run round a

couple of sticks by the stream and end up linked through a tent peg to the back of Simon's bivvy. At the end of the line would be a small bushy branch. When lying on my bedchair I could pull on the line, causing the branch to rub up against Simon's bivvy and make a scratching noise. Gary would depart (giving me a wink!) and we would retire to the bivvies for the night.

I'd wait for some time until everything went very quiet and I guessed Simon would be starting to nod off. I'd then give the line a little tug. Within seconds, I'd hear the startled noise of Simon shooting off his bedchair. His torch would spark into life and I would see it being flashed around the bivvy. It was very painful laughing hysterically whilst trying not to make a sound! He'd often come down to my bivvy with the torch and say, "Paul, I think there's a rat in my bivvy. Will you come and have a look?" Sometimes I would, but often I'd say, "Don't be daft, Simon. Go back to bed they are more frightened of you." He'd go back to bed and I'd give him ten minutes or so, before giving the line a good old tug again. He'd shoot off the bedchair again, frantically search the bivvy and, after ten minutes or so, retreat to the big willow separating the two pitches. He'd spend all night standing under the willow until it was light, with his torch going on and off from time to time, investigating any nearby sound. He'd retreat into his bivvy once it was light and safe and sleep for most of the day. I'd dismantle my apparatus as soon as he went to sleep so he was never any the wiser. Gary and I wouldn't let "the rats" torment him every night - just the occasional one now and again - for it would have been just too cruel.

Poor old Simon as far as I know no longer carp fishes - for I never saw him again after I could no longer fish Rodney. Perhaps his fear of rats became too much for him to stand in the end?

. . . .

After the fish were taken from Rodney, the lake quickly filled up again and John Stent introduced hundreds of fast-growing "Dinks" into the water. Those fish have thrived and prospered and I am pleased to report that Rodney Meadow as a big carp fishery is on its way back. Some of the remaining original fish have also grown. It is not what it was, but it is getting there.

I think in the not-too-distant future I will tread the lovely banks of Rodney again, and fish for those wonderful carp. If you decide to have a go too, look out for me. I'll be on my beloved Corner.

A fat twenty, taken at dusk. A busy night of carp-catching ahead!

The Tip Lake
The Ecstasy and the Agony

*"A man who fishes habitually for carp has a strange look in his eyes...as if he had
been in heaven or in hell."*
Arthur Ransome

In 1990, Jim Hindle, then the General Secretary of the BCSG asked if I
would write a specially commissioned article for the forthcoming 5th
BCSG book. I'd started to draft out an article that I felt I had to write at
the time about my recent experiences on Darenth Tip Lake, and I felt that
this might make a suitable chapter. I extended the article and it was duly
accepted.

My reaction on receiving a copy of the published work was somewhat
mixed. Whilst I always appreciate seeing my work in print, I was a little
surprised to find that my name was missing from the acknowledgment list of
those who had submitted specially commissioned articles for the book.

Still, I suppose it was a reflection of those still political times. I was the
General Secretary of the Carp Society at the time, and I suppose the new
leadership of the CAA and BCSG at that time in the shape of John
Gaze/Alec Welland were still finding it hard to break with recent traditions.
I was more concerned to find that the book had been paginated wrongly
and that two pages of my article were mixed in with someone else's chapter!
For obvious reasons - as you will see - this piece meant a great deal to me and
to see it butchered in this way was upsetting.

Funnily enough, many BCSG members including the new more liberal
leadership that emerged, regarded the article as the best thing in the book
and I received many phone calls and letters of congratulation, as well as
positive comments at meetings. I wasn't quite sure how to take this as clearly
many hadn't spotted the fact that there were two pages missing!

When deciding what to write about my Tip Lake days, I felt it would be
fitting to set out my original chapter in the BCSG book as it should have
been and to add some more technical points.

I don't think a completely new chapter would have been much more
definitive in terms of my memories of the Tip Lake.

One important point about my time on the Tip Lake. I experienced
spectacular results in the relatively short period of time I fished there. In my

first summer, I caught eight fish over 27lb from this difficult water, with four thirties. But that result was mainly down to one factor: bait. I had originally intended to go on the Tip Lake with a quality milk protein, Nutrabaits' Hi-Nu-Val. However, when I heard about what was going on at the lake with the nutritional fishmeals and oils I realised that I was never going to compete with this bait - unless others were baiting heavily with milk proteins too, which they weren't. For the second time in my carp fishing career (Hawk Lake being the first occasion) I jumped on the bait bandwagon. Thus, my captures were down in large part to the fact that the carp were already onto the bait I was using and everyone fishing the lake was putting it in. Results on that bait were getting stronger and stronger. Bait is one of the few areas where it doesn't pay to be different on waters where it is very significant. Remember that Fred Wilton said that carp will always take advantage of the best available food source. That is a great truism.

The other big factor in my success was that I had my unlikely Guardian Angel from Rodney Meadow, Albert Hayes, to help me again. Albert, in his own inimitable fashion used to secure a good swim for me, just as he did on Rodney. I was focussing on the Dry Dock and Albert would arrive a couple of days before me and secure it for himself and then for me by hook or by crook. If anyone happened to be fishing the swim (and there usually was) Albert would engage the poor chap in his own version of psychological warfare, in which he was always victorious. They invariably went home with high blood pressure, shaking their heads. A great, great friend, who sadly passed away a couple of years ago.

Wherever you are, Albert, I hope you are still saving a swim for me...

. . . .

There was the odd sign of fish over the bait and I knew they were about to have it. It was one day into the session in the Dry Dock, a quiet, interesting swim from which a number of areas where the carp sometimes feed can be covered.

This was my second serious session on the lake and I had already gained a feel and affinity for the place and, in particular, this swim. My instinct and experience told me that it was just a matter of time and application. The fish would come.

I had fished in the Dry Dock for five nights in my previous session - my first session on the water - when it had unexpectedly become vacant, thus

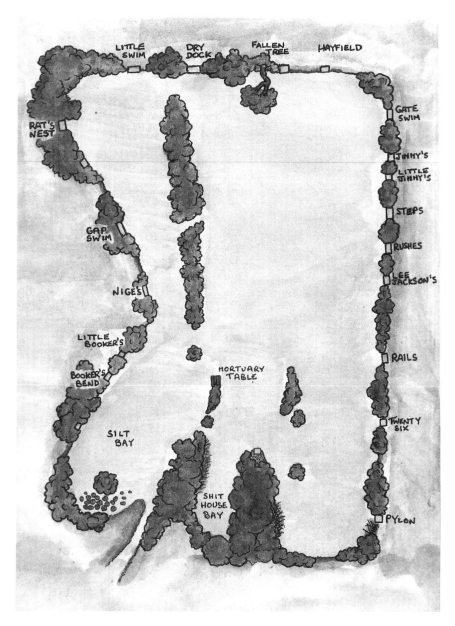

ending a frustrating two nights in a heavily weeded Jimmy's Pitch on the Fence Bank, with little sign of any fish. Although the lake is small at nine acres, the fish can be very localised, hanging around just one or two areas.

The Dry Dock is a pitch with many options. To the left of the pitch lies a small island, and the area between island and bank is the resting place of a huge fallen tree, its weed-festooned branches rising out of the water. Running out from the island is the second bar from the Fence Bank which runs down the length of the lake. The bar is heavily weeded along its length and in places rises to only inches below the surface. To the right of the pitch is a long tree-lined island which starts two hundred yards out from the pitch and is around 60 yards long. Then there is a gap before the island re-appears and continues on for 100 yards or so. Between the second bar and the island is open water, the bottom being silty in places. The channel between the pitch and long island enables one to fish the back channel behind the island (weed allowing), and this is a quiet, overgrown area which the fish sometimes move into when the main section of the lake is heavily pressured.

The first night of that first session had produced a 22 pounder from a gravel patch in the back channel by the dry feeder stream - a victim of the heatwave being experienced that summer. The second night produced a 14lb and the loss of a big fish from the same area. The other rod had been fished tight to the long island, the bait presented on a smooth bottomed area under the canopy of the trees - a tricky cast. Any fish moving either side of the island had been covered but it was not until the final night that this particular rod saw any action. The fish finally moved into this heavily baited area and mirrors of 19, 23 and 29lb resulted. I'd been intimidated by the reputation of the water and felt it was a real test. This opening catch of five fish really boosted my confidence and I felt comfortable on the water.

Needless to say, these were the two feeding areas I was again concentrating on in this my second session.

I mentioned heavy baiting. Some people's idea of this, from observation, differs from mine. I learned very quickly when I started to make the long journeys to the South that bait application on the really big fish waters was crucial. In a nutshell, in the summer months, more bait means more fish. That's a brash statement and it's a generalisation, but it is the case more often than not. You're seeking to precipitate heavy pre-occupied feeding from some of the fish. I use a lot of bait compared to most, and big ones too!

The plan for this session was to introduce a 24 egg mix topped up each night depending on developments. To cater for any eventuality I usually make up this amount each day. I had done this in the Dry Dock with the results already described. Some carp anglers might recoil in horror at the thought of such an amount of bait. Big fish can consume a huge amount of bait very quickly and, on this lake, this quantity of bait per day - where the average size of the 40 or so fish is over 25lb, with 10 over 30lb - is not excessive. These fish are bait fish - they have grown big on bait - and so they instinctively recognise good bait and are looking for it.

Applying bait like this entails spending the daylight hours in the chore of bait making, since it is impossible, unless one lives locally, to take this quantity of fresh bait each day to the lake. This type of fishing is hardly glamourous. One sleeps, eats, makes bait, sleeps, eats, makes more bait - the relief from the routine being the snatched chats with friends, a visit to the shops to buy eggs and supplies and, of course, the captures.

This is not everyone's idea of the essence of carp fishing, but it is a necessary approach to lakes like this one. Every reasonable swim on the lake is occupied day and night, seven days a week from June to October, and a take every three to four days is considered a result. This is one of the few lakes in England where there are a number of "residents" - anglers who have decided just to fish - and will spend the whole season on the bankside.

One side effect of bivvy bait-making is that my boilies tend to get larger as the session goes on. I generally start out with bait the size of a ten pence piece but invariably they end up about the size of a tangerine. They make impressive little waves when they hit the water. When you're using large baits and large beds of bait you're not dependent on rigs to a critical degree. You're aiming to get the fish down on to the bait in a determined "I'm having this" mood, so that the cautious inspection of each bait which we've instilled is eventually overcome by greed.

The rigs I've placed either side of the long island are simple. A size 4 Drennan to a 9" 15lb Silkworm hooklength (original version) to a 3oz lead and on to a 1mm diameter rig tube with the hooklength tied to the swivel running over the tube "helicopter" fashion. (See Fig 1) I have found this set up entirely tangle-free. The bait is presented on my own version of the hair which I whip Domhoff fashion to the shank, enabling significant variation in the length of position of the hair and bait in seconds. The hard bait is

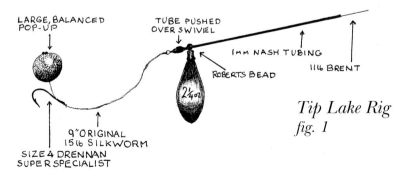

LARGE, BALANCED POP-UP

TUBE PUSHED OVER SWIVEL

1MM NASH TUBING

ROBERTS BEAD

11lb BRENT

2½oz

Tip Lake Rig fig. 1

9" ORIGINAL 15lb SILKWORM

SIZE 4 DRENNAN SUPER SPECIALIST

packed with polystyrene to provide buoyancy, lead wire inserted into the bait to achieve a slow-sinking, just-off-the-bottom effect. When fishing on gravel, I am always obsessed with the possibility of the straight-pointed Drennan being damaged. I always tie with PVA a poly ball to the bait to keep the hook well clear of the gravel while the lead is worked into position. The poly ball, on surfacing, satisfies my paranoia but also serves as an initial marker for baiting up.

The bait is a high quality blend of quality fish meals with added milk proteins, birdfoods and with a feed-inducing fish oil.

I'd used fishmeals in the early 1980's - primarily Rod Hutchinson's Seafood blend - but this particular bait I'm using is nutritionally light years ahead of that and responsible for something of a revolution on the Darenth complex and I'm certain it will spread out from here. The mix I'm using (and virtually everyone else on this lake is using a similar one), is as follows:

Premier Fish Base Mix

5ml per egg Fish Feed Inducing Oil

5ml per 6 eggs Premier Peach Melba

10ml Minamino

1ml Premier Sweetener

6 eggs

It might seem a contradiction to use a fruit flavour and a sweetener with a fishmeal bait but it seems to work. Others on the lake are using similar types of fruit flavours. I'm not sure the bait wouldn't work just as well without the flavours as the base mix and oil has a distinctive smell all of its own. However, I think that all carp anglers feel more confident when they add a smell or flavour to a bait and this psychological aspect shouldn't be overlooked. Geoff Bowers designed this bait with the emphasis on digestibility and nutritional roundness. It certainly seems to be working as all of the fish in the lake have shot up in weight since this bait has been going in.

Fish oil I haven't used before and this is a very interesting ingredient. I've used a lipid source in my baits for years but the concept of a bulk food oil supplying a massive source of attraction is a clear winner. In addition, not only does it provide the carp with nutrition and energy like other lipid sources - such as sesame and olive oil etc - the fatty acids it contains has other beneficial effects. Geoff Bowers' early experiments were with Cod Liver Oil which was successful as a fish catcher but this Fish Feed Oil is even more so. The oil is a good source of Omega 3 and 6 unsaturated fatty acids, which are known to be beneficial to both fish and humans. This particular oil I'm using is used in commercial aquaculture. It is used in trout and salmon rearing to stimulate growth at the correct rate and the omega fatty acids help repair damaged body tissue. The oil is perfectly safe as the host salmon and trout are for the table and thus are in the human food chain.

The oil is a definite pull, particularly in this hot weather, and in my first session I began pouring the oil neat onto the baits - both hookbaits and freebies. This helped stop the baits spoiling in the heat but I'm also certain that the carp - and all of the other fish in here - are hitting this wall of attraction as it rises up from the bottom and then they are going down and looking for the source - the bait. Every living thing in this lake is eating this oil and this bait.

Kent big fish man, Alan Smith came round for a chat around tea-time. We discussed this and that - setting the carp world to rights, as you do. He left for home after an hour or so, remarking, "You'll have them tonight, Paul, there's a lot of fish on your bait now." To have one of the best carp anglers in England agree that things were looking good was inspirational. In went the hookbaits around eight, followed by just enough bait to keep them interested.

At 11pm I took a 21.7 off the long island and lost another of considerably larger size about half an hour later. At 2am the right hand rod to the feeder stream was dragged off the rest and I connected with a big fish which ran down the far side of the island. This tends to make playing a fish difficult because the line runs around the tip of the island and only indirect contact with the fish is achievable. To continually feel the line pinging through the trees, underneath roots, etc. is stomach-churning, but after landing two fish in the previous session in this predicament I knew that if the hook held the fish could be bullied around the island and into the channel. Once around the island it was necessary to wade into the water, parallel to the fish, to prevent it charging into the undergrowth and snags. There I was, waist high in water as the fish came from around the island and into the channel. Heavy pressure brought it to the net and when the nose touched the spreader block I lifted gently. This was a big fish.

Two friends, Ollie and Gary Verity, wandered around from the Fence Bank during the commotion and they helped me to sort out the inevitable chaos. Ollie recognised the fish as Scar Bar, a famous old fish which was the thirty most often caught, and one which I had wanted as my first thirty from the lake - to get out of the way, so to speak. Scar went 32.04. The rest of the night was quiet although Gary had a low 20 from the Steps Swim, which was encouraging.

The next day was spent making baits (as normal) in the blistering heat, with the rods reeled in for most of the time due to tench activity, which indicated to me that little bait was remaining in the two spots. I baited up heavily late afternoon through to tea-time. The night that followed was quiet save for Gary who again had a low 20 from the Steps.

Ian Selby arrived Friday morning, and the only reasonable swim left on the lake was the Rats' Nest in the back channel which clearly posed problems for the right hand rod. I opted to re-position this and fish the left hand side of the pitch by fishing a smooth area at the back of the second bar. I had seen little fish activity during the day here, but I had heard a fish crash out in this vicinity two nights previously. Ian had to leave on Sunday morning and I decided to bait the second bar lightly with only 50 baits and then concentrate again on the back channel on his departure. Due to the pressure on the lake, I was sure some fish were temporarily resident in it. There was a lot of weed on the second bar and weed seemed to attract the tench which, given the chance, were really on the baits, however big. This was confirmed at dusk when a big tench of about 7lb picked up the bait at the back of the bar. I was a little annoyed at having to reposition and re-bait accurately as darkness fell. Afterwards I climbed into the fish-oil impregnated sleeping bag and fell into a deep sleep.

It was some time around 8am when I woke and the sun was already beating down. I put on the kettle and switched on the radio to hear that the forecast was for a hot 90 degrees, and no wind. I was just into the second coffee when a buzzer sounded - a take on the bait on the second bar rod. Tench! Too late in the day to be a carp. Scrambling reluctantly off the bedchair, I picked up the rod and came into contact with the fish, which was definitely a tench as the rod tip knocked in typical tench fashion. This tench was heading mischievously for

The problem with Darenth is that you wake up and find things like this have set-up next to you!

the dead tree and so I gave it the butt to stop the little beggar snagging me. I expected instant submission but was surprised when a tremendous boil on the surface told me that this was no tench. The carp looked huge as it passed in front of me in a run towards the long island. I turned it before it hit the trees overhanging the island and suddenly it was in front of me boiling in the margin. I grabbed the net and bullied it into it. On lifting, I was surprised at the weight and on the unhooking mat the fish was long and lean and looked about 27lb. The Avons went right round to 32lb. I was astonished! I called Ian, who had been unaware of the action, to come round with

Big H - first capture 31lb 14oz.

his scales because I thought the scales were way out. Ian's scales confirmed a weight of around 32lb and, after consideration, we agreed a weight of 31.14. After photographing the fish we had a good look at it. Sudden recognition came from memory of all the magazine and book photographs I had seen of this fish at my knees. This was Big "H", a large-framed fish and a famous one, a target for all who fish the lake as it is normally the biggest and not often caught. I had been very lucky indeed - two thirties in two days.

The rest of the day was spent chatting, re-living events and, inevitably, bait-making.

Saturday night, and I found myself again in contact with a fish alongside the island. After a long fight with an alarming weed-festooned line which eventually I could not reel in, the fish inevitably dropped off the hook as I tried to bring it over the second bar. This gutted me, as does any loss on a lake containing such big fish.

After recasting to somewhere near the baited area, after an hour I was away again and a 21.8 resulted. One other fish was caught on the lake that night and this was the Parrot at 30lb plus, caught by Joe in the Rushes. This worried me a little - were the fish moving down the lake? If they were, there was no way of moving onto them as every swim was taken.

Ian left on Sunday and, as usual, people came and went throughout the day, but fortunately no one moved into the Rats' Nest. My old mate Del arrived, and moved into the Steps, following Gary. John Buckley, who fished Rodney Meadow with me, arrived for the week and settled into Jimmy's where a couple of fish could be seen in the weed in the scorching conditions.

Sunday night was overcast and thunder rumbled in the distance. This was encouraging, for I knew a storm and rain could really get the fish feeding. The rumbling got louder - there were tremendous flashes and cataclysmic bangs. Lying on the bedchair, expecting torrential rain at the least, something suddenly flashed past the bivvy door and crashed into the lake fizzing and steaming. On investigation, I discovered that the on-coming storm was, in fact, a firework display in the grounds of a nearby football club! Feeling silly, I climbed into bed and fell asleep. At 2am the island rod was off again and a 23 was netted fairly quickly. I re-cast and this time the bait was spot on. At 3am this was away again and a considerably bigger fish ran out towards the gap. I had been playing the fish for about five minutes when I heard John's deep voice behind me, "I thought you'd had a take, Paul, so I thought I'd better nip round."

Now those of you who know John Buckley will know that he's a lovely bloke but likes to rub it in, so to speak when he's had one. So I suspected that John hadn't really come round to see me catch a fish. I kept quiet deliberately. After a minute or so of silence John said, "I've had a 25."

"Well done, mate," I replied, chuckling to myself after predicting the real reason Buckley had come round. With a sense of mischief I said, "I've had a 23."

"How do you know?" enquired John, mystified. "You haven't got it in the net yet."

"I've one in the sack, mate." I replied triumphantly.

John went all quiet. The fish out there was going crazy charging left and right and then right and left in the open water. Eventually, it ran under the island tree canopy and I could feel the line grating against the branches. I gave it some stick and soon it was boring and swirling in the margins. John dropped into the margin and sank the net. I walked up the bank, pulling the fish into the net. "It's a big one," said John in the torchlight. "Looks like another thirty."

Two sets of scales later and the fish refused to weigh any more than 29.14 - but who cares?

Early in the morning before the sun rose over the trees we photographed John's fish first - a chunky fit looking fish. On its return the fish waddled round the surface for a few seconds, causing initial concern, but it righted itself and swam off strongly. I got out the 23 and recognised it as the 22 from my first session - an ugly bull-nosed fish, which I was to see regularly from then on. I got out the big fish and Hippy Paul immediately recognised it, "The Old Pilgrim; it looks different but it's definetly thc Pilgrim, it was thirty last time." This was a lovely original fish and one. which had its life saved in the 1970's when just prior to a big fish kill on one of the lakes on the complex it had been moved into the lake I was fishing. Then it was a low twenty.

I returned the fish and we adjourned to John's swim for a chat and the usual good humoured wind-ups. When I passed the area where I had released the Pilgrim on my return to the Dock, he was still sitting in the margins. I watched the fish for a couple of minutes thinking how big it looked in the water. I cast a shadow over the fish and still it stayed in the margin, upright but reluctant to move, its gills and mouth moving slowly but showing no desire to swim away. I summoned Paul and John to have a look at the fish. We watched it for a few more minutes, wondering why it didn't swim off. After a while we splashed water around its face but it just stayed there, breathing, its fins moving very slowly. We touched it and still it would not swim away. We wondered what to do - we had all experienced problem fish before but they had usually responded by now. John got into the water with the fish and gently moved it backwards and forwards. There was some response but the fish still seemed unable to swim away. Paul commented that when he had photographed the fish it had looked very pale and yellow, but he had thought this was just a trick of the light. The fish was normally very grey; had it had a heart attack or something?

Still the fish remained in the margin, breathing, its fins sometimes moving. The problem was its tail : which did not seem able to move although everything else did. We were all very experienced carp catchers, but we were limited in our knowledge of dealing with a potentially critical fish problem like this one. In hindsight, we should perhaps have left the fish alone and not stressed it further by handling it - but how could we know? We continued to try to revive the fish by simulating swimming movements - again some response but not quite enough. Eventually the fish responded sufficiently for it to move out of range, whereupon it went lower in the water and remained static. We sat and watched it for a while until the sun rose too high, a warm breeze sprang up and it was lost to sight.

We all thought it would be alright. What had happened was very worrying, particularly as the lake had lost several fish recently, including a thirty-six pounder which Hippy Paul had found. I was worried sick, but as the day wore on with no sign of the fish in distress, the anxiety cleared and I got on with the chore of bait-making in the unbearable heat.

The night was quiet but I was troubled. I couldn't settle and slept only fitfully. Half asleep as the sun climbed again, I heard footsteps and Del stuck his head round the door. "Paul's found Pilgrim in the margins. He's gone, mate. They wanted me to tell you - it's not your fault, mate."

I cannot describe how I felt at that moment. Devastated, empty, numb, sick, gutted are words that could be used together to try to describe how I felt. I muttered some sort of reply to Del and he sensed that I wanted to be alone. It was an hour before I could face the world. We buried the Pilgrim at the back of the Dry Dock, so that he would return to the water he had lived in, grown in and died in, in respect and reverence of this fish that had given so much pleasure to so many over the years. I considered packing up there and then as I had no desire to fish and didn't even know if I could ever fish again.

We were worried about the rumours that could be circulated by the uncharitable and the envious and we all decided to keep the fish's death quiet to all but the regulars. We were also worried about a bailiff digging the fish up and merely dumping it or a trophy hunter digging it up. We felt the fish belonged to the lake. I was inconsolable and had to talk it through. No one, at least to my face, blamed me. I was glad that John had been with me at all the stages of the capture and release. Between us we had caught well over a hundred 20+ carp and a number of 30's. If I had been alone the uncharitable would have had a field day.

I decided to stay in the swim, basically to protect the grave. I fished only half-heartedly, my thoughts elsewhere, chucking out just two hookbaits into the baited areas. Early morning saw me catch a fish of 20.5 which came from the back channel. This was photographed straight away for I had vowed that I would never use a carp sack again - even if this might not have been to blame due to the short time it was sacked - in the summer months save for the few seconds required to set up the camera. After all, if we think about it do we really need to sack a fish with modern aids to night photography readily available? Is it necessary to even remotely put a fish's life at risk for the sake of a slightly better photograph?

During the day something happened which put the cherry on the cake. While talking to John and Paul, I spotted what looked like a dead bird in the heavy weed near the Gate Swim. Paul looked through the binoculars and realised it was another dead fish. He swam out and returned with a fish that was around the mid-twenty mark, quite dead and evidently had been so for several days. None of us recognised the fish, not even Paul who has an encyclopaedic knowledge of all the fish. This time we sent for a bailiff in case we had something on our hands besides obviously low oxygen levels. As it turned out this was luckily not the the case, although a couple of other fish turned up over the next few weeks.

As the bailiff took the fish away I'd had enough. I packed my gear away and made the long trek north feeling totally empty. I'd gone from the heights of ecstasy after a tremendous catch which was one of the highlights of my carp fishing career to the depths of despair and agony in a few short hours. I came very close on that dreadful drive home to giving up carp fishing for good.

....

Postscript: I was at a Carp Society Junior Fish-In at Farlows in September when Rob Maylin came bouncing into the cafe to tell me that "H" had died at 37.8. On my return home there was a message telling me to contact John Bevan, one of the regulars, as soon as I could. John told me what had happened. A lad had caught the fish from the Gap Swim - the first time in the season it had been captured - and it had shown distress from the moment of capture. The lad did nothing wrong but the fish was very pale and seemed paralysed. All sorts of things were tried including a desperate search for oxygen supplies, but to no avail. The lad had been devastated and had not even photographed the fish; it had been laid to rest at the back of the swim.

After some time I have managed to come to terms with the Pilgrim's death. We're fishing for live animals, the bigger of which are sometimes old and tired like race horses. But we are not really able to put them out to grass. When we put a metal hook into any carp we subject it to tremendous, unnatural, physical stress. It's wrong of us to assume that the old big boys can take it forever. They can't. As long as we take great care of them we can minimalise the stress and the pressure. But there are bound to be casualties, occasionally, which we can do little about.

Having come to realise this it's still very, very hard to come to terms with when it happens to you. I hope it doesn't.

*Never Mind The B*ll*cks. . .*
here's the sensible guide to using rigs...

Anyone who bought this book expecting to see the latest "secret rig" exposé will have been greatly disappointed. There is more nonsense written about rigs than any other subject in carp fishing. When putting this book together, friends have told me that for it to be more commercially viable I must "put loads and loads of rig drawings in it - that's what they want!" What on earth for? There are rig drawings in this book but they show rigs which have been demonstrably successful. There are no fantasy rigs within these pages. Yet I see others recommending rigs they have "created" which can't possibly work as claimed or present a bait to a fish underwater as shown in the said diagram! I've fished with guys on the waters were they have claimed to have used such rigs with success - well, I didn't see them in use! Perhaps I wasn't looking?

The hair rig was the giant leap forward. It turned what had become known as twitches into runs. Dave Powell told me about this thing called the hair rig. He was fishing with Kevin Maddocks on Ashlea, who had shown it to him. Dave didn't show me the rig or tell me anything about it. I just had this name - the hair rig. I turned it over in my mind, day after day, tying up rigs and trying to work out what it was. I just couldn't bring myself to ask him what it was. One afternoon, whilst fishing at Gorsty Hall, an idea just came into my head of what it might be. I tied a loop of heavy nylon to the bend of the hook and threaded a block of luncheon meat at the end of it so it hung free. Within two minutes, I had a blistering run and I knew I must be nearly there. I was using a size 1 hook so I wasn't quite there yet! I showed Peter Ray, one of Dave's BCSG mates this rig, and he told me where I was going wrong. The fish didn't know what had hit them for a time. Inevitably, things slowed down and so we tried to adapt the rig, improve it and make it more difficult for the fish to avoid being hooked. But none of those adaptations have been anything like as revolutionary as the hair - nor can they be.

On the next page is the rig I was using back in 1982 and the rig I use now in open water fishing in 1997. Not all that different are they? The key thing is that my 1982 rig would still catch fish on any water in England today, although it is not as good as the 1997 rig. How little things have changed - and I don't see how resorting to a drop rig, anchor rig, bent whatsit or sliding wedding ring rig or whatever, would make the slightest difference in

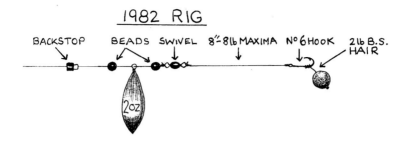

1982 RIG

BACKSTOP   BEADS SWIVEL   8"-8lb MAXIMA   Nº6HOOK   2lb B.S.
                                                        HAIR

2oz

1997 RIG

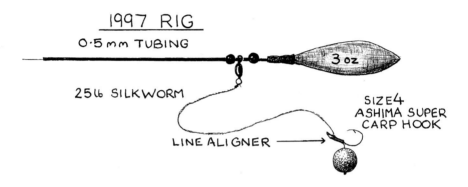

0.5mm TUBING

25lb SILKWORM

3oz

SIZE4
ASHIMA SUPER
CARP HOOK

LINE ALIGNER ——————→

the fish-catching stakes. I saw recently in *Carp-Talk* reports of anglers catching on a "Cuckoo" rig. Others were catching on a so-called "Harrier" rig. What the hell are these? They must think we're all cuckoo! I don't catch any less fish than guys around me who are using the latest so-called wonder rigs. Usually, I catch a damn sight more!

The least important thing in carp fishing to be worried about is the latest

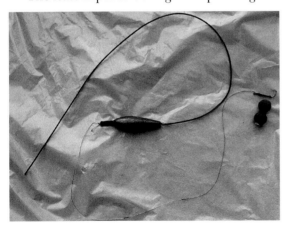

wonder rig. Providing your rig is neat and sensible, has a good sharp hook and you are confident in using it, your rig is as good as anyone else's out there. Realise too, that a rig isn't just what goes on around the hook but includes everything you cast out. This is very important.

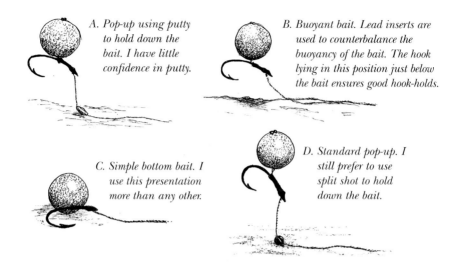

A. Pop-up using putty to hold down the bait. I have little confidence in putty.

B. Buoyant bait. Lead inserts are used to counterbalance the buoyancy of the bait. The hook lying in this position just below the bait ensures good hook-holds.

C. Simple bottom bait. I use this presentation more than any other.

D. Standard pop-up. I still prefer to use split shot to hold down the bait.

The first factor I take into consideration when deciding on any rig I cast out is how I am intending to present the bait. This generally means choosing between a pop-up, a critically balanced/buoyant bait or a bottom bait. I often use double baits and this often also involves deciding on what combination of these three types of baits to employ. The decision to use one particular type of bait presentation will affect my set-up to a degree. For example, if I use a pop-up, I will employ a shorter hooklength than when using a bottom bait. I will normally use a lighter hook and possibly a smaller one, and so on.

I'll look at some aspects of rigs in turn.

Hooks

Since they have been available, I have always used chemically sharpened hooks, since I can't manually get as sharp a hook as that obtained by chemical etching. Hook sharpness is the most important aspect of any rig. I've seen advice written that argues that even chemically sharpened hooks should be touched up with a sharpening stone. I regard that advice as poor, as the whole point of chemically sharpened hooks is that they have already been sharpened sufficiently. Messing around with a sharpening stone leaves chemically sharpened points more brittle, more likely to fracture and turn inwards. I've used chemically sharpened hooks straight out of the packet for years and have never experienced any problems with lack of sharpness.

All hooks should be inspected closely before use and discarded if they look a bit 'iffy'. Check the eyes and the size of barb. Out of a pack of fifty, I probably discard half a dozen on appearance alone. One thing I have always done is to change my hook after every fish. I've drawn some criticism for this, but I feel a hook is subjected to great stress when playing a carp and thereafter is much more prone to springiness and thus likely to fall out. A hook that has penetrated a carp's flesh is never going to be as sharp again, and tidying it up with a sharpening stone etc. is a recipe for disaster. Modern hooks cost a few pence and I'd rather put on a fresh hook than lose that big thirty because I was too lazy to ensure my rig was 100% efficient. Some of the modern braids start to unweave and show stress areas too after playing a heavy fish. I probably have up to 50 ready-tied hooks for every session, and I can change a complete hooklength and hook in the dark in about thirty seconds! At the end of the day, confidence is the vital factor. I'm confident when I change my hook after every fish, and you can't fish well without this vital psychological factor.

My choice of hook is a limited one through experience. I've tried most brands and types of hooks, but keep coming back to the same ones. Over silt, I have mostly used Drennan Super Specialists. I relate hook size to bait size - using a size 4 mostly, but going down to a size 6 when using smaller baits in winter. They are strong, sharp and reliable. Over gravel, I use the Drennan Boilie Hook in size 4. The size 6 Boilie hook doesn't seem as strong or reliable as the size 4. When fishing pop-ups, I like the original Gamakatsu in size 6 or 8, but this hook is increasingly difficult to get hold of. More recently, thanks to Julian Cundiff and Richard Skidmore, I have switched over for all my fishing - except on gravel pits - to the Ashima Super Carp hook C310. These are similar to the Gamakatsu in appearance, but are much stronger making them ideal for both pop-ups, bottom baits, clear water or heavy weed. These also have a slightly inturned eye. For me, these are the best all round hooks on the market and I have gone over to them completely, moving away from the Drennan range, save for pits where I need the beak point of the Boilie Hook to stand up to gravel. Ashima produce a number of different patterns and I'll also be trying one of their barbless range on one of the waters I now fish where barbless hooks are compulsory. This is the C145 model.

Bait presentation

Over much of the period this book covers, I've fished baits from a mid-shank position off the hook which I still think is the most effective form of presentation, providing as it does, an effective angle of separation between boilie and hook. In the last couple of years, I've gone over to the line-aligner form of presentation due to its neatness and plain efficiency. I use 1.6mm shrink tube for the line-aligner which I shrink using steam, a method which damages braid the least. Whether it provides the hook-turning effect which is regarded as so important to others is debatable, however, hook-holds for me have been good and deep - but having said that, they were with the mid-shank position too! I don't think this testing for hook turning with the "finger" or "palm" test is particularly meaningful. What is meaningful is the positioning and extent of the hookhold in the fishes mouth itself, and I'm currently happy with what I'm getting from the line-aligner, although I'm also sure bending the eye inwards to achieve an offset eye would have the same effect. Incidentally, I must be one of the few anglers in Britain who has never caught a fish on the old bent hook presentation. I played around with this on the Tip Lake but was put off by its crudity and the possible detrimental effect on the strength of the hook caused by amateur bending with pliers. In the end, I discarded it completely. Others around me on the so-called rig sensitive Tip Lake persevered with it and caught - but it didn't exactly set the world alight.

In terms of length of hair, I favour a shortish one. I like the edge of the boilie to rest against the bend of the hook, although I have played around and varied the length of the hair from time to time. As with a lot of rig experiments, results were inconclusive. I have always pierced my baits and have used sundry "boilie stops" - I am an abject failure at trying to tie baits on with dental floss etc. They always fly off when I cast them in, which is not to be recommended!

Hooklengths

This is very important in two related aspects. I guess the standard length of hooklength in use is around nine inches. That should tell you something. I very often start on every water fishing a standard length hooklength but see what happens. A tell-tale sign that there are problems, is the number of fish that simply drop off and the number of times the hook comes free of the fish when it is netted. That tells you to look at the length of the hooklength. On the Mangrove, I found that by the autumn of 1996, virtually every fish I hooked I was getting in, but the hook would invariably fall out of the mouth as soon as things were not under tension in the net. Earlier in the season, hookholds were deep and required forceps. I was using the bog-standard nine inch hooklengths. I increased the length of the hooklength by only 3 inches but the difference it made was remarkable - with deep hookholds resulting again. Similarly, shortening the hooklength might have achieved the same effect. The basic lesson is to avoid stereotyped presentations and be adaptable once you come across problems.

The type of hooklink material can also be critical. When fish are feeding heavily, any type of hooklink will catch fish. When the fish are more cautious feeders it may be necessary to think about hooklink material. My bog-standard hooklength is 25lb Kryston Silkworm which I rate very highly, but there are times when I'll resort to good old fashioned nylon if it will increase my opportunities. Nylon has a different feel to the fish when it is testing baits, it is springier and I suspect more difficult to eject. The success of stiff-rigs demonstrates this. Whilst everyone is using a variety of different materials, nylon has a long productive life - if everyone gets onto it then a braid will outfish it in time again. I remember something Dave Powell said to me once in the late 1970's, "In the early '70s, I had a big edge. Everyone was on nylon, so I went on braid and I caught lots more fish than anyone else. Now, everyone's on braid and I've lost my edge." That comment interested me, and I've always tried to be flexible in terms of hooklengths and try to use things a little bit different to that which most are using on a particular water. For example, a lot is promised by Kryston's new Snakeskin material. It is excellent, and I tested some of the prototype versions out. If just a handful of people were using it they would clean up everywhere they went. But of course, Dave Chilton has to make a living and so makes it available to all - which is why it will never realise its true potential. It will catch lots of fish, sure, but through over-use it will be short-lived in terms of success, because everyone will be using it - except me. You lose the edge because so many are using it. It could be argued that because Snakeskin can be adapted in a dozen different ways this is never going to happen. Well, thousands will be trying those different ways of presenting it on every water in the land. Sounds like a good time to stay on the 25lb Silkworm to me!

Try to be flexible on the hooklink front and, if you find something unique in terms of material, keep it to yourself for as long as you can.

When using braid, I tend to make it lie flat by applying a few blobs of Magma or lead wire. This avoids the "looping effect". However, I still caught many carp without doing this, before I realised this might be a problem. I'm not sure the "looping effect" is a problem in terms of spooking fish at all really - I've seen no hard evidence. I have seen instances of small nuisance fish pecking at a looped line. (I once had the mad brainwave of soaking my hooklengths in amino acids - there was frantic small fish activity - until a pike bit my hooklength in half!) I have also watched how a bait can be eventually moved by pressure on the looped braid due to strong undertows. I don't think these are anything but minor points. The bottom line (excuse the pun) is that I'm more confident when having the braid down on the bottom and in a sport where so much depends on frame of mind that is sufficient justification.

Swivels

Only one choice for swivels, these should be the Berkley type and, crucially, have round eyes. Diamond eyed swivels can cause excessive knot strangulation under pressure, leading to line breakage. Swivels need to be checked regularly, particularly at stress points around the eye and where the shank runs into the main body. Swivels that are slightly bent should be discarded. Similarly, swivels roughened by gravel should be instantly replaced.

Leads

These are very important. They should not be simply regarded as aids to get your bait out and the weight that causes the hook to prick in the mouth - although these are crucial functions.

Firstly, ensure leads are reliable. There are some very poor ones on the market, with poor quality swivels, and staples and have little bits of ironmongery sticking out of them. These are best avoided. I use leads made by Mark Shirley of MOD Developments, but there are good leads being manufactured by Roger Smith and Kerry Barringer, Mike Willmott of Essential Products and Korda Developments. Some of these boys have made lead principles into an art form. I tend to keep things simple, using three basic types. One is a Zipp-shaped type for open water fishing and pits, the second is an in-line lead for weed work, the third a fluted tri-lobe type for very soft silt (they won't sink as far as conventional shaped leads) or for situations where I want a fast rising lead to flip over weed or steep bars.

I don't coat my leads for the idea that carp are frightened of a lump of old lead is just plain daft. Coating leads would also inhibit the other purpose I have for them - to act as a guide as to what I am fishing over. On pits, they will scour which will give me an indication of the sort of gravel I'm fishing on. Over silt, they will discolour and take on the smell of the silt I'm fishing

From left to right, in-line tri-lobe, in-line standard lead, tri-lobe, Zipp-type.

in. I scratch a few lines into the lead to get silt samples. Coated leads can't be read to the same degree at all - my leads are a source of vital information.

In terms of lead size, flexibility is important. On Hawk and Capesthorne, as you will have read, I had tremendous success on two waters where the carp had got accustomed to encountering heavy lead resistance by using light leads. I got a lot more takes simply because the carp had developed a method of dealing with/testing baits presented on very heavy set-ups. Hookholds on the light leads were tremendous. On most lakes today, most are using leads of between two and three ounces. Using one ounce leads or smaller can really make a difference. A small lead in the middle of Redesmere would be deadly. You can go the other way too. For example when fishing margins, I tend to use very heavy leads because a lot of people use light ones.

Two other ways I use lead. I use lead inserts in pop-ups as a counterbalance, to make a buoyant bait - just about held down by the weight of the hook - or to reduce the amount of weight needed on the hooklink when using pop-ups. This is perfectly safe, because the carp doesn't eat the hookbait. I don't favour putting too much weight on hooklinks which I think might inhibit natural behaviour when a carp is sucking in and blowing out baits. I aim to put the smallest shot possible on the hooklink to hold the pop-up down. Notice I don't use putty for this task. A lot of the putties

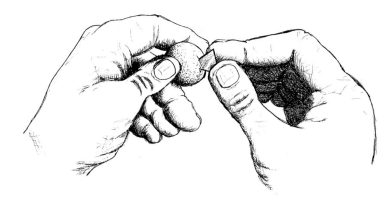

around are not all that trustworthy in terms of adhesion. I use a lot of liquid foods and oils in my baits which obviously get onto my hands and make putty difficult to work with. I use putty to pin down anti-tangle tubing and sometimes as a stop on tubing when using a helicopter set-up. I use small non-toxic shot - usually a size 4 maximum - to hold down pop-ups. These don't come off even on the hardest cast and are also more discreet than putty. I am certain carp can smell putty - tank fish will suck it in and try to eat it, but this isn't the reason I don't use it on the hooklink, it is simply that I don't trust it to stay on the link. That confidence factor again.

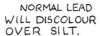

NORMAL LEAD WILL DISCOLOUR OVER SILT.

SCOURED LEAD WILL DISCOLOUR BUT ALSO TRAP SILT IN RECESSES FOR ANALYSIS.

Anti-Tangle Tubing

I use this for all my fishing today, as I want to achieve a certain no-tangle situation. Only some form of anti-tangle tubing will guarantee this. Only on a couple of waters in the past, have I suspected that there was a problem with using it - because others not using it were getting more takes, although even then I was sceptical. I would concede that in very clear margins in daylight conditions, possibly some carp can react to tubing, rigs and hookbaits generally. Some carp are more cautious than others and get caught very rarely as a consequence. These carp - a minority - tend to get caught at night or early morning or in coloured water conditions. On the waters I currently fish, I don't think tubing is a problem at all, and they range from very clear to very cloudy. I still prefer, though, to keep the tubing as discreet as possible and rarely go above 0.5mm diameter for open water fishing. This is also pinned down with putty. For weedbed fishing, I use the tough Robustatube material as the soft open water tubing I use is cut to shreds in lily pads and other tough weeds.

The PVA bag. The fish have been over-exposed to these on many waters.

PVA

One thing I always incorporate into my rig presentations is a PVA stringer if I can. The stringer guarantees the rig will be tangle-free and having a couple of baits right next to the hookbait ensures it is emphasised amongst a bed of baits. I've fished a single bait against a stringered bait

The PVA stringer. Much more variable forms of presentation are possible than can be obtained by using a PVA bag.

amongst a bed of baits and the stringered hookbait consistently takes more fish. I've used PVA bags very extensively for years with tremendous success, but I've shied away from them in the past two seasons due to their sheer over-exposure. Few people are using stringers as they are considered old hat and are filling up those PVA bags instead.

M y rigs are pretty standard then, although if you ever see them you will notice that they are very neat and ordered - unlike the rest of my bankside paraphernalia.

I am certain that in the future a rig will come along that will be as revolutionary as the hair rig was. Several times, I've locked myself in a room, with pen and paper, all the rig bits etc and tried to force myself to come up with something. I have come up with rigs that would be deadly but they were unethical and would be banned! I've not come up with anything that people would accept and which would still be a major advance. They have just been variants or adaptations on a basic theme, like all the other rig advances since the hair.

But one day perhaps.....till then, cuckoo, cuckoo.

The Pilgrim from Tip Lake at 29lb 14oz.

The Tip Lake Big Linear, 30lb 12oz.

*Looking out from The Pallets on the Tip Lake on the only occasion
I managed to fish the swim.*

Chubby Chops from the Tip Lake - my second capture at 31lb 4oz.

My home at the Tip Lake, the Dry Dock. Inset: The Brown One - a favourite big fish of mine.

Tip Lake. Scar at 32lb 4oz.

The Hump looking into The Mad at Harefield. My baits are by the swans - in inches of water.

Slug's Bay at Harefield.

A 'goldfish' of 21lb from The Mad.

Maurice the Mirror at 28lb from Harefield.

Bitemark at 31lb plus - caught from The Mad.

A classic common of 27lb from the Stick Bar at Harefield.

Fat bloke with a big, fat Redesmere common.

A Mangrove sunset.

An old 25 plus known as the Animal from The Mangrove.

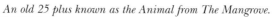

My first capture of the rarely-caught Mangrove Cream fish at 31lb 12oz.

The fabulous Mangrove Scaley at 35lb plus.

Conan The Barbless at 34lb 4oz from The Mangrove.

Three Little Capesthorne Lessons

In the late 1980's, I fished a number of summer evening sessions on Capesthorne Hall, an estate lake in the heart of beautiful Cheshire, which contains a good head of pressured, cute carp. It was a popular day-fishing only water and so it was necessary to concentrate very hard on the water to succeed. Each day, a different cast list of anglers turned up at the water. I learned a great deal during those barmy summer evenings at Capesthorne and I have applied the knowledge I gained there elsewhere with considerable success.

One particularly hot July evening, the carp were up on the surface and were interested in taking the odd floater. The notorious Beachcaster Rig had been used extensively on the water for a couple of seasons, but the club had banned the method due to the damage being done to the fishes mouths and due to the fact that it had made a previously prolific floater water very difficult. I agreed with the decision, for in my view the method causes a decline in both fish and fishing wherever it is used and de-skills the whole art of floater fishing.

Despite the ban, the fish were very suspicious of any floating baits, although they clearly wanted them. Occasional floaters would only be taken at some distance from the bank and only after they had drifted a good way away from where they had been initially catapulted in. For a quarter of an hour, I tried to increase their interest to see if I could tempt one. Steady feeding seemed to inspire confidence, and, after this time, more fish were taking more floaters, but individual fish only seemed to take one or two each before spooking. After another ten minutes, one or two fish were feeding more confidently. Out went the controller and it was allowed to drift down in the gentle breeze to my right. The hooklink was 9' of 7lb Drennan

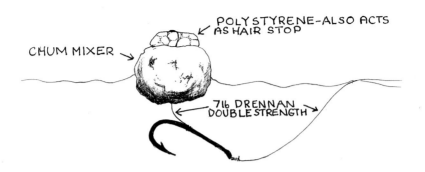

POLYSTYRENE-ALSO ACTS AS HAIR STOP

CHUM MIXER

7lb DRENNAN DOUBLE STRENGTH

WHEN USING MIXERS ENSURE BAIT STANDS HIGH IN THE WATER SO THAT IT LOOKS LIKE THE FREE OFFERINGS. USE POLYSTYRENE OR CORK. OTHERWISE, THE WEIGHT OF THE HOOK PULLS THE BAIT DOWN MAKING IT LOOK SUSPICIOUS. THIS ALSO ENSURES HOOK IS CORRECTLY PRESENTED TO A TAKING FISH.

Double Strength, the hookbait being presented on a size 8 Super Specialist with a piece of cork or polystyrene acting as a hair stop but also to help lift the bait, so that it appeared to rest on the water at the same height as a free offering.

The controller seemed to have a very detrimental effect. The carp disappeared completely from its vicinity, even when it was allowed to drift at the same speed as the free floaters. In fact, whilst carp refused to feed wherever the controller drifted, they fed enthusiastically on floaters quite close to me and about where the controller had been initially cast to. A group of carp were also picking off floaters beyond the current position of the controller to my right. There was a definite no-go area around the controller and hookbait. I tried a number of different ploys, like shortening and lengthening the hooklink and casting the controller in all sorts of different areas, but couldn't raise any interest wherever I cast it to.

An old friend of mine, Andy Talbot, popped into the swim for a chat. He wasn't fishing but just looking around. I was telling him about the problem with the floaters when an idea occurred to me. I fired out a trail of Chum Mixers so that they would drift down in a continuous stream to my right. I cast the controller right out in front of me, where the carp had fed when I had allowed the controller to drift down a good way. This time, I would not allow it to drift with the free offerings. Free offerings were catapulted to the left of the controller which would ensure there were free offerings around the hookbait when a carp took it - providing that is, my ploy worked.

Floaters which had drifted about 40 yards to my right were now being taken well by carp. I asked Andy to creep up to this area and cast out a spare rod which had a standard bottom bait rig on it, in the general area of these fish. Off he went and he did exactly as I instructed. The fish immediately disappeared from the area. Within a few minutes a group of carp were feeding on the free offerings around the controller and the hookbait was taken and a good double landed.

After that, I started using two controllers when floater fishing at Capesthorne, one actually fishing, one being a "dummy" for frequent casting. The one I caught fish on, was always the one that had been cast out in the water for a significantly longer period of time than the other.

....

Over a period of a couple of weeks, I had a good run of fish and in short evening sessions in one particular swim I was catching four or five fish a trip. The bulk of these were coming to the same rod, despite the fact that the rods were fished at an identical distance from the bank. Exactly, the same bait, rig and fishing technique was being employed on both rods. The bottom felt identical and leads coming back didn't read differently, and the hook didn't produce bloodworm from one spot rather than the other. Neither spot produced any worms. There had to be a difference, though, to explain why carp preferred to pick a bait up from this particular spot and not the other one. One evening, I sacrificed valuable fishing time and plumbed that spot with a very light lead and float. That small area of about five square feet was four inches deeper than the surrounding lake bed, including the lesser successful spot. Insignificant? Not to the carp. Since then I have found that minor depth variations have been critical in silt on several waters.

. . . .

One particular season, the controlling club, Stoke-On-Trent AS, passed a rule that the maximum lead size that could be used was three quarters of an ounce. There's usually a way around silly rules, but in this instance there were rumours that the then Chairman - who took no prisoners - would be walking around the bank with a set of electronic scales, checking leads. I thought I'd better comply with the rule but still had daft ideas about using 2oz back-leads or several three quarter ounce back leads! In the event, I decided to just stick the three quarter ounce bombs on and await events.

Stalking in a quiet corner at Capesthorne

I had takes fairly quickly and the interesting thing was that hook holds were absolutely incredible and it took delicate forceps operations to get the hooks out. Previous hookholds with more standard rigs, incorporating a heavy lead had been nothing like as good.

It occurred to me that the fish had become educated to test for the heavy lead, by picking up the bait, extending the hooklink and, on feeling strong resistance ejecting the bait causing light hook holds or none at all. It also seemed logical to presume that the lighter lead didn't sink into the silt as deeply and made more of the hooklink available to be tightened before resistance was felt. The longer the hooklink, the more confidence is

The lake biggie, the legendary Moby.

inspired in the fish because it uprights and moves further before hitting resistance. It also seemed fair to presume that baits were presented better on the lighter rig over what was fairly deep silt.

I took the light lead approach on to different waters with success,

A common caught on the two controller method.

particularly in situations when everyone else was using heavy leads. I still use them today, too, when I think the carp have begun to behave like those spooky Capesthorne fish. My one regret is that when I fished Redesmere where it was often necessary to fish at ranges of over 100 yards, I did not spend time developing a rig that would put a light lead at that distance. A rig with a one ounce lead at extreme range, surrounded by rigs utilising three or four ounces in weight just might have cleaned up!

A twenty pounder caught from a small depression in the silt at Capesthorne.

Harefield Lake

"Don't forget to smell the hops along the way."
Rod Hutchinson

By 1990, my fishing on Darenth Tip Lake was drawing to a close. Rule changes on the complex had been introduced in an attempt to give everyone in theory a fairer crack of the whip. In reality, the major problem was simply too many members. The big weight increases of the Tip Lake fish had attracted a lot more anglers. The rule changes imposed a 7 day occupancy on swims, but on the Tip Lake this led to the understandable practice of friends swim-swapping every seven days. New swims had been cut into the lake by the management against the wishes of the anglers on the lake and their close proximity to established swims was causing tension. Swims were at a premium, and for me as a long distance carp man life was made very difficult. By the end of July, I'd caught a new thirty from the water but I had lost interest in it. I'd planned to fish right through, but decided I needed a break from the busy waters and retreated with my family to France for a month for some laid-back fishing with Jon Burrows.

On my return, I started to think about where to fish next on the southern scene. I'd planned originally to move onto Longfield after the Tip, but Leisure Sport's decision to close it down had put paid to that. It was looking like Yateley, but some of the Tip Lake regulars had moved there as well as some of the Longfield lads. I expected a lot more angling pressure down there, particularly on the Car Park Lake which I was interested in. Beyond these options, there were not many other waters to consider because there are not many accessible big carp waters in the south east for a bloke from Manchester.

There were changes going on within Boyers. Dougal Gray had been brought in as head bailiff and there was a more relaxed atmosphere. I had a long discussion with John Stent about our differences over Rodney Meadow at a Carp Society conference and I was invited back into the Boyer Leisure scheme. I was placed on the waiting list for Harefield and was invited to join for the following season. That solved the problem of where to go after the Tip Lake.

I knew Harefield would be a challenge and possibly more difficult than any other water I'd fished. It was a largish water with legendary gravel bars. Despite recent stockings, it was still a very difficult water to consistently catch carp from. In addition, it was being heavily fished by some of the most experienced carp anglers around. From memory, the cast list in that first season included Zenon and Rael Bojko, Phil Harper, my old mate Steve Allcott, Rob Maylin, Dave Whibley, Steve Briggs, Pete Jones, Travolta, Essex John, Isle of Wight Paul, Paul Boyd, Martin Clarke, Dave Courtney, Bob Sammett, Simon Day, Kevin Gulliford, Hampshire Chris, Simon Lavin and Chris Ladds. These guys had been around.

There were no rota's then and I knew the lake would be busy. The main difference between Harefield and the Tip was that most Harefield swims were well spaced out - in some cases very well spaced out. On the Tip Lake, many of the Fence Bank swims were only five yards apart which I hated. Each Harefield swim had a large amount of exclusive water in front of it which made for better fishing generally. Although it was busy, one could still fish how one wanted in relative peace and quiet, without having to live on top of other people.

My first trip was in early July, and I found the lake was very busy when I arrived on Friday afternoon. There were very few swims free that I fancied and eventually, I set-up in a swim half-way down the Road Bank. In front of it was a small, bare island called Dougal's Hump about 90 yards out. This represented the surface of the first main bar, the water between the bank and the island consisted of a deep boat channel and a few minor clay and gravel mounds. I elected to fish both baits some distance apart at the back of this bar. I wasn't mentally or technically geared up to try and fish any further out, although others were thrashing out. The "Famous Five" were on The Causeway although they seemed to be on the move. There was also activity on my bank, with two chaps literally running past with gear down towards the Bottom Bank. The guy fishing next to me I discovered to be an old mate from my Rodney days, Eddie "Ham and Egg" Lancaster.

"What's going on Eddie?" I enquired. It was like Piccadilly Circus in the rush hour.

"All the fish are showing off the Bottom Bank and The Stick Bar. I don't know whether to move myself," said Eddie.

"Well mate," I replied "with all those going round there, I reckon they'll spook the fish and we might just be in the right spot when they move. I'm staying put."

After five minutes another old Rodney mate, Jim Rich, set-up next door to Eddie in the Island Swim.

He'd just moved off the famous Harefield Point. I couldn't quite believe that. I asked him why he'd moved off reputedly the best swim on the lake.

"I've been on there three days without a touch. I've seen no fish there either. I know I'm probably mad to move, but I was cracking up."

I knew about the Point and contemplated moving there myself. Through the binoculars I saw two guys moving in so that option was gone. They bagged-up later in the week!

Just before dusk, Zenon moved in on the far side of the island to Jim. The wind had been gradually getting up and so I didn't re-cast before dark in case I couldn't get to the spots I'd baited. I was using 8lb line with a short 15lb leader and 100 yards was the limit with my little Cardinal 55's - in fact there wasn't much more line on the spools!

On dark, the two lads who'd earlier run past with all the gear re-appeared only to set-up in the same swims again. They were called Nick and Nigel.

"What's going on?" I asked.

"Well, the fish are moving up. There's too many fishing down there - there's leads flying everywhere - and the fish are moving. No one's caught. There's a few showing in the middle now, right out in front of Zen," said Nigel.

This was a right old pantomine. I settled down for the night. Harefield was a day water and I didn't expect much to happen.

I was up fairly early and put the kettle on. I sat on the bedchair looking out across the water. I saw Nelson roll ten yards to the left of Dougal's Hump on the nearside of the bar. I know it sounds unbelievable, but I'd seen it roll and caught so many times at Rodney Meadow that I recognised every feature of the fish. When Albert Hayes caught Nelson, it surfaced fifty yards out when hooked next to the Big Island and I shouted, "You've got Nelson, you jammy so and so." That set the old boy really shaking!

If the fish was on this side of the bar it had to go over it and down and find my bait. Nelson liked beds of boilies! It crossed my mind that I was

Nelson. I tried hiding behind him when someone said, "Your round."

about to catch Nelson at last.

Ten minutes later, I had a run and bent into a carp. As it came over the bar, I pulled it quickly towards the bank, winding the little reel handle frantically. Eddie came running up, "You got one?"

"Yes," I said, "I've got Nelson."

"How do you know?" enquired Eddie.

"I just know, he'll be in the edge in a minute. Will you get down and net it for me?"

The fish came straight into the bank, did one slight backward and forward movement, then gave up. Eddie scooped him up. Nelson either goes or he doesn't, this time he decided not to bother - it was pretty undramatic stuff.

"It's Nelson," exclaimed Eddie, peering into the net.

"I told you it was," I said. Cool.

Amazing really. I'd netted this fish several times for others and probably put a hook in him myself at least twice on Rodney yet failed to land him. I'd come down to the difficult Harefield, made two casts and within 12 hours had caught Nelson - the biggest known fish in the lake at that time. Pure luck.

We hoisted the one-eyed boilie machine onto the scales and settled on a weight of 37lb 8oz - twelve ounces lighter than Rob had caught him at during opening week. The crowd gathered round to take the photographs, most of which didn't come out very well. Zen came up to take the mickey and then congratulate me. "The drinks are on you tonight then, Paul," said Zen with a wink.

Now, it is a long standing tradition on Harefield that the captor of a big Harefield carp gets in a round at the *Horse and Barge*. It was a tradition I had mixed feelings about, particularly as there were a lot of anglers on the water and I reckoned the thirteen quid I had in my pocket wouldn't stretch very far! Towards early evening, Dougal popped down to see me. Congratulations and all that. "See you soon at the pub. Don't forget the drinks are on you," said Dougal, with a far more sinister-looking wink.

I didn't feel very well.

I put off going to the pub as long as I could. I was the only one left on the lake by the time I got scrubbed up, shaved and changed. I walked at about 4 miles an hour along the lake and then down the gravel road to the pub. As I stood opposite the pub, there was a huge cheer and what seemed like hundreds of carp anglers spilled out. Dougal had been busy! Not only the Harefield lads were there, but so were some of the Savay lads. There were lads from Harrow, Pit 4, Farlow's, The Con Club and the Fisheries - from everywhere in the valley. I put my hand in my pocket and felt the two crisp fivers in my pocket. I'd left the three quid in the bivvy in case I ran out of petrol on the long drive home. I needed a miracle on a par with the five loaves and two fishes. Salvation was at hand. Grinning at me with pint in

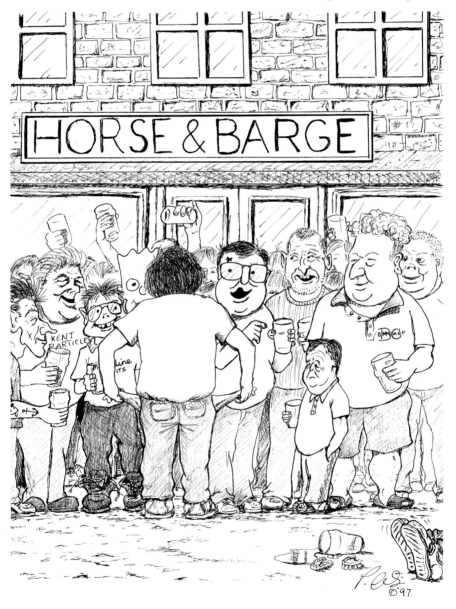

hand was an occasional employer of mine, "Fatty" Bainbridge - who owed me some money and was always "wedged". He was fishing nearby and couldn't miss out on the fun. A quick word in his shell-like secured an advance. In we all piled, only for me to find another load of carp anglers already ensconced within. Isn't it strange that blokes who normally drink lager suddenly develop a taste for double brandies and Black Russians etc, when someone else is in the chair?

By the end of the evening, I'd secured a substantial loan from Lenny Bainbridge too. The inevitable mass Indian invasion followed - what a surreal scene that was.

I had a head like a box of frogs in the morning. I wish I'd never caught Nelson. . .

. . . .

A conversation with Steve Allcott on the Sunday morning (once I'd sorted out the disaster of a bivvy and eventually cast out for an hour or two), set me thinking about how I was going to approach the water. We were sitting drinking coffee and looking out and talking about the water. Steve pointed out into the lake and said, "We've done all right on that spot there."

"Whereabouts?" I asked, keen to find out where.

"Where that far tuftie is - there," replied Steve, pointing to a black speck way out.

I guessed that it was about 170 yards out.

"I can't cast that far, Steve."

"Get the right gear and you will," said Steve.

I doubted if I could ever cast that far even with the gear. Steve could - easily - but he was twice my size!

The other thing I wondered about was that even if I could reach that spot, how could I ever hook a fish and bring it in safely over all those bars? I'd seen Zen getting out to the middle that weekend on light line, and I'd heard he'd had takes but landed nothing so far that season. In the middle "zone" there were always plenty of fish - they showed there at certain times of the day almost constantly and they were being caught from there - but it just wasn't me.

I realised I needed to upgrade my tackle and buy some bigger reels and rods, but fishing a single bait in the middle of nowhere just wasn't what I was confident with. It seemed like the needle in a haystack approach. My strengths lie in applying bait and fishing for carp within baiting range. I

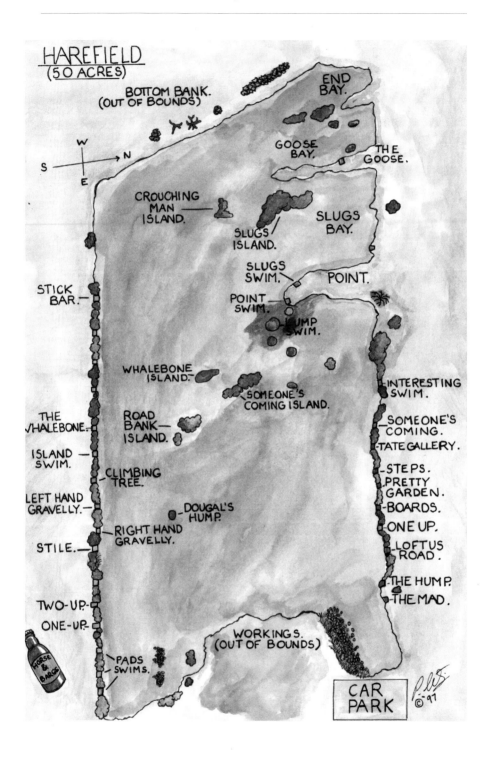

always believe anglers should fish to their strengths.

The two most successful anglers on Harefield in recent times had been my old Rodney buddies, Simon Lavin and Chris Ladds - Frogger and Carebear. I knew how they fished on Rodney and there was no way they were fishing in the middle of Harefield. They were into 100% efficiency and applying bait. As it happened, I bumped into the pair of them later that Sunday as I was walking around prior to going home. They were fishing around the Pads area - a long finger off the main body of the lake. I had a chat with them and it served to confirm what I thought their approach was. They were fishing swims on the lake where they could fish quite close and use bait. They were not interested in that thumping it out to the middle zone mark business - nor could they do it. They had been catching loads more than anyone else - Chris in particular.

When I got home I thought long about things. Carebear and Frogger were not strictly session men. Sure, they would fish for a few days whilst on holiday but they were basically weekend anglers. Yet they were outfishing virtual full-timers on the water. They were obviously keeping closely in touch with the water all the time like on Rodney and finding fish in quiet areas, away from the main body of the lake where the constant pressure was. They were fishing close, applying bait. I knew that the Harefield fish moved a great deal most of the time, and Carebear and Frogger would be moving with them. Hit and run type fishing.

I'd obtained a very detailed map of Harefield which had been thoroughly echo-sounded and charted. I had a good look at it. The main body of the lake ran from Someone's Coming across to the Island Swim, along to Jim's Swim and across to Loftus Rd - a central square. These were generally the range swims. The remainder of the lake were swims where one could fish at medium range and bait could be applied. Judging by Carebear and Frogger's results, these were the areas where multiple captures could be achieved. On my walk around, I'd had a good look at these areas. The Pads, The Stick Bar, the Bottom Bank swims, The Goose, The Point, The Lump, The Hump and The Mad. These had to be the swims to look at, depending on the wind and conditions, although it seemed to me that The Point and The Lump being outcrops in the middle of the lake would be productive under any conditions - hence their popularity. In these swims I could use a small-water approach and be efficient - with pin-point baiting and rig placement. I wanted to forget about the central square if I could, but would force myself to fish there if my preferred swims were all taken. In those

A view from Someone's Coming.

circumstances, I would prefer to fish The Causeway as the second bar was quite productive and it lay only 70 yards out. It still seemed a little bit like fishing in a line and trusting to luck, but it was preferable to fishing the Road Bank where very long range fishing with single baits was the norm. I'd caught Nelson from there on a fairly close cast but I didn't like it at all. All those big leads crashing around!

I'd invested in some big Daiwa PM4000 reels on the return from the first trip - just in case - but I guessed they would also help me fish at medium range with heavier line to avoid cut-offs and they would be useful for fishing on Redesmere where long range fishing was going to be necessary, although nothing like the ranges people were fishing at Harefield.

On my walk around, I'd been very interested in the two swims known as The Hump and The Mad. These lay at the Workings end of the lake. There was a fair bit of weed around here and - crucially - they were the two swims that warm south westerlies would end up in. I quite liked The Pads but guessed that the proximity of The Pads to the entrance would make these swims popular with short session men. The Point and Lump were head and shoulders above everywhere else as swims went, but I decided that I would concentrate the rest of my efforts on The Hump or The Mad if the winds were right, and if I couldn't get The Point or Lump.

One final consideration came into my tactical thinking. I couldn't be anything like as mobile as Chris and Simon. Living locally, they could take

The Island swim - the base of it was a productive spot, which was ignored by most.

the minimum of tackle. I'd have to take all the necessary paraphernalia with me for a four day trip, including food and bait and bait-making equipment and so on. Whilst I would not hesitate to move if I thought it worthwhile, I would be more dependant on getting a good swim and anticipate fish moving into it during my stay. It seemed to me too, that it was possible to move too often, which can be exhausting on a water as big as Harefield.

. . . .

I learned an important lesson on my second trip. The Mad and Hump were occupied, as was The Point. I wandered down to The Goose and found fish - a lot of them. I hurriedly set-up camp behind a large bush. I crept down the Goose Spit with the rods and banksticks. There was a lot of fish to my right in the Goose Bay - a frightening amount of fish really, with a lot of big ones. With shaking hands, I cast out two stringers and retreated to the bush. I could still see the water clearly and, for the next half hour, fish after fish rolled, crashed and head and shouldered. I estimated there was over a hundred fish, with some of the very big fish amongst them - Nelson, Black Spot, Orange Fish, The Fully Scaled, Little Pecs and a common that looked bigger than them all. I was certain I would get a take but nothing happened. After three-quarters of an hour, I had a rush of blood to the head. I thought I would fire out just a few boilies to maybe get a fish feeding more confidently for I thought they might be suspicious of the stringer. My lines were slack and I was sure they were not suspicious of the lines. I crawled down the Goose Spit and by hand I tossed out about half a dozen baits and then half a dozen further out by catapult. The baits were pretty well spaced out. I crept back into the bush to watch events. It was amazing. Within half an hour, the surface activity had ceased and every fish had just melted away. If I'd have had a piece of rope, I'd have hung myself from the bush. Those fish just wouldn't tolerate baits being put in over them. Why hadn't I just left the stringers out? I stayed in the swim for the rest of the night and I woke up at about 2am. I heard and saw fish rolling in the Slugs Bay on my left. I reeled in the rods from The Goose Bay, tied on stringers and flicked them into the Slugs. Ten minutes later, I hooked a fish which kited into a little bed of pads behind the spit I was set-up on. I had to strip off and go in for it which created a lot of disturbance. It was a fish of 17lb or so. The other fish disappeared again.

People had told me how easy it was to spook the fish into moving, but I hadn't realised how nervous they were.

I then realised that one of the secrets of cracking Harefield was to have the traps set before the fish arrived. If I'd have had the rigs and baits out before those fish had arrived in the Goose Bay I'd have caught. It also occurred to me that finding the fish moving and then casting to them could be seductive but counter-productive, it would be better to work out where they were moving to and get there before them. Really, I suppose, I should have pieced that fact together on my first trip when I caught Nelson.

The following morning, I moved into The Hump on the strength of the weather forecast which predicted strong south-westerlies were coming. I had a 22 common and lost another fish. I fished either of these two swims on my next three four day trips which made up that first season. These two swims were very close to each other but they were like chalk and cheese.

The Mad really was a tiny swim. A decade earlier, it had been the fourth swim or so along the bank and got its name due to the difficulty in landing fish because of the severe bars that used to lie out in front of it - which could drive carp anglers insane. The gravel workings gradually spread along the bank, burying previous swims and due to wind action vast amounts of silt were deposited on the notorious bars. The Mad today is a swim consisting entirely of deep and very soft silt deposits and averages about a foot in depth or less in terms of actual water. The deepest area - about the size of a small dinner table - is 18 inches which makes this a real hot spot.

On warm days, particularly in south westerlies or southerly winds, carp love to get right into the swim in numbers. It adjoins the gravel workings and a long cast could put a bait on the edge of a largish bay at the far side of the Workings which couldn't be reached from any other spot. The fish liked to hang around the Workings, for it was a quiet spot from an angling point of view and the gravel and sand was often being worked, dug out with a sling digger and then unwanted spoil dropped back in again. This attracted the carp. Bernard Loftus once told me that when he fished there, a 26 pounder had been caught in the sling bucket as it grubbed in the torn-up bottom for food. The water in The Mad was always coloured a reddish/brown which meant that fish would come in very close unaware that an angler was present. The other big advantage with The Mad was that if you hooked a fish, there were no bars to worry about. I never lost a fish in there.

There were three disadvantages. If there were no fish present or going to drift in, it could be very frustrating having such a limited amount of water to go at. Many left it alone or regarded it as completely insignificant because of that. Secondly, in the first season I fished the water, John Stent allowed bailiffs to fish the Workings and this was a massive edge, as they could fish very close to the fish which regarded the area as safe. If you were in The Mad, it was depressing to find a bailiff perched on the Workings right above the carp and the rig you were trying to catch one on! Thankfully, this was stopped for health and safety reasons in the end - but it caused some friction whilst it went on. Finally, with the area still being worked, gravel was constantly being removed or dumped into the swim. You never quite knew what the swim would look like from week to week. Once, I cast out and flaked out in the heat of the afternoon sun on the bedchair. I woke up to find both rigs buried under several tons of gravel. I wonder what archaeologists in a thousand years time will make of two carp rigs with fossilised boilies still attached under the gravel if they dig them up and find them?

The Hump was more typical of the rest of the lake, containing severe bars and several gravel "humps", hence its name. Soft, but extensive weed, covered the humps. A small island lay in front of the swim at about 100 yards. This was a nice casting marker (it had a good spot right in front of it) but it also separated the two swims. The bars which begin in the swim run the length of the Causeway. The fish came into the swim via the water between the Workings and the island or from along the bars. The bars as they move right are pretty severe and cut-offs are common. Fish come right into the bank in both The Mad and Hump, but I found they preferred to feed further out - at least 60 yards out. They seemed to just cruise along for the hell of it closer in.

I caught on every trip from one or other of the swims and the fish were all twenties. I'd had southerlies for all those trips and fish had drifted in. On one occasion, a mass of fish drifted in but just didn't feed, driving the guy in The Mad to distraction. I caught a twenty as they moved out across The Hump. The fish could be like that often. My catches were steady rather than spectacular, but I didn't see all that many fish caught whilst I was there, although generally a fish would come out somewhere on the lake each day. Chris and Simon had a big catch from the same area which I saw the tail-end of, and Martin Clarke had the magnificent Fully-Scaled from The Mad shortly afterwards. No one was taking the place apart, and many were not catching at all, so I was happy with my results that first season. I finished fishing the water in September, so I missed Rob's big catch off The Point later that season and Steve's capture of the Fully Scaled. I was so pleased for Steve - such a tremendous fish.

Baits and rigs were straightforward that first season.

Bait-wise, I'd settled on using the same base mix I'd used on the Tip Lake, but had altered the attractors slightly and was using a new oil for me:

Premier Fish Base

1ml Premier Peach Melba

1ml Premier Sweetener

1 drop per egg Nutrabaits Black Pepper essential oil

30 ml pure Salmon Oil

6 eggs

I'd take a 24 egg mix with me which would all go in in the first 24 hours and, after that, it was rolling time each day in the bivvy. I'd make what I thought I needed to each day. I was using big baits - far bigger than anyone else on the lake. Most were using small 15-18mm boilies and I wanted to be different. I also wanted to avoid the bream, which could be frightening. There were a lot of doubles in Harefield - you could do a week for a twelve pounder. I caught very few doubles and they were all over 16lb. I caught a high proportion of twenties. I think the big baits contributed to that statistic like they did on the Tip Lake.

One thing that I hadn't counted on in relation to bait application was the Harefield birdlife. There were masses of tufted duck, pochards, Canada geese, mallards, seagulls and coots and they were all boilie-eaters. There were also swans which lived on boilies. The birds could wipe you out completely in terms of bait very quickly and baiting during daylight could be fatal. I took to baiting after dark to avoid a wipe-out, and frantic landing-net waving during the day to try to keep the birds at bay. Sometimes, the only safe method in The Mad was to fish a stringer. In truth, I think on Harefield, more bait is eaten by the birdlife than the fish.

I'd spoken to Paul Boyd at length about rigs - he'd fished the water for years. His advice was to keep things simple and that he'd done best on bottom baits. "If they come past, and they stop to feed, they'll eat every bait around them and you'll get a take," I remember him saying. With my big boilies, bottom baits would be just fine as it would take a one ounce lead to hold them down if they were popped-up! I used PVA blobbed size 4 Drennan Super-Specialists as usual, with the new 25lb Silkworm from Kryston which was good stuff and superior to the original 15lb Silkworm I'd got used to using. To help the Silkworm sink flat, I used a couple of coils of fine lead wire as used by trout anglers on the hooklink to pin it down - a method I sometimes still use today. Kryston Magma had yet to arrive. I'd started to use the helicopter rig by this time and quite heavy leads for me at 3 ounces.

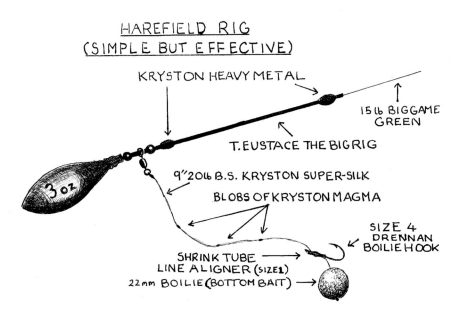

HAREFIELD RIG
(SIMPLE BUT EFFECTIVE)

KRYSTON HEAVY METAL

15lb BIGGAME GREEN

T. EUSTACE THE BIG RIG

9" 20lb B.S. KRYSTON SUPER-SILK

BLOBS OF KRYSTON MAGMA

3 oz

SIZE 4 DRENNAN BOILIE HOOK

SHRINK TUBE
LINE ALIGNER (SIZE 1)
22mm BOILIE (BOTTOM BAIT)

A couple of points about presentation.

Most of the lads when fishing The Mad fished pop-ups straight off the lead to try to ensure as much as possible of the bait was visible. Martin Clarke was emphatic to me about the importance of this. Martin is an exceptional angler and I listened to him, but I've always believed in going my own way and fishing with things I have absolute confidence in. A silly little pop-up swirling around above the soup I had no confidence in. The Mad is the siltiest swim I've ever fished. A big carp in the swim has its head pushed right down into that silt, grubbing and foraging for food, like a pig in a trough. I wanted my baits in that silt, where that carp was looking for food. A big bottom bait, with a three big-bait stringer is going to seem very safe to a carp lying deep in silt, and give off food signals far stronger than the natural food it is searching for. Irresistible. I wouldn't have caught any more carp on a pop-up, quite the reverse, I believe. To use my pig analogy again, it is like a wild pig finding truffles as it roots around in the soil. There is no testing of baits in silt. The carp is submerged in that semi-liquid ooze, totally blind and relying purely on its senses. The primary requirement of the rig is that it has a good sharp hook. That is all.

I keep reading articles today, where writers emphasise the importance of using pop-ups to avoid baits being contaminated by silt and masking the smell/flavour of the bait. Utter bunkum. The sense of smell a carp possesses is hundreds of times more advanced than our own - which is pretty poor. Carp feed in silt for natural food that live in or on it - bloodworms, tubifex worms, caddis, snails etc. These very same natural food items will reek of silt to our senses. So will our boilies. So what? They will scream, "I'm food, eat me," to the carp even though they might smell repulsive to us. As I've said before, think carp not human.

When fishing The Hump, I experienced one or two hook-pulls which is frustrating on a water containing so many big fish. The hook pull occurred within seconds of bending into the fish, which suggested that my favoured straight pointed Drennan Super Specialist wasn't penetrating the carp's tough mouth as it should. I was PVA blobbing the hook point to protect it from damage whilst being pulled into position. The bars were much more severe than those in Rodney and ate rigs. It seemed possible to me that once the PVA had dissolved, the hook might

PVA STRING BLOB

METHOD OF PROTECTING HOOK POINT ON GRAVEL

sometimes come to rest against flint or sharp gravel. As a carp sucked in the bait, this might cause the hookpoint to brush against the coarse material which wouldn't cause it to blunt, but which just might take the edge off the chemically sharpened point. It is difficult to describe the problems at Harefield to people who have never fished there. In many swims, if you cast out a three ounce lead you are lucky to get two and a half ounces back. Delicate things like hooks and hooklinks are easily chewed up. I was convinced this was the problem, but was at a loss about what to use having absolute confidence in the Drennan and my alternative the Gamakatsu, which were both straight-pointed. It was Simon Lavin who provided the solution, by suggesting I went onto the same hooks he and Chris were using - the beak-pointed size 4 Drennan Boilie Hook. I wasn't convinced at first, but I went over to them in the end and they proved strong and reliable and (touch wood) I haven't experienced a hook pull since on the lake.

They still need checking regularly on reeling in and I still PVA blob them for peace of mind. If only I could cure the cut-off problem!

Being surrounded by some of the very top anglers rubs off, and I learned a great deal from them. Rob and Co. amazed me, to say the least. They caught fish but when you take into account the actual time they fished each day, it was miraculous that they caught anything at all! A typical Maylin itinerary was as follows. Up at dawn(ish), fish till around 10' o'clock. Reel in to go to the shops, then the cafe for a good fry-up breakfast. (I found cafe time the most productive time at Harefield - that's why I had to be dragged kicking and screaming to the cafe, rather than due to my supposed "tightness" which the gossip columns have claimed!). Fish from around 12 noon to 6.30 pm. At 6.30pm reel in to go to the pub. Out at closing time. On to the Indian to return to lake after 1pm. There was often additional itinerary items at weekends! I'd like to include Essex John's daily itinerary here, but I don't want the book banned! I'm not criticising Rob or anyone else here. I'm not heavily into the social scene, but as long as people don't interfere with my fishing and what I want to do, I don't have a problem with those who greatly enjoy the social side. "The Five plus whoever," enjoy their fishing as much as anyone else, but believe in catching fish very much on their terms. My social involvement in the virtually nightly Harefield scene, was the occasional one night a week lake/rota night out, which I enjoyed. I don't think it cost me a fish at any time for it was basically a day water with only odd fish caught during darkness.

Rob and Co. were good anglers - no question about that. Rob himself is certainly the best long range caster I have ever seen anywhere. Others could cast as far as Rob - by using light line - but Rob was casting with tow rope and intoxicated! One of my vivid carp fishing memories, was seeing Rob cast across the lake in the moonlight in the early hours after he'd got back from a local night club. I was on the opposite bank. As he let loose with a fearsome thump, he cried in that Bedfordshire dialect, "Blindin' caarrsst....!" The bait landed between the third and second bar on my side of the lake - The Causeway side. I still wonder today if he really had a bait on - for that was one incredible cast!

I learned a lot about the fish that first season. One of the things that was very interesting was the number of Harefield fish which just never got caught. Simon always carried around with him a photo album full of prints of Harefield carp for recognition purposes. There was from memory, 65 different twenties in the album, including fifteen thirties. When a fish was caught, it was invariably one of the album fish. However, we knew that there was at least the same amount of twenty plus fish in the water that just never got caught or had been caught so infrequently that there was no photographic record. Just why these fish evaded capture was open to debate. I think those 65 fish that get caught are fish that move around the lake, and those that don't get caught are territorial and mainly resident in certain swims or areas of the lake. Moving fish and resident fish are two very different animals. Resident fish are more difficult to catch than fish that move a lot. This is because they are so familiar with the environment in which they live. If you cast a lead and a bait into it they notice a difference - a foreign object - and they become suspicious and cautious. If I put a cardboard box in the middle of the floor in your living room you'd soon think, what's this? If I put a cardboard box in the corridor of a building you only visit now and again, you don't worry about it, because as far as you know it could have been there for some time. It is exactly the same with carp. When fish are on the move and they don't get used to a small area which they know intimately, they are much easier to catch. When the Longfield fish went to Horton, they got caught easily because they didn't know their immediate environment and so the rigs and baits worked easily. Now they know their environment they are hard fish to catch.

Swims on many lakes have resident fish that live, or spend most of their lives in the vicinity of them. They are sometimes moving fish, but more often than not live in a certain area. Just a couple of Harefield examples. The big Fully Scaled lives around the Goose Island - most of his time is spent there.

On a big south-westerly he'll move with other fish down to The Mad, where he'll occasionally get caught. I saw him in The Mad once when the carp were spawning and the angler fishing there cast too close and spooked him. I watched him swim on the surface in the calm water all the way back to Goose Bay. He might feed on The Point en route to The Mad and get caught there. He'll mostly get caught around The Goose though, where he lives. If you want the Fully Scaled you've got to fish The Goose, The Point or The Mad - forget about anywhere else. He's got so familiar with his environment in recent years that he's avoided capture for some time now. He's there though, and often seen. A fish bigger than the Fully Scaled, known as The Italian - considered to be well over forty pounds - has been seen many times but always around the unreachable bay against the workings. Gutbucket was caught once on introduction at 33lb, but hasn't been landed since. Seen though, several times in Harefield - in the same area. This fish disappeared in Rodney Meadow for two years and has clearly become territorial. I could cite many examples of resident fish from many waters I've fished and it seems the most plausible explanation as to why at least 50 of the lake's population of twenty plus fish evade capture.

My second season on Harefield was not a good one and it was a poor one for most Harefield anglers. It was the year of Rob's video success on The Point and Stuart Gillham's record-breaking season. The opening fortnight captures on The Point can never be repeated, due to the enormous advantages Rob and Stuart had, although Rob showed what a good angler he was. Not many would have caught so many fish, even given the same circumstances. Stuart did ever so well that season, but he had massive advantages which mere mortals couldn't hope to have. He was able to fish a great deal. He was able to retain The Point swim week after week. When he moved swims, bait was introduced by miraculous means on his behalf, for it was impossible to introduce mass baits or boilies at such ranges without a very large helping hand. He was pulling major league strokes that no one else could possibly attempt because if they did, Stuart would have had to confiscate their ticket as he was head bailiff! Stuart has never hidden the strokes he pulled or the massive edges he had. But it still could all have gone wrong. Stuart had observed the Harefield carp extensively and had hit on a method to catch them. He knew exactly how much hempseed and boilies would hold them in his two spots, The Point and off the Workings. His baiting technique and pattern were spot on (well, they should be in a floatation suit, flippers etc, with a bait bucket or with Dougal pulling "strokes". Get it?), and so the rest of us could only sit and watch really.

Stuart showed again though, that a mass bait feeding area as commonly used in the north for so long would hold the fish on gravel pits too. I'd already proved this on Rodney on a smaller scale, and Stuart had proved it previously on Harefield when he'd applied hemp by using the gravel

company's tug boat! Makes a little bait dropper seem insignificant doesn't it?

It was a pretty miserable season for my rota. I caught a few fish, but nothing like I expected to. The reason was pretty obvious. Stuart had the bulk of the fish pinned down in front of him, week after

A gentle "Monster" I met one day on the bank. Any resemblance to anyone alive or dead is purely coincidental.

week. We were fishing for the crumbs off the table. On the big fish waters I've fished, there are roughly the same amount of takes forthcoming each season and a fairly consistent number of big fish (thirties) caught. Rob and Stuart collectively, probably had 75% of the total number of takes that season which meant that the rest of us (well over a hundred people - for some 'unofficial' members had been let into my rota) had to share 25% of the total takes that year between us. A lot of people paying good money blanked, or just caught one or two fish.

. . . .

The new management at Boyers lasted less than a year, which wasn't surprising. Rota's were retained, but a lot of the famous faces had moved on - back to Savay, the Cons, the Fisheries or onto Yateley and Wraysbury. Harefield was very much quieter - my rota in particular. Everyone was equal again in terms of access to the lake. That third season was the one where I was able to put together everything I'd learned and it was a memorable and very successful Harefield season for me. A lot of my success that year was simply due to the fact that the lake was so much quieter. Mid-week, there were at most six anglers on the lake instead of the thirty or so I'd had to put up with before. One could move. A fair rota (more or less - bailiffs still had priority) meant that if you put yourself out you could be first in the queue for swims on Monday. I'd travel down in the early hours of Monday to arrive first light. Generally, I'd be first but one or two wised-up and started to beat me to it. Ollie was one particular pest, as was Colin "Gaylord" Nash. There was little angling pressure and everyone got on well with each other, with no competitiveness. It was tremendous. The other rota was much busier though, and had a number of full-timers fishing.

Things had moved on a little on the fishmeal bait front. Geoff had been playing around with some pre-digested ingredients, both with his tank fish and in fishing situations, one of which was an interesting fishmeal derivative. Other ingredients had been tried out, including one potential biggie but it couldn't be made to work in boilie form. The pre-digested ingredient interested me. Geoff formulated a base mix which he'd christened Aminos. He felt it was a definite progression due to the pre-digested ingredients - which would aid digestibility and speed passage through the carp's gut. The pre-digested fishmeal had a protein content of 85% with a high biological value. It was 80% water soluble which had proved to be a problem when trying to mix it with various types of ingredients. It proved best in a favourite combination of CLO birdfood, casein, lactalbumin, sardine meal, anchovy meal and a koi carp feed - algae extract. In addition, a powdered amino acid ingredient was added. This included an ingredient called betaine which seemed highly effective as a fish attractor. With various minerals, vitamins and extracts, the base mix looked a significant advance on my standard fishmeal mix.

A number of new fish oils had been looked into, and I'd been playing around with a couple myself as had Geoff. There was one particular human grade oil christened Hi-Vit Oil which looked promising. This was a blend whose primary constituent was Halibut Oil. The data concerning this oil showed high levels of Vitamin E and D and a good spread of others. Vitamin E itself, is a natural anti-oxidant. Oxidation is a problem with fish oils and can turn them rancid and therefore potentially harmful. All of the oils we had used were developed for the purposes of aquaculture mainly (salmon, trout rearing, some cyprinids), and all contained anti-oxidants. All were human grade or accepted as suitable to enter the human food chain. The famous Nodd Oil, for example, is available on prescription in the NHS for the treatment of heart disease! The Hi-Vit Oil had a distinctive smell and taste, was very clean, pure and thin. In tests, it seemed to work best at slightly higher levels than other fish oils in use. I stuck to my usual big baits which had served me so well - most on the water were still using small baits also. The successful recipe was:

6 eggs
8 ml per egg Hi-Vit Oil
10 ml Minamino
1 drop per egg Nutrabaits Black Pepper Oil
Aminos Base Mix

The rig I settled on that season was virtually the same as before, although I'd begun to use a line-aligner by now on the size 4 Drennan Boilie Hook. I'd also started using the Kryston Super Silk in the 20lb version which was strong stuff. I'd tested out a prototype of this on the Tip Lake but had experienced problems with getting it to knot securely. This had been sorted out and the new braid was more resistant to the Harefield gravel. The only problem remaining was that because it was so supple, it had a slight tendency to tangle when cast out or pulled into position - it twisted making it more springy. Within range, I used stringers to prevent tangles but also stiffened the braid using Kryston Super-Stiff gel prior to casting. The other change was that I'd started to apply a few blobs of Kryston Magma to the hooklink to sink it rather than lead wire loops.

My approach that season was the same as before, but the fewer anglers on the water meant that I had the chance for the first time to really have a choice in terms of my favoured swims.

That season I fished only four swims - The Mad, The Hump, The Lump and the Stick Bar. I caught consistently from them all in the four five day sessions I had available to fish.

The previous season, I had begun to get interested in the Stick Bar. In my first season, this swim hadn't been productive and was largely left alone, and being opposite The Point during the Haulin' season it was not popular because you had to witness the slaughter going on across the water each day! During that season though, my old mate John Bevan fished in the swim a fair bit. Now old Bevo - lovely bloke that he is - is hardly the most efficient or prolific angler, in fact, he tended to fish on the Road Bank side simply because it was on the same side as the pub. Bevo had a drink problem - he couldn't get enough of it! When he lived in The Pallets on the Tip Lake, I used to listen out for fish jumping after dark. A couple of times, I heard real monsters throwing themselves out of the water. Unfortunately, on both occasions, it was old Bevo falling in, after forgetting where the bank ended when he got up for a pee! Bevo greeted every dawn with a "tttcccssshhhh"....as the first ring pull bit the dust.

He kept going in the Stick Bar and, over the course of one of his week long sessions, he'd winkle a fish out. He had one or two good ones too, up to 27lb. I thought if old Bevo was getting them out of there then there must be a lot of fish around that area of the lake! So, I made it my second priority if I couldn't get The Point, with third priority being The Goose or The Mad and Hump, depending on wind and conditions.

I started my opening trip with a bang. I was first in the queue and intent on the Lump but saw a big fish roll in The Mad. Fortunately, no one else saw it. The Mad was rapidly shrinking at that point due to a lot of gravel being dumped in it, so I opted for The Hump to give me more options, but elected to fish both rods in The Mad. I hoped no-one would notice the build-up of fish activity in the swim. A gentle south-westerly was pushing in and forecast to do so for the next couple of days. I cast out two stringers, one just outside the little gravel bay which had formed in The Mad, and one further out and more towards The Hump - both in heavy silt. No free offerings to avoid spooking any fish - I'd learned my lesson. Within five hours, I'd had a thirty and a twenty from The Mad. In the photo session which followed, I had to emphasise they were from The Hump because I didn't want anyone to jump into the Mad! Dinnertime the following morning, saw me land a 25 pounder and, within an hour, someone on the Road Bank came right round and plonked himself in The Mad. After an hour of him casting, re-casting and baiting, all the fish disappeared from the area for the rest of the session. I'm certain if I'd managed to keep The Mad free I'd have caught steadily. I could have moved into The Mad myself, of course, but then someone would have definitely gone into the more popular Hump where one always had a chance because odd fish drifted into it because of the weed. There are so few fishing options in The Mad that if the fish move out you are really snookered. There are a couple of residents in the swim but these are small commons which are not worth catching. Matey left after a day or so, wondering why the fish had moved. I had a 21 common from The Hump from against a weed bed on the final morning. I'd fished a rod again in The Mad, trusting to luck, without further success.

The second trip was very memorable. I managed to get onto The Lump which was a pitch I had wanted to fish for some time. There are a huge number of fishing options on The Lump - it is an incredible swim and to my mind, a better one even than The Point. I had just two spots to choose and opted to fish the rigs in positions which I thought covered most of the fish

Stripes at 31lb. One of Harefield's few remaining originals.

One of the large number of Harefield twenty pound commons.

moving in or out of the area. The first spot was tight to the Someone's Coming island, which marks the edge of that swim, which would cover any fish gaining access by that route. When watching people fishing The Lump they rarely fished this spot. It seemed so logical to me and fishing tight to any island is always a safe bet. The other spot was slightly to the right of the gap in the Whalebone Island, which would cover fish moving directly into or out of the centre of the lake, or moving along The Whalebone from the farside of the island on the Road Bank. I could have concentrated this rod right in the gap, but felt that this was too obvious and the fish might just have got used to rigs being presented there and feel somewhat pressured. There were other potential spots and the two I opted for may not have been everyone's favourite choices, but I was confident I'd chosen wisely. The judgements were proved right, for over the next two days I had some incredible action. In one morning, for example, I caught fish of 19lb, 21lb, 23lb, 25lb, 26lb and 28lb, which just shows what can be achieved on Harefield if you get it right. That particular session was very interesting, because others watching were amazed at my tactics. I was baiting my two spots quite heavily each evening, with the expectation of fish from dawn onwards. Although I'd caught fish off The Point at night in the past, encountering dark-feeding fish seemed to be just one-off occasional occurrences. After I caught a fish, I topped-up the spots with bait immediately. On the morning of six fish, five came from The Whalebone spot and I was banging out bait between fish. Normally, this would have spooked fish out of the area. There were two reasons why I took this course of action with absolute confidence. Firstly, there was a fresh wind and the water was turbulent and colouring up against the features I was fishing to. This helped disguise the bait introduction greatly. Secondly, I was certain that fish were moving up from the Slugs, Goose and Bottom Bays in little groups. I had wandered round these areas before casting out the evening prior, and the fish I saw were in little groups and not mobbed-up in one or two big shoals. When they were moving past they were in little groups, in procession. From each little group, I was picking off one fish. It was then some minutes before the next little group moved past, allowing me time to re-bait with safety before they arrived. With all this action going on in my swim, it was interesting to note that Ollie next to me in The Point was having no action whatsoever, despite the fact that these fish had to be coming past The Point to get to me. Now, Ollie is a stubborn bloke and he always does what he wants to do. In this session, he just wasn't putting enough bait out - in fact, in all of his Harefield fishing he rarely, if ever, put much bait out which I think was a big mistake. I was constantly going on at him about it. The catchable Harefield carp are all bait orientated fish. He was full-time Ollie, and didn't have much money to spend on bait. But having said that, if he decides to fish in a particular way he sticks to it. He's not bothered about what others catch even if they are within a few yards of his baits, because he's so easy going and laid-back - me, I would have been tearing what was left of my hair out! But that is Ollie, his attitude is one of the things that makes him a great bloke to fish with. There simply wasn't enough bait in The Point to interest them enough to stop and feed and it was only when the action died completely in my swim for some hours, that Ollie caught his only fish of the trip - the well-known Long Common at 26lb.

There was an interesting "happening" one morning during that session. I'd just returned a 26lb common when I had a run, picked the rod up and bent into something special. The clutch on the PM4000 was screwed down but instantly, line was torn off the clutch as whatever it was ran off towards the Road Bank Island. I could do nothing with this fish which just kept going and going, taking line at an alarming rate. After a minute or so, the fish was threatening to run round the far side of the island. I had an incredible amount of line out and I thought, "I've got to stop this fish." I grabbed hold of the reel spool to prevent any more line being taken from the reel, and the rod was pulled down with such force that it was almost pulled from my grasp. I can't describe the power of that fish adequately, it was like I'd hooked an express train. Within seconds, the 15lb Big Game parted like cotton about 100 yards out, and I was left reflecting on an incredible experience. Funnily enough, I'd had a similar, though shorter-lived experience when fishing up against the base of the Road Bank Island the previous season. I hooked a fish at shortish range on very heavy line and tried to stop it as it threatened to go round the island. It parted the 30lb Drennan Sea line I was fishing with - in open water! Several members have had similar experiences. Geoff Bowers, for example, once hooked a fish at close range in the Stick Bar and couldn't get the rod above level with the water due to the power of the fish. This broke him too. These incidents have led to speculation that there is a big cat in the water, but I don't think that is the case. I've caught cats and some good ones and the two fish I hooked didn't run or fight like a cat. The clue, I think, comes from a big water I joined for a couple of seasons in Berkshire. This contains some very big carp which have not been caught or fished for before. In fact, I think this water will produce a record carp. When members started to fish the water, they just couldn't do anything with these big, very long, virgin carp. They were tearing off, charging through weed beds and smashing everyone up. The water has produced some big thirties and two forties, but most of the fish have been lost. I think these unstoppable fish in Harefield are just big, previously uncaught Harefield carp that don't like being hooked - probably big long commons with huge tails. All of the Harefield carp fight incredibly strongly, the commons especially so, but I think a carp that has rarely experienced a hook and fight just goes crazy. Unknown carp on Harefield with that angling pressure? Yes, absolutely loads of them. Only very recently, for example, two completely unknown fish of over thirty pounds were reported to the press - Colin "Gaylord" Nash had an old-looking common of 31lb, and John Meecham had a long, skinny, heavily-scaled mirror of 30lb.

The two other trips which I made to the lake that season, were spent in The Stick Bar which old Bevan had been fishing the year before. There were three bars in front of the swim. The Stick Bar itself, which was 100 yards or so out, the second bar at about 70 yards and a bar running just past the marginal boat channel. I concentrated on the second bar, as I felt that the Stick Bar itself was obviously the pressured bar, and few would have bothered with the second bar. Some of the Harefield lads just are not happy unless they are thrashing out! The first bar looked promising, as fish often showed there, but I have found that to be illusory - they didn't feed there. I fished a snide on this bar at night and into morning and only caught one fish on it, despite the spectacular Carp Crashing, Jumping and Rolling Show.

There is no way the Stick Bar is ever going to be as good as The Point or Lump, but to my mind it is a very good swim and it covers areas the fish pass through when the two aforementioned swims lying opposite are getting some stick. It is more of a steady swim rather than one from which spectacular catches can be made. In my trips that season, I caught a fish a day from the swim - which is very good going for Harefield, and it seems to throw up the big ones too. This pattern has repeated itself on my trips since when I have fished it. The much-neglected second bar proved to be very productive when heavily baited and landing fish proved un-problematic.

So, by my third season, I felt I'd really sussed the water out and could catch from it consistently. The example provided by Frogger and Carebear of fishing the edges of the lake and fishing over bait for real success, had an enormous influence on me. That third season, I caught 16 big carp in twenty days. That is some going for Harefield which is a very difficult water, especially when not given the ability to pull strokes which have been the major factors leading to the heavily publicised mega-hauls on the water. So I'd done well. That period probably represents some of my most successful and enjoyable fishing ever.

. . . .

I've stayed in Harefield - for I have a great affection for the water - but I've only fished it very occasionally in recent years. I've caught on every trip, so I'm confident on the water. The fish in the water have continued to flourish and it now contains a forty pounder, with other catchable fish looking likely to exceed that magical mark in the near future. I think the water has always contained a couple of big uncaught monsters but whether they will ever be landed remains to be seen.

I'm going to go back onto the water, for I want more of those tremendous fish and a forty pounder would be very welcome. I miss the friendly laid-back atmosphere and camaraderie found there which is so rare today. It would be nice to sit in 'Angler's Corner' in the *Horse and Barge* again. I know I'm going to catch and catch well.

I shouldn't have said that, for fate has the habit of being rather cruel to those who tempt Providence!

Redesmere Lake

"What sort of people live about here?"
"In that direction," the Cheshire Cat said, waving his right paw round, "lives a
Hatter; and in that direction," waving the other paw, "lives a March Hare. Visit
either you like: they're both mad."
"But I don't want to go among mad people," Alice remarked.
"Oh, you can't help that," said the Cat: "we're all mad here. I'm mad. You're mad."
"How do you know I'm mad?" said Alice.
"You must be," said the Cat, "or you wouldn't have come here."
Lewis Carroll Alice's Adventures In Wonderland 1865

For four years I applied for membership of the club which controlled the fishing on the Capesthorne Estate where the mighty Redesmere was situated, and for four years my application was rejected.

It was rumoured that known carp anglers - particularly members of the local BCSG branch - were not welcome. The unofficial policy was changed when two of the club stalwarts - Geoff Hayes and Liz Shapley - pointed out to the powers that be that the club would have less trouble with a known carp angler who was so keen to join, than an unknown one who was simply more likely to be accepted because no one had heard of him. At least you knew what you were getting. Geoff and Liz supported my application, and I will always be grateful to them for fighting my corner. The long awaited membership card came through.

I became an occasional enthusiast at Capesthorne Hall almost straight away, but Redesmere itself had little immediate appeal. On visits, many of the regulars didn't seem to be too welcoming or prepared to talk about the fishing, the water itself looked a little intimidating and the rules in operation at that time seemed to be a potential minefield I'd have difficulty crossing. I'd got used to very relaxed and laid-back fishing elsewhere, and I wasn't sure I could put up with some of the restrictions. Having said all that, there were some very big fish in Redesmere by any standards, and I really fancied getting amongst them.

For the first year of my membership, I didn't fish Redesmere at all. In my second year, I fished it just the once. One Saturday afternoon in June, I caught my target fish from Capesthorne, the lake monster, Moby. I'd caught a lot of the Capesthorne fish along the way until the big one had decided to succumb to my attentions and, as Moby rolled into the net, I felt I had no ambitions left on the water. In sheer arrogance (and stupidity), I decided to ride my luck by opening my Redesmere campaign the following day.

I parked my car in the only car park provided by the club, as the parking was mostly on public roads surrounding the lake which were susceptible to car break-ins even though this was a leafy and very affluent area of Cheshire. This was a small red ash-type car park some way from where I felt like fishing, which was the noted Stream area. I thought the car would be a little bit safer than if it was parked on the quite busy roads. That was my first mistake. The second mistake was that I had chosen a Sunday to open my campaign and the lake was dotted all over with yachts, skippered by lunatics in sailing caps all completely oblivious to anyone else who might be enjoying the beauty of the lake - particularly the anglers. Casting in from The Stream swim without actually implanting a 3oz Zipp lead into the cranium of one of the would-be Francis Chichesters, Captain Blighs and Captain Pugwashes was the first priority, the second being to get the lines back-leaded down as quickly as possible, to avoid the line being picked up or cut-off by a rogue dagger board.

This wasn't my idea of enjoying myself and I contemplated the possible strategy I would have to employ if I actually hooked a carp and had to try and get it safely in. One of the Pugwashes capsized, fell out of his boat and bobbed up and down right over my hookbait. I began to wonder - head in hands - what on earth had compelled me to attempt to fish Redesmere on a Sunday?

Andy Talbot turned up in the afternoon for an overnight session so at least I had someone to talk to for the rest of my stay, and we sat and watched the Bedlam being re-enacted in front of us. For amusement, we did a spot of cloning, matching up the yachtsmen who threatened to sail right into Andy's bivvy to various celebrities and giving them marks out of ten. We identified two Kenny Everetts - one an eight and the other a nine - a Bruce Forsyth, a Dickie Davis, Bobby Charlton and, disturbingly, considering the size of his boat, a ten-scoring Pavorotti. Lord Lucan was there too, which wasn't surprising in this part of Cheshire.

By tea-time, I'd seen enough and decided to pull up stumps. I said my goodbyes and good lucks to Andy and trudged tackle-laden the half mile to the car park. When I got there, I found the passenger window had been smashed and I'd been robbed. What a perfect end to a perfect day!

I'd been deprived of the use of a fake gold Rolex watch. My one consolation is that the thief probably thought he'd made off with a two grand watch, instead of which he'd done a runner with a two quid Singapore special. That ended my Redesmere campaign for the rest of that season and for the next two.

The following week I went down to Harefield, only to find I'd left my landing net at Redesmere! I borrowed a spare net off a fellow Harefield member and somehow contrived to break it within half an hour of assembly! Fortunately, for me, Andy Talbot spotted my net lurking in a bush on The Stream and took it home with him.

....

For the next couple of years, people kept asking me why I didn't fish Redesmere. My standard reply was that I'd fish it when it produced a fish of over 35lb in weight - never thinking it would. Unfortunately, the big common it contained got bigger and bigger to spite me and came out at over 35lb. With the major excuse for not fishing it gone I suppose I felt I had to get over there.

I had always kept in touch with the goings on at the lake and before starting to fish it, I spent some time wandering around and gaining a feel for the place and trying to suss out what was going on.

Redesmere is a fairly largish lake of about 40 acres. It is a breathtakingly beautiful lake which is heavily wooded on several sides, lying as it does at the bottom of a steep valley. It contains areas of shallows, depths and rush-lined bays. It is stream-fed, with the exit stream causing a considerable undertow at times. There was little or no weed in the lake when I started to fish it although there had been substantial lily beds dotted around the lake in the 1970's and 1980's. The demise of the lilies had been blamed on the multitude of Canada geese on the lake, but I always suspected this had been caused by the then club policy of heavily bone-mealing the water to make it cloudy to avoid weed becoming established - after all, the Canada's had always been there and it seemed odd that they should suddenly acquire a taste for lilies! It is a very silty lake and it presents to the angler the problems that fishing in silt create, made worse here by the necessity of having to fish at long range at times, requiring heavy leads. The margins at Redesmere are shallow and it is necessary to wade out a fair way to cast out and land fish. This means that thigh waders have to be used for fishing in - which I've never liked, being a mocassins and slippers-only man. Still, when in Rome.....However, I did draw the line at lying in a sleeping bag wearing waders as some of the lads were prone to do.

I mention lying in a sleeping bag, rather than dozing in one because when I started to fish the lake, sleeping whilst fishing had been made a capital offence by the controlling committee. The Committee didn't take any prisoners. Rule breakers, regardless of mitigating circumstances, were hauled before the Chairman and his mates on the Committee and dealt with in a manner that Judge Jeffries would have been proud of. In his wisdom, and in yet another attempt to put carp anglers off fishing the water, the lovely Chairman dreamt up a unique interpretation of the water authority by-laws. If you were asleep and cast out fishing, you were not in charge of your rods, thereby you were in breach of the water authority by-law which states that baited rods should not be left unattended. Clever, but bizarre thinking that. It's a bit like saying that when you go to bed at night you are leaving your house unattended! It ignored the reality of carp fishing: that very few of us sleep deeply or normally and sleep with one ear cocked. Most sleeping carp anglers hit a run in seconds. People tried pointing this out but were told to shut up and sit down.

The "no-sleeping" rule was enforced by the bailiffs even though it had never been voted upon. Of course, it didn't have to be: it was merely the enforcement of a water authority by-law. Clever that. If you wanted to sleep, rods had to be reeled in. People did sleep whilst fishing, of course, but only during the hours of darkness when bailiffs couldn't see you - not that they ever dozed off, of course. Until dark and at first light, when binoculars were functional, you had to be sitting bolt-upright on the bedchair with eyes wide open, or risk being grassed-up and publicly humiliated. If the Chairman had had access to night vision binoculars I'm sure he'd have issued them to bailiffs.

I wasn't sure I could live with this rule and it was one of the reasons I'd avoided the lake. I thought of all sorts of silly ways round it. I wondered whether it was worth hiring the services of a local artist to paint a life-size image on the bivvy door of a wide-awake Selman sitting on a bedchair - perhaps even sticking my tongue out. I thought of blacking-up like Al Jolson, to make the whites of my normally blood-shot eyes more significant. I had a good look in the local joke shop for a pair of artificial eyes (no pun intended). Unfortunately, the most life-like were attached to springs and bobbed up and down horrifically, which I was sure most bailiffs would suss out eventually. I did find a pair of spectacles of the National Health variety with open eyes painted in the frames which I decided to purchase and try out. I looked like Kevin Clifford! The first bailiff that encountered me was not amused and started to become aggressively more interested in other features of my tackle and kit and so, sadly, I gave the spectacles away. The only way to get round the rule was to do what everyone else did - to try to sleep for a couple of hours a night with the constant guilty fear preying on the mind of the after-dark torch being shone in the face.

"ZZZZZZZ z zz"...

There were other rules which were less problematic, the main one being that it was only possible to fish in a swim for 48 hours, then it was necessary to move at least one swim away or go home. Swim-swapping in any form was banned. This rule had been brought in to prevent the monopolisation of swims which had occurred in the past. In some respects, this was a good rule. The lake by this time was starting to get crowded with competition for swims, but the constant moving in and out gave everyone a fairer crack of the whip. It meant you had to maximise your fishing effort for that period in the swim and think a lot more about what you were doing. I never really enjoyed fishing the lake much, due to the rules and the manner of fishing which had to be adopted, which I will come to shortly. Forty-eight hours was about all I could stand anyway. The downside to the 48 hour rule was that it was not possible to apply bait properly. You couldn't sit in a swim for several days and work it up, knowing the fish would have to come sooner or later. This would have been the way to really catch a lot of fish. You had to think hard about bait application and about putting just the right amount of bait in to produce a fish during a 48 hour stay - and not a fish for the chap who followed you into the pitch. If you caught a fish, invariably, someone was waiting to come in - sometimes halfway through a session, in a pitched bivvy at the back of the swim!

. . . .

As usual, before fishing the water, I did my homework. The consistent catches in recent seasons had come from the central body of the lake. The swims on The Stream seemed obviously good ones as one could cover a large expanse of water. The other likely area was The Meadow, with some swims covering more area of water than others. Two in particular took my fancy. The first was known as The Snag and this had been a noted spot for many years, as a large sub-surface snag lay out in front of it at about eighty yards range. A lot of the snag had been dragged out by a working party due to fish losses on it - but not all of it was removed with odd bits remaining. This created an area of difference and I have always found that any objects or variation of any sort on the bottom attracts carp. Fish like the re-assurance underwater features provide. The Snag was also the most generous in terms of bank space and water acreage too, providing many options for the two rods allowed. It was more like the sort of swim I like fishing with most of the other Meadow swims being close together with people fishing in a line. A long cast from The Snag could also put you off the front of The Stream which was often productive. Two other swims took my eye.

The first was called the Left Hand Hollybush, which lies to the right of

The Snag. This enables quite a lot of water to be fished including, with a long cast, the area being fished off the left of The Stream. You could also get close to The Snag from here. The second was called Solomon's, because the land adjoining it was owned by Mr Solomon who lived in the lakeside house. No fishing was allowed on that stretch of land which meant an unpressured stretch of water - I thought fish would find this a retreat.

I discounted the New Bank due to the extremely long walk and the fact that the car park was a public lay-by half a mile from the swim. If the fish were in that vicinity it would just have to be tough - and I felt the same about The Shallows and its car park. Once bitten, twice shy.

The Floating Island was more accessible. This was a boggy and treacherous piece of bank which had once been on the the other side of the lake. In a very rare naturalist book published in 1948 by the late Fred Tunnecliffe there is a fascinating description of what happened: "Many years ago, so the story is told, on a night of roaring wind and storm, the island which was at that time part of the opposite shore of the mere, broke away from the main bank and sailed across to the Fanshawe side. And the tellers of the story insist that, on that same wild night, "th'ould squire died." But now, I think, alder and willow roots have a firm hold on the bed of the mere and the island's travelling days are over." I helped construct a walkway and platforms to tame the swampy Floating Island and make it fishable, but I didn't like the look of it still. Besides, the mosquitoes were as big as bats! The most convenient bank for avoiding back-breaking walks was The Wood. Here though, I felt one was restricted in terms of fishing options and it was popular with tench anglers and 'bit' men, so I felt it best to leave them to it. First choice then was The Stream, then The Snag, then the Left Hand Holly, then Solomon's in summer feeding situations. Looking back, that initial judgement doesn't look a bad one. I rarely got on The Stream due to it being more or less permanently occupied, but it turned up the goods consistently. The Snag and Left Hand Holly proved very productive for me, with The Snag being the swim the regulars began to associate me with. Other Meadow swims, like the Right Hand Holly and the Oak, also produced for me when the fish were feeding in that area. Solomon's didn't prove as productive for me as I thought it might be, but others had a few fish from the area. The Stream and Meadow were definitely the two areas to fish for consistent success on Redesmere as I thought they would be - and that remains the case today. A vast amount of bloodworm was located in that main body of the lake, but I suppose that most of the artificial food in the shape of boilies was always being introduced there and, when the fish decided for whatever reasons to feed on bait, they knew where to find it.

In terms of bait, I knew that a good fishmeal/fish oil bait would be successful, as fishmeals - some supplied by myself - had been going in for a couple of seasons with success. I felt though, that I wanted my bait to be a little bit different than the others the fish were sampling. The bait I eventually decided to use was as follows:

Premier Baits "West German Special" Spiced Fish

5ml per egg Ses-Marine Oil

10ml per 6 eggs Minamino

1ml per 6 eggs Premier Peach Melba

1 drop per egg Nutrabaits Black Pepper

This was a very good bait and I was convinced very different from others being introduced. The base mix incorporated a higher percentage of West German Lactalbumin to make the bait rock-hard for throwing stick use, and the base mix also had a higher than normal percentage of Robin Red. The oil was a combination of Chinese roast sesame oil and a marine oil which gave the bait a distinctive sausage-like smell and taste, which the Minamino complemented. The other liquid ingredients were based on a combination I'd had success with and were mainly included for my own confidence rather than for any practical fishing purposes. To be honest, simply the base mix and the oil on their own would have been just as effective, particularly as the oil was so pungent. I think a lot of the time we only use a smell additional to inherent smells for confidence reasons - we feel happier if they are there - and confidence is critical.

Redesmere is a biggish lake, with no pre-baiting being allowed and I wanted that bait established. I also had limited time on the water as I was concentrating more on Harefield. There was a virtually full-time angler fishing the lake called John who was basically skint and welcomed the opportunity for a load of free bait to fish with. So with John fishing it too, I knew it would be going in on a regular basis, at least for a time.

The more a good bait is introduced, the more its effectiveness improves. I see so many people using what is good bait but they don't give it a fair trial by giving up on it after a few sessions if it doesn't catch. What they should be doing is to keep putting it in even if at first it seems useless. If it is a good bait it will produce in the end and get stronger and stronger. On today's waters, I do believe that more bait does equal more fish, providing that bait is nutritional and balanced. I have seen people trying to cut corners by using very poor baits in massive quantities and whilst they have caught one or two fish, they have caught nothing like they would have done if they had used a good bait in the first place! You cannot skimp on bait and get away with it.

Choosing a rig to sort out the Redesmere carp was quite easy but was also closely linked to the bait. From observation, the vast majority of anglers were using very small baits - often a pop-up - of about 14mm. There was a particular group of anglers who fished in a very similar way to each other with some success. This included Dave Sawyer, Brian Bevan, Paul Hook and Graham Trickett. These are very meticulous anglers (although if you look at Sawyer, you wouldn't think so) and they take great care with their bait and their rigs in particular. Everything is down to the last detail. Rigs are super-critically balanced or ever-so slow on the descent pop-ups. Hooks are small and honed to perfection with a jeweller's eye-glass. Ever-so neat counterbalanced hooklengths and sleek terminal arrangements are their trademark. They are expert distance casters - pin-point and accurate, placing stringers at 150 yards and all that jazz. Good anglers, and I thought them to be the main opposition on the water.

In a thousand years, I couldn't be as organised as they were. But the Redesmere carp didn't know that. So I went against the trend. I decided to use a big (by comparison) bait of about 20-22mm. A big grappling hook in comparison - a size 4 Drennan. Bog standard undignified braided hooklength. A standard hair whipped on the shank. Baits were standard bottom baits or pop-ups, but I used very crudely weighted down pop-ups without the usual finesse of the Redesmere rigs. My rigs were appallingly simple. (see next page)

Now I didn't exactly take Redesmere apart - no one does - but the lads will tell you I did very well in relation to time fished and in terms of the size of the fish I landed. Was part of this down to the fact that I bucked the trends a little? I like to think so, but I don't know for sure.

I don't know anything for sure about Redesmere. I'm not alone in that for it is a very curious place, perhaps the strangest lake I have ever fished. Let me explain further.

The first session I fished the water I certainly found the fish. They were at 80 yards in front of the High Bank swim fizzing and bubbling en masse and so I set up in that swim. At dawn, what seemed like every fish in the lake was rolling and leaping over the baits. Get the sacks ready lads! Nowt. Fizzing and bubbling all through the day. Crashing all through the night. Rolling in numbers again at dawn. Nowt.

Now I remember talking to some of the older Redesmere regulars in the 1980's, who had said that if you cast to rolling fish at Redesmere at dawn you caught one. Clearly, this was no longer the case. The angling pressure or whatever had changed the carp's behaviour.

Second trip, they were again in numbers in front of the High Bank. There was someone fishing the pitch, who was clearly frustrated, as he was throwing a rope over the branch of a nearby oak when I arrived. I set up in the Left Hand Holly. My old mate, Dave Fletcher, was in The Snag and he'd seen nothing. There were no signs of fish in the Left Hand Holly either. During the night, I landed my first Redesmere carp - a nicely scaled fish of 21lb or so. Fletch moved out of the Snag and I moved into his pitch. "You

SIMPLE BOTTOM BAIT RIG

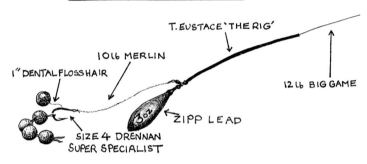

LONG RANGE POP-UP RIG

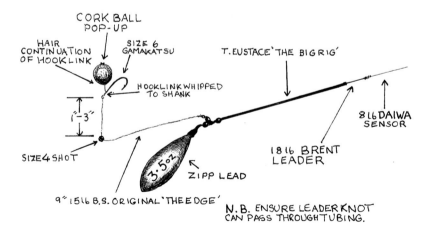

must be mad to move off fish," said
Fletch. It was an irresistible hunch -
but I had to move and would have
regretted it if I hadn't. That night
in The Snag, I had my second
Redesmere fish - a clonking great
mirror of over thirty pounds.
"You're a jammy beggar, Selman,"
said Dave Sawyer (or words to that
effect) as I packed away.

The fish were still in the High
Swim. As I walked past it there was a
different angler in the swim. He was
dousing himself in petrol.....

It seemed to be the case
throughout my time on the water,
that where the fish showed and
where they fed on bait were two
different places. Mass fizzing and
bubbling represented a number of

Typical Redesmere common of 22lb.

fish feeding in a preoccupied manner on bloodworm. You might have
caught the odd fish in this situation, but I think it occurred mainly by
accident when the carp sucked in a bait along with the worms and silt.
Leaping, crashing and rolling clears the gill covers prior to more
preoccupied bloodworm feeding. But the Redesmere carp weren't
interested in baits when they were behaving like this. So, if you saw a lot of
rolling fish in a swim you generally didn't catch, because they had already
fed. If you fished a swim with no fish showing or just one or two - you had a
chance - for those were the potential bait feeders and were still catchable.

It was important in Redesmere to keep an eye on the bloodworms. They
were reeled in often on the rig somewhere and it was important to check
both the colour, condition and size of the worm. If you wound in big, red,
juicy wrigglers from an area where there were few carp it could possibly
indicate a future feeding area. If the carp were fizzing elsewhere but the
worms coming in from that area of preoccupation contained an increasing
proportion of dead, grey or weak-looking worms that could be important
too. That could signal the depletion of one bed by the fish before they
moved onto the next - which could be the one you had found. I found that

I caught fish on quite a few occasions from a bed that was clearly becoming depleted which had previously been very rich - I reeled in grey, clear and dead worms when previously they had been the big, red wrigglers. Could it have been that I caught the fish on bait as that bed became depleted and they were still hungry - until they moved on to the next natural larder? I thought that a strong possibility at the time.

The issue is still confusing though, which is typical of Redesmere. The pattern of fishing was as follows. There would be nothing out for weeks except for a couple of fish, then, bang, it would switch on for a couple of days. Then it would go back to normal for a few weeks with just one or two out, then, bang, it would switch on again for a couple of days, then go back to normal. When you fish Redesmere between the feeding sprees it can seem to be the most difficult water in the world. If you are there when it kicks off it can seem to be the easiest.

Just why the carp behave this way is beyond understanding. It doesn't relate to weather conditions at all, for it can fish badly or well in the same conditions. It doesn't relate to angling pressure which is fairly constant but has a tendency to rise when the telephones start ringing after a feeding spree when the world and his wife try to get a swim. It's too late then, though!

I have heard it said that you don't catch the Redesmere carp *they catch you*. That is very true.

I adopted a very flexible bait-fishing approach to the water. For a session, I would take about 500 18ml boilies. These were of this size so that they would fit into a steradent tube bait dropper (see below) and were a little smaller than the hookbaits. I would lay down a bed of about 200 baits of about 5 square yards with a few odd baits scattered around this area. This would be at ranges of 70-90 yards. I would fish a hookbait in this baited area with a stringer of three or four baits. I would also cast out about a dozen three bait stringers with a rod in the general vicinity of the hookbait. On

THE REDESMERE SCUD

PLASTIC STERADENT TUBE

3cm

16cm

1cm

SHAPED AND PAINTED WINE BOTTLE CORK. ARALDITED TO TUBE.

PLASTIC WINGS ARALDITED ONTO TUBE

SLIDING KNOT

30-50lb LINE

reflection, I made a potentially big mistake by tending to bait up when everyone else was ie. evenings. I should have tried baiting up and getting the rigs out perhaps in the early afternoon to allow the baits to settle more and appear safer than those all put in at evening/dusk. The other bait would be a single bait fished singly and away from the main feeding area. This tactic was developed at Longfield where the single bait fished apart from, but close to the feeding area, was often the banker.

I learned an important lesson from Dave Sawyer here, who had a terrific season when I went on the water. Dave was doing most nights before going to work and weekends, and he often arrived on dark. He would thrash both baits out 130 yards or more and then bait up as far as he could at 70-80 yards. He caught fish using such tactics and there had to be a method to his madness. There was, of course. His bait was still going in and carp were eating it - risk free for most of the time. So if they then came across a bait again they would wolf it down - only this time a hook would be attached to it.

Back to my method. A take on the first night from whichever rod determined my tactics for the remainder of the session. If the take came from the single bait outside the feeding area, then this was topped up and the single hookbait placed just outside it. The hookbait in the feeding area I moved to a new spot fished singley in the middle of nowhere to give me another catching option. If the take came on the feeding area I moved both hookbaits into it for the rest of the session. Instinct determined whether I topped up the existing feeding area. If I decided to, I didn't put as much in as I would if the take had come off the single bait away from the bait bed. I had no fear of topping up a swim at night, but never, ever topped up in the day if the fish fed in the day. Night carp and day carp are very different creatures.

If Dave Sawyer, two swims down, suddenly got a take at 130 yards, then the pre-conceived plan could go out of the window. Re-casting to this mark in the dark was worth a gamble on a very hard water where a fish a session is an unachievable dream for anyone. Consistency from the water over the seasons is the best possible aim. If that swim next to Dave Sawyer was free, then it was tactically appropriate to move if you hadn't caught - whether day or night, regardless of conditions. You must move, when you know you should, without hesitation - never be a bedchair potato. In my experience, anglers who aren't prepared to suffer physical and psychological hardships will never be successful carp anglers. I have suffered both many times.

The silt in Redesmere had a very important role in the fishing. During the summer months the silt became rancid all over the lake and contaminated the baits very quickly. Even pop-ups would take on the smell of the silt very quickly and would smell repulsive to human senses and the original smell of the bait would be completely masked. I have never encountered this to such a degree on any other water. I'd found areas in lakes where baits became contaminated by rancid silt but had always been able to find plenty of clean areas. Here, I couldn't find any. Initially, this worried me because I thought this would detrimentally affect the bait. This was illogical though. We still got takes with these contaminated baits and, of course, everything in the lake - including the natural food - would also smell like the silt. The fact that we were still getting takes meant that the carp's olfactory senses - far superior to our own - could still identify food signals from the surrounding background.

Depth of silt seemed to be critical. The silt in Redesmere was generally quite deep and leads needed to be pulled out of it with some effort. I noticed quite a few anglers pulling the lead out of the silt in order to ensure the bait and as much as the hooklink was clear of it. I've rarely done this and prefer not to - and I never did it on Redesmere. You run the risk of picking up a leaf or a twig or other flotsam and jetsam on the hook. You run the risk of tangling the rig. I don't generally mind if the hook and hooklink are actually in the soupy surface layer of silt anyway - for that is where a feeding carp would naturally find its food. My rigs are cast and simply left alone when fishing silt lakes.

There were areas of silt though, that were much deeper than others and I found these unproductive.The lead could only be pulled out of this deep silt with extreme force by the rod. These areas tended to be also where the silt was what I call sour - blackish, with decaying matter of all sorts present. How did I discover this? This is where the lead is an important aid to fishing. I have never coated my leads because that would inhibit one of the jobs I want it to do. Lead will become affected by its surrounding medium - whether that be silt or gravel. The lead will tell you a great deal about the nature of the lake bed. I call it 'reading the lead'. In silt, it will become discoloured by a sour medium - it will become darker. A lead placed in these deep sour silt areas in Redesmere became virtually blackened. If the lake bed smells, then that smell will be discernible on that lead. The lead is also the only fishing tool that can provide you with samples of the lake bed it rests in. Since my Rodney Meadow days, I have routinely mutilated my leads

Looking across to The Spinney and Meadow

by scraping grooves and holes in them. This is to allow some of the silt - or in the case of Rodney, clay - to become trapped. I can then smell this, rub it between my fingers and taste it.

It certainly seemed best at Redesmere to avoid the areas of deep silt and any area where dark-looking silt was found - I watched or worked out where every fish was caught from when I was there (there weren't many of them!), and they came from the same old spots time and time again. Generally they were areas of not excessively deep silt. In addition, the takes I had and others had always came in 11-12 feet of water, with the shallower and deeper water unproductive.

In the summer and early autumn months, the fish were quite spread out throughout the lake, although at certain times more fish were concentrated in certain areas and in front of particular swims. As the water temperatures dropped and winter began, the fish moved and became very highly concentrated in one particular area. Anyone who has ever kept carp or goldfish in a garden pond will have observed this. This has occurred to a degree on many of the waters I have fished but Redesmere was an extreme example of this. On Redesmere, winter localisation effectively meant that swim choice could be reduced to as few as three in terms of any realistic chance of a fish. This made winter fishing a hair-tearing experience of course, if you couldn't get into one of those three swims. Worse still for me, was the fact that in winter I am generally a Friday through to Saturday night or Sunday morning man. By the time 'old Selman' got down to the lake, those swims would be gone and so would the others near to them. It was a case of getting into any available swim - knowing that there were no fish anywhere near - and praying for someone to move out of a better one. Not that anyone did at weekends.

Complete and utter lunacy.

....

In my second season of fishing Redesmere I had a remarkable run of luck on the water, which to this day, I cannot totally account for - which implies I have at least a partial understanding of the reasons for what happened. It was late September and I was struggling to get a decent swim. At Redesmere, as I mentioned earlier, the carp which were being caught as the season wore on could be very localised and the swims that could reach the fish were very busy. To have a chance of catching these localised fish, I decided to go down to the lake on Sunday afternoons when everyone would be packing up, get one of the good swims and fish Sunday night leaving for work early the following morning.

Posing with my first thirty from the water - can you spot the matchsticks keeping my eyes wide open?

I knew where the fish were - hence my partial understanding. The bulk of the carp were in front of The Stream, which was more or less permanently occupied. My best chance was to get into The Snag, the Left Hand Holly and the Three Oaks and cast across at extreme range to the front of The Stream. I spooled up the big PM 4000's with 8lbs Daiwa Sensor line and a 20lb leader!

I arrived the first Sunday afternoon, to find the usual

Did I mention the ducks?

head-shaking Redesmere regulars having experienced a total weekend's blank. Going into The Snag, I cast out a single pop-up off the front of The Stream over 130 yards out. Twenty minutes later, I was photographing a big grey mirror of 25lb plus. I decided not to bother fishing Sunday night and packed up and went home.

A fortnight later, I again made my way down the Meadow for an overnight session. Again, The Snag was free and I dropped in and cast a single bait a very, very long way at The Stream. Half an hour later, this was away and even at this range I was having to give line and I knew I had something special on the end. "You've got one of the big linears on," said Paul Hook. I doubted Paul's words but hoped that he was right - particularly if it was the rarely caught Original Linear - a superb looking, big shouldered fish - the best mirror in the lake. I was a long way out playing a potential monster and hoping the coned leader knot would take the strain it had always coped with before. This was a special carp, and I was so far across that, after playing the fish for 5 minutes, it picked up Tim Bottomley's line on the far bank giving him a run. Anxious shouts across clarified the situation and Tim opened his bail arm - I was now playing an animal and his rig too. Twenty five minutes later I was posing with that highly prized fish of many Redesmere angler's dreams - the Original Linear at 31lb 12oz. I packed up and went home to celebrate.

Deja vu a fortnight later. A linear again was the result but not one of the big two but the next one down - the Little Linear - a good mid-twenty nonetheless. The bizarre thing about these three captures is that they followed complete blank days on the water and all of the takes came from an area that had been constantly fished without success by anglers better than me. All three takes came to my single bait within half an hour. As Alice cried "curiouser and curiouser." Answers on a postcard please to...

I prefer to put it all down to luck, which is the only angling skill I possess to an inordinate degree.

. . . .

Redesmere got more and more crowded, and less and less enjoyable as a result. I don't enjoy anglers bivvying up behind me waiting to get into the swim. I had to move on to preserve my sanity. I had one major result before I decided to call it a day - catching three good twenties in 24 hours from The Stream - on the only occasion I could get a swim there. Even then, I moved from one swim I'd caught in to the next one down on an instinct that paid off in the shape of two more fish. Three twenties in such a period is an incredible result, for some don't achieve this in a season.

I'd gone there to catch the big common which haunts my dreams still. I

First Redesmere carp - a cracking twenty plus mirror.

decided though, that I might have to spend a lifetime trying to catch that fish and still might not succeed, even though I've always been very lucky. Life is too short to chase one fish. And when you do encounter the fish of your dreams, fate can still get the better hand as Ahab discovered when he finally caught up with the Great White Whale.

I think I actually did put my hook into the mouth of the great, magnificent common one cold winter's morning. Fate played its part to deprive me of that golden-flanked prize. I was in The Snag, it was dark and bitterly cold and I sought the sanctuary of the sleeping bag. Before getting into the bag, I tested my buzzers and found one to be completely dead. Bill Warwick, one of my Liverpudlian friends, lent me one of his new Delkims but it kept going off in the howling wind and the blackness. In the end, I got Bill to set it at its lowest sensitivity, and before it bleeped quite a bit of line had to be taken. Satisfied that I wouldn't be disturbed, I crawled into the bag. I fought to stay awake as I knew I was in the right place at the right time. I must have dozed off (cough) because the next thing I remember was that my face was burning. I had somehow contrived to knock over a candle and my canvas bivvy was ablaze and the intense heat in my face had been caused by melting plastic dripping from the umbrella! I managed to get out of the burning bag and bivvy, grabbed my big water bottle just outside the door and poured it over the burning bivvy extinguishing the flames. I quickly re-filled it in panic and extinguished the little fires in the bivvy. I then spent half an hour in the margin of the lake choking and vomiting due to the plastic fumes I had inhaled. Fortunately, John was next door and helped me sort myself and the bivvy out as best we could. I spent a cold, wet, miserable night in my mini-bivvy being rained on. Despite offers of help to pack-up and go home, I resolved to stay as I knew something special was going to happen.

Somehow, I must have dropped off to sleep again, for the next thing I remember was a slow bleep, bleep of a buzzer in front of me. I was very disorientated by the events and in my mind thought it must be Bill's borrowed buzzer playing up again. I ignored it in my suffering but it persisted. I stuck my head out of the bag to see that it was daylight and my bobbin was flying up and down the needle! I flew out of the bivvy and bent into the fish. That fish gave an account of itself every bit as spectacular at long range as the big linear had done. In my mind, I knew it was the common, and felt the lake was paying me back for the intense suffering of the previous night.

After a good ten minutes, I began to make progress and the fish was coming in. Bill Warwick donned his waders and entered the water ready to net the fish - my first one for months. Everything was going fine then suddenly at about 60 yards out, everything went solid as the fish found an unknown snag. I made a fatal mistake - which I put down to my general weak physical state. Instead of giving some slack line and allowing the fish to possibly swim free of the snag with the pressure eased off, I bent the rod and I felt the hook pull-out.

I can't describe the feeling of that moment. To this day, I still think I lost the common.

. . . .

The Chairman, accused me of lighting fires on the water at the subsequent AGM of the controlling club. I'm pleased to say though, that he eventually fell from grace like all dictators do. The club is now a democracy, with a humane Chairman and a member-supporting committee.

The Redesmere carp can be as frustrating as ever and the lake today is even more crowded than it was when I was an occasional visitor.

There are some very good carp anglers on that water, but they are all quite mad you know.

The Gentleman's Guide to Gaining an Edge

(or how to pull strokes and get away with 'em)

__Stroke-Pulling__ (Orig. unknown but believed to have originated in Kent) To gain an advantage in carp fishing by devious means. In the most extreme form, this involves systematic rule breaking, at a basic level a form of gamesmanship.
The Carp Angler's Dictionary 1997

All successful carp anglers have had to resort to pulling strokes of one sort or another to gain an advantage over others. Stroke-pullers generally fall into two main types, major league stroke-pullers who have no scruples or concerns for the fishing of others whatsoever, and minor stroke-pullers who merely bend the rules a little and whose stroke pulling is just an extension of that quaint thing called "watercraft." I am not adverse to the odd stroke, but I must confess to be a very minor player in stroke-pulling terms. I'm too much of a gentleman, due to over-education and plain simple cowardice.

It has been my privilege (or misfortune, depending on one's point of view) to have known some of the greatest stroke-pullers in the entire history of carp fishing. I am too much of a gentleman to name them - although one or two have appeared in this book. Their

Stroke-pulling on the Mist.

deeds would - at the very least - shock the reader if I were to recount just a fraction of them. Some of the most compulsive stroke-pullers are some of the biggest names in the sport, and I would not want to shatter the mental picture - possibly heroic - that some readers might have of them if I spill the beans.

How do you get to be a major league stroke-puller? Well, without doubt the best approach is to become a head bailiff or the controller of a water. If you can achieve this lofty position, you can break all the rules yourself willy nilly, but ban for life anyone who even commits a minor infraction. Of course, this has never happened in carp fishing...

No, to be a major league star you have got to be an ambitious, aggressive, downright rude, don't give a damn, I'm gonna stitch you up, big and bold, baseball-cap wearing sort of fella. Any correlation between this type of angler and the county of Essex is purely coincidental... As I said earlier, my minor stroke-pulling is a form of gamesmanship, a gentleman's approach to gaining a devious edge. The one rule I admit to breaking on a regular basis is the odd extra rod that somehow appears magically in the swim, usually during the hours of darkness. Not particularly a dastardly deed that, is it? My stroke-pulling is about being somewhat crafty and careful. Being crafty and careful I have made into an art form.

I learned my stroke-pulling on the banks of a notorious water in Warrington known as Grey Mist Mere. The club deliberately promoted stroke-pulling by only allowing one rod to be used during daylight hours. What genuine carp angler is going to be happy fishing with just one carp rod?

A big Grey Mist winter mirror.

No one, of course, which is when the fun and games begin. The club and the bailiffs know the carp anglers are not going to be content to fish with just one rod. The carp anglers know the club and bailiffs know they are going to try to fish with more than one rod. Everyone knows the score. The game is to fish more than one rod without being caught. So, you get rods on the ground, or split in half, in the swim next door, or minded by the wife, girlfriend, mother-in-law, child or the bloke who just came round to collect the rent. Rods up trees, in bushes, in the rushes, fishing underwater, reel spools not connected to rods lying on the ground, rods on the roof-rack of the car, in the baby's pram or as the girlfriend might say "are you glad to see me, or is that a rod in your pocket?"

One of the bailiffs on Grey Mist was old Henry. Now old Henry is over eighty years of age and he's got 50 years of catching stroke-pullers under his belt. He's a real challenge, is our Henry. For years, our respective intellects were in mortal combat whilst he tried to gain sufficient evidence to confiscate my ticket and I tried to keep that one step ahead of the Committee Room door. Many times he came close to catching me, but always I managed to bluff my way out or keep that one step ahead. I had one big advantage in that I always took my little dogs with me and Henry was fond of little dogs. They were against the rules too, but providing they were terriers of whatever sort, Henry was likely to turn a blind eye. He'd sit next to me and play with the dog and, providing he couldn't work without a lot of fuss and bother where I was fishing the extra rod, he didn't seem to mind a great deal, although if a Committee member hoved into view he'd bristle into action to check the swim - after telling me to hide the terrier in the rucksack or wherever.

Two rods in use - but can you spot the third?

I'm very proud of the fact that I am the only well-known carp angler locally to ever survive Grey Mist. I never suffered a ban or loss of ticket. Others were not so lucky. Sandy Smith, Bernard Loftus (no less than two life bans plus sundry suspensions), Peter Dean, Disco Diddy and Corky all had their disciplinary problems, and fell prey to Henry's attentions. They slipped up because they didn't play the game fairly. Henry liked stroke-pullers, providing they were clever and didn't take the mick out of him too much...

My favourite stroke was to pretend I'd fished at night when two rods were allowed, although I never did. I'd keep the second rod on the pod, with a rig hooked up on it - still fishing, of course. Henry would come round and say, "Oh, you have it reeled in then?" He'd sit down next to me, which was the cue to get the terrier out. Often I'd get a run on the snide rod, but I had the old routine down to a fine art. I'd leap up when the buzzer sounded, knock the snide off the rest with the old leg and strike the rod which didn't have a fish on with some force. "I've missed it Henry," I'd complain. I'd watch the line peel off the spool on the snide. Sometimes, Henry would wander off or get on his bike and cycle off - almost as if he knew - but often I'd have to invent a reason for him to go so I could play the fish in. Ironically, the best tactic was to say, "that bloke opposite is fishing two rods, Henry." He'd be off round the lake like a shot, after patting and saying his goodbyes to my little dog...

The carp fishing was cut-throat on Grey Mist. It was the ultimate circuit water. You were under constant surveillance. There was a paranoid, back-stabbing carp angler in every swim. As you played a fish, leads from all points of the compass crashed into your swim. If you went for a pee, people dived into the bivvy to try and get a bait or rig sample, or, followed you to see what

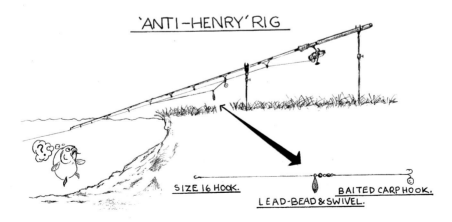

'ANTI-HENRY' RIG

SIZE 16 HOOK.

LEAD-BEAD & SWIVEL.

BAITED CARP HOOK.

you were up to. People cast over you deliberately to reel in your rig and bait if you were catching. I once had litter planted in my swim, which was reported to Henry. Everyone slagged everyone else off. Aggro' of all sorts was a daily occurrence in the summer. To keep ahead, you had to be more devious than everyone else and develop your own little tricks.

. . . .

Here's my rough guide on how to successfully fish waters like Grey Mist - and to keep smiling!

A Gentleman's Guide to Pulling Strokes

1 When using simple bottom baits, always test them in the margins or a jar in clear view of everyone, so giving the impression that you are using pop-ups.

2 When using pop-ups, never test them openly. Test them in the confines of the bivvy well out of sight. Place putty or shot on hooklengths very discreetly.

3 Always leave samples of the bait you are not using in strategic places around the swim.

4 Always fish a snide rod (or three), but try to be discreet at all times. Remember, you can't really enjoy yourself unless there is an element of fun.

5 Never cast out or reel in when you have company. When landing a fish, shield the rig away from prying eyes. Leave an example of the rig you are not using on a bait bucket or similar container in clear view of everyone.

6 When fishing single baits only, cast out a stringer but make sure it consists entirely of pop-ups. Throw a bit of bread into the margins to explain away the seagull activity in your swim.

7 When standing behind someone who is about to cast out, as they release the line and propel the rig, flick a small pebble into the margins. A remark such as "I think your bait has fallen off mate" will guarantee paranoia in your victim as you walk away.

8 You may find the simple phrase, "that's tangled," will sometimes be sufficient to guarantee paranoia should a pebble not be easily to hand.

9 Don't cast out or bait up to where you are really fishing until it is dark.

10 If you intend casting into someone else's swim, only do so after dark and you are sure they have gone to sleep. A simple "Sorry mate, but it has kited into your swim" will cover you, should you hook a fish. Should you by

"Sorry lads, it has kited into your swim."

some freak accident reel in someone else's rig and bait, you should check it to reassure them that it isn't tangled and you can still smell the bait's flavour. This is what friends are really for.

11 Always arrive at the water's edge at least two hours earlier than you told people you were going to.

12 Never tell downright lies about anything, particularly about fish, because you will get caught out in the end - as one or two famous carp anglers have discovered to their cost and reputations. Gentle "blinds" about what bait you are using, how long you are staying for, exactly where you caught a particular fish from etc. is acceptable behaviour.

13 Be friendly at all times. The true gentleman helps carry tackle, offers food and drink and gives poor advice freely when asked. This is also the best strategy to employ to really milk others of all of their secrets.

14 It is perfectly acceptable to suggest to enquirers that you have seen fish jumping down the other end of the lake, even if you haven't.

15 Keep rod tips well below the surface so no one can see where your lines are going.

16 Never sleep with a fellow carp angler's woman, regardless of how attractive or enthusiastic she might be. This is unsporting. A suggestion that "I'd keep a close eye on her, mate" often frees a swim up for a couple of weeks, and is in keeping with the gentlemanly approach.

"You'd better keep an eye on her, mate."

17 If you suspect someone is using a particular rig but you can't tell, make up a copy of the rig you think is in use. When you have caught a fish, take the rig down to the unsuspecting angler you are trying to suss out. A simple, "Excuse me, mate, I've just caught this fish and it had another rig in its mouth. Is it yours?" should confirm the facts one way or another.

18 Sporting a "Gay Pride" badge will guarantee that you are left alone on most lakes. However, this strategy is not recommended if you are a member of the Harefield syndicate.

"I've just caught this twenty and it had another rig in its mouth. Is it yours?"

19 If someone gets next to you and casts out right on the line where the carp are feeding, a simple suggestion that they are "short" or are casting "too far out", should have the desired effect. If not, shake the head and draw in a sharp intake of breath, muttering loudly "Well, I tried to tell him." If this still doesn't work, accuse the chap politely of crossing you. If that doesn't work, thump him.

20 To prevent encroachment into your water, remove some large branches from the nearest tree and plant them in the margins of the swims either side of you. Don't forget to remove them on leaving the water - just to wind everyone up further.

21 Always keep a supply of largish ball bearings to hand. They are useful for deterring swans, ambitious bailiffs and cormorants. Should you get a show-off with a catapult, they are a useful aid to really teach the guy what long range baiting is. Should you get a real show-off long range caster, recruit an accomplice to fire out a ball bearing whilst you pretend to cast out.

22 Be polite to bailiffs at all times and do everything they ask. Just think how fortunate you are that you don't have their personality problems.

23 One of the best ways to ensure that no one copies your successful method, is to be absolutely honest and open about what you are up to. Tell them your exact bait recipe, rig etc. and the spot you are catching from. People will naturally assume you are a lying, two-faced, deceitful so and so, and consequently, do exactly the opposite.

The Mangrove Swamp

*"There is a placidity about it which you find in no other kind of angling. Having
laid out your rods (you may just as well use two while you are about it, with a
different bait on each), you are at liberty to smoke, meditate, read, and even, I think
sleep, if all goes well. Nothing will happen to disturb you. You and the rods and the
floats gradually grow into the landscape and become part of it.
It is like life in the isle of the lotus."*
H.T. Sheringham Coarse Fishing 1912.

A small boy fishing his local ponds for roach, perch and tench dreamt
for many years of fishing Redmire for the huge carp written about
in hushed tones by B.B. and Dick Walker. When that small boy grew
into a man and began fishing for carp he still dreamt and wished that one
day he would be a member of the Redmire syndicate. Not only because of
the monster carp that lived and breathed in those magical depths but also
because Redmire was so private and mysterious. No ordinary Tom, Dick or
Harry could fish there.

I was that boy and that man.

I lost interest in Redmire when it passed out of syndicate control and it
could be fished on the "rent a week" scheme. Any old Tom, Dick or Harry
could fish there now. One winter's night, one of the great influences on my
life, Tim Paisley, rang me and said, "We've got Redmire." We being the Carp

Society. I was genuinely pleased as it was now in safe hands. The pull of the place overwhelmed me when I visited the water for the first time. I intended staying for only an hour. My emotions were overwhelmed and it was several hours later when I forced myself to leave the water and for my pains I got a scolding from those who were worried about where I'd got to. I joined the winter syndicate on the strength of that visit. But it was not the same place I'd dreamt about. For it was no longer the exclusive province of the fortunate few, something a mere mortal could barely aspire to except in his dreams.

All of the waters I've written about in this book are wondrous in their own right - some are very beautiful - and I have enjoyed fishing them all. But none of them were very private or exclusive and anyone could, if they were prepared to put themselves out a little bit, fish them. Today, in England, there are very few waters left like Redmire once was. Most of our good carp waters are crowded and over-fished.

With the image gone of old Redmire, a new Redmire haunted my dreams. The Mangrove. The very name is mysterious for, of course, it is a nom de plume. It was not far from my home but it seemed out of my reach and only fished by a dozen devotees who were as reluctant to leave as I was to leave Redmire when I first visited it. Dead men's shoes.

The water has been written about with great feeling for over a decade by Tim, but it is still shrouded in mystery even for those of us who live quite near to it. I had friends who had fished the water since it was discovered but they said little - so anxious were they to protect it from the harsh world of the outside carp circuit. For a variety of reasons, I didn't fish it when it was an unpublicised day ticket water, although I could have done. I fished nearby Birch Grove instead. I kept hearing the stories of the place and its marvellous fish. It became my Redmire, and I badgered Tim whenever the occasion seemed right to consider me as a suitable member.

One day I was informed by telephone that "I was in." I felt like the luckiest man on earth.

A little bit about the water. As I said earlier, like all classical carp waters its real name cannot be mentioned. It is situated in a remote and beautiful area of Shropshire, but like Redmire's situation in Herefordshire not too far from civilisation. There are few clues as to what century one is fishing in - the rumble of a distant train in the night or the odd tractor working a nearby field do sometimes give the game away a little. The Mangrove is timeless.

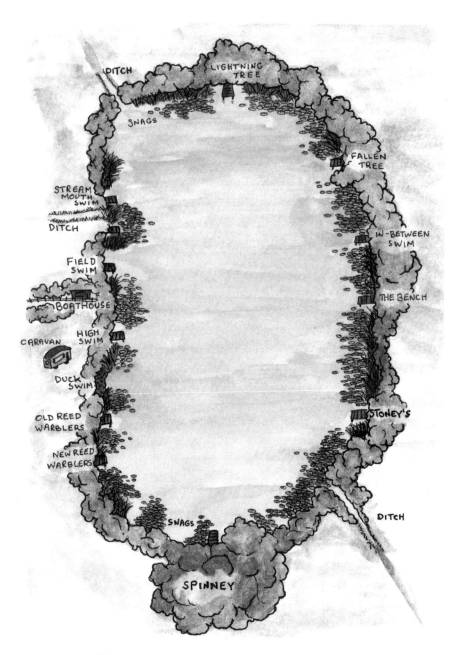

At around 18 acres, I guess, the lake is ringed by large beds of Norfolk reeds fronted by big broad-leaved lilies. Willow, alder and ash grow profusely on its somewhat soggy banks. Anglers fish from well-constructed platforms with access to one side being by boat. Of all the waters I have fished, it is perhaps the most beautiful and certainly the most tranquil. To quote B.B., "Here indeed could the weary man find peace and quietness, far from the turmoil of this troubled world."

Then there are the fish! Hundreds upon hundreds of mirror carp of all types and shapes and sizes and golden flanked commons as pretty as any that came out of Redmire. A few friendly fish have names - the big fish that feature regularly in the press - but most don't and there are those fish that get caught and then vanish for a few years and reappear a little bigger. There are the mythical monsters and when that run occurs a pleasant surprise could always be on the end. The Mangrove grabs you by the throat and once you begin to fish it it casts a spell over the angler that it is difficult to break. I know, because I am afflicted with the Mangrove spell and one has to force oneself to contemplate fishing anywhere else. For years I have climbed into the car late on Friday afternoons and rushed off at a hundred miles an hour to the water. On the journey my head would be swimming with thoughts of what swims might be free and often if I would be able to actually secure one. Now, I get in the car and take in all the sights and sounds on a relaxed journey, knowing that at the end of the road is a choice of swims and all of them interesting, offering a number of fishing options and all capable of throwing up a memorable capture.

I'm writing this chapter after returning from the Mangrove after spending opening night there. In the late morning the three anglers present on the water gathered in my swim to talk about the new season. We'd all caught a fish but the sun had crept up high in the sky and in those conditions the Mangrove carp take a siesta. Dave Philips, a down to earth, long-time carp angler, not noted for his emotion, remarked as Tony Baskeyfield and myself gazed out at the magnificent sights and sounds in front of us, "Isn't this a magical place? Where else in England would there only be three anglers fishing such a beautiful water on opening morning?"

The water has changed significantly over the last few years. Until a few years ago the mass of eels the water contained caused problems when fishing with boiled baits. Then the bulk of them were netted out by a commercial eel trapper and this made it easier to apply bait. As a consequence the water has become a bait water to a significant degree as Tim himself predicted it would. Another development is that the head of doubles the water contains has greatly increased due to successful spawning and the number of fish between 16-18lb is incredible. These are clearly fish of the future that will gradually replace the original stock but they can be something of a nuisance when one is setting one's stall out for twenties and thirties, but also very welcome when the water is in one of its dour moods!

The Mangrove carp feed mainly at night and early morning, particularly during the warm, summer months. In fact, after dark all of the fish in the water seem to come alive and the sounds of fish swirling and leaping about on the surface, the kissing smack of fish sucking on the undersides of the lily pads, and the singing of the reed warblers dominate the nights.

During the day, many of the carp retreat into the lilies and the Norfolk reeds to lie up and then they emerge after dark. In any given swim the angler has the option of fishing down either side on the edge of the pads and has a considerable amount of open water in front to fish. Not surprisingly, there is a historical tradition of multi-rod use on the water - if the angler limited himself to two rods he could only scratch the surface of the options available in every swim. Most opt for a rod down a favoured side and a couple out front. Fish can be caught during the day if the conditions are cool and breezy and as the season wears on, but the Mangrove is essentially an after-dark water with everything having to be geared to the nights.

Baits fished just off the pads are likely to be picked up as the fish move in or out of them. On being hooked the carp more often than not charge off into the pads to seek sanctuary and they can be difficult to extract. In swims like the well known Lightning Tree where the beds of pads and reeds are extensive the tackle is really tested to its limit. The lilies are well rooted and carp can easily be lost as they have the uncanny knack of leaving the hook in a lily root and making good their escape. Fish hooked as far out as 80 yards in open water sometimes deliberately kite on the long line into the pads on either side of the angler despite heavy pressure exerted on the fish. I hadn't fished extensive lily beds since the late 1970's when I fished Gorsty Hall in Cheshire and I had to amend my thinking on terminal tackle arrangements somewhat.

I'd been lead to believe that the Mangrove is a very silty water. It is, but the silt is nothing like as deep and clinging as it is on other meres I've fished such as Redesmere. For example, if you cast out a marker float the lead will plummet into the silt and requires a pull to release it. However, it then glides quite easily along the bottom. If you cast out a baited rig and check it as it hits the water the lead can be felt hitting the bottom. It's as if there is a fragile surface crust on the surface with very deep silt underneath once it's penetrated. So the silt on the Mangrove is very manageable compared to other places I've fished. In addition, the lake isn't entirely featureless. Leading and plumbing around reveals vast beds of swan mussels adjoining the pads which have a nasty habit of opening and closing around leads and blunting hooks. Certain areas seem to attract more detritus and rotting vegetation than others which are cleaner. The latter areas I've tended to concentrate on.

My thinking on rigs when I started to fish on the water ran in several directions. Firstly, there is the pad problem. There are a number of rigs one can utilise when having to think about getting fish from pads. One rig involves fishing the lead on a very fine "rotten bottom" so it will break thus depositing the lead on the bottom and allowing the angler to play the fish on a lead-free line. Another rig involves fixing the lead to the rig by means of a plastic leger stop which comes apart under pressure thereby achieving the same effect as the rotten bottom rig. I wasn't happy about resorting to using rigs designed to allow the lead to fall off. Besides the cost, it's not environmentally friendly to leave dozens of leads lying around on the bottom just for the sake of landing a couple of extra fish. I felt that an in-line set-up which allowed more direct contact with the fish and playing the fish under pressure from a high position would probably be equally effective.

I felt that a light lead would assist in getting the line up quickly from the bottom which is important when using heavy line (15lb Big Game) and in a situation where most of the members were using quite heavy leads I thought light leads might offer better presentation in a situation where the carp are feeling heavy resistance quite quickly as the hooklink tightens. I settled on in-line leads of 1.5oz presented on 18 inches of rig tubing. In heavy pads, soft rig tubing doesn't stand up to much stick and in this respect Alan Smith came to my rescue by sending me some really tough tubing to try out. This is the tubing marketed as Robustatube and I found it perfect for the job. In terms of hooks I've found the Ashima Super Carp (C310) reliable, and these I use in size 4, line-aligned with size 1 shrink tube. Syndicate members reported that double baits were taking a lot of fish and so I have opted for two 14mm boilies to complete the set-up on the pads' rods.

In terms of fishing out in open water, I decided to use larger single 18mm boilies. I've found I can't bait accurately with 14mm boilies over about 50 yards with either stick or catapult. A dropper is the solution of course, but I had reservations about using these all the time. I use a dropper sometimes when baiting up for the night, but I'm reluctant to use one after dark, if for example, I think there is a need to top-up after I've caught a fish. Bait droppers are fiddly things to use at night and I like to see exactly what is going on when I cast one out, which is difficult after dark. I'm much more confident topping-up with a catapult or a stick in the dark. On the Mangrove, I have found it very important to top-up the swim after each fish. The fish can consume an awful lot of bait quite quickly and I liberally top-up the swim after each fish - if it is dark. At night, I think you can get away with doing so without disturbing the fish. In the daylight, when there is more risk of spooking fish, I just stick to fishing stringers, but if it is rough and windy I'll add a few free offerings. Initially, I used a marker with an isotope taped to it for accuracy in the open water at night but I dispensed with that fairly quickly, as I was sure a couple of fish were spooked on retrieval. I now bait up and hope that the baits are landing close to the hookbait but if one or two fall away from it it doesn't worry me. Whilst bait is in the water the fish will continue to look for it - a lesson I learned at

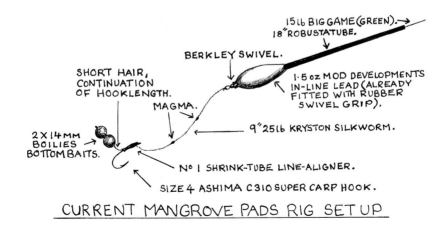

15lb BIG GAME (GREEN).→
18" ROBUSTATUBE.

BERKLEY SWIVEL.

SHORT HAIR, CONTINUATION OF HOOKLENGTH.

1.5oz MOD DEVELOPMENTS IN-LINE LEAD (ALREADY FITTED WITH RUBBER SWIVEL GRIP).

MAGMA.

9" 25lb KRYSTON SILKWORM.

2 X 14MM BOILIES BOTTOM BAITS.

Nº 1 SHRINK-TUBE LINE-ALIGNER.

SIZE 4 ASHIMA C310 SUPER CARP HOOK.

CURRENT MANGROVE PADS RIG SET UP

Redesmere and Hawk. Like all waters where I can confidently catch fish at less than 80 yards, I invariably use a stringer all the time to draw attention to the hookbait.

Takes have been about even between the double 14mm bait fished against the pads and the single (though stringer-fished) 18mm bait out in open water, although I have caught most of my big Mangrove fish in open water with more doubles being caught against the pads. I've still caught a couple of thirties from against the pads though, which still makes fishing the margins an irresistible proposition. I had to amend the normal method of playing fish to deal with the pads. The conventional "pumping" style is inappropriate in pads, as every time the rod is lowered this gives the fish line. I keep the rod high with the fish under pressure with the aim being to keep its head (and the hook) upwards. Line is retrieved in that high rod pressure situation by keeping the fish on the move and clearing a way through the pads on its own. Even very big carp can be extracted from pads this way with no damage being done to the fish, providing the tackle is strong and you don't lose concentration. If despite the pressure everything does go solid, I allow the line to fall slack for a few seconds which fools the fish into thinking it is free. The fish moves off, altering the angle of pull, and it is then a simple matter of getting the fish on the move again. Although I lost quite a few fish whilst perfecting the technique - particularly in Lightning Tree - my success rate in terms of landing fish is about 95% (touch wood!). When fishing open water, it is important to keep in control of the fish. I lost my first couple of fish when they kited on the long line into a bed of Norfolks to my right where they got off. Off went the little reels and on went the big PM4000's, and on pulling into the fish if there are signs that it is starting to kite, I retrieve line very quickly to keep ahead of the fish. If pressure is maintained the fish are less likely to kite and more likely to fight.

Where do you start if you have acres of open, mostly featureless water in front of you? This is the $64,000 question on the Mangrove. The carp will be caught in open water from a small area of perhaps one square yard, whilst a bait fished outside of this area where the features are exactly the same will not produce. Why the carp choose to feed in one particular spot at one moment in time and not another identical spot is a mystery. Bloodworm don't seem to be the significant factor for I've only reeled in one or two and from unproductive areas too. The secret of successful fishing here is to be efficient at pin-pointing these spots every session. If you do find a productive spot, it can soon die after a few fish have been

Swamp Bay from Lightning Tree - an area which puts tackle to the test.

caught off it and remain unproductive for months. One such spot produced two thirties and some big twenties in two trips last season. Yet after those two trips I couldn't get a take on it again and still can't. It can be very frustrating thinking that you have found a hot-spot only for it to go cold after a few fish. I'm currently fishing three night or two night sessions on the water and spots where you might pick up a couple of fish on the first night fail to produce thereafter during that session, but can produce again on the next session. The spot that was dead for one or two nights can suddenly spark into life, but then completely die off for weeks. There are some nights on the Mangrove when you wouldn't think there was a single carp in the lake so dead can it be, but then on another night with identical weather conditions the carp can be coming out everywhere. The Mangrove is not an easy water, because you are faced with the constant puzzle of identifying the few places in a swim where the carp are likely to feed compared to the numerous places where they won't. You have to work hard at finding those hotspots and time on the water and experience is vital in terms of getting it right. People fishing other waters in the North West often forget that the 12 members fishing the Mangrove are amongst the most experienced carp anglers there are. This is reflected in some of the fabulous catches that are achieved. As an indication of this, this is the only

Marking the line to ensure pin-point marker float finding of a hotspot

syndicate I've ever been a member of where I am the youngest member!

How do you find those hotspots?

The fish can themselves identify them for you, although they rarely show in the day. The Mangrove carp often show just before dark and a carp head and shouldering, rolling or swirling just below the surface can betray some feeding activity which might identitify a natural hot-spot. A re-cast and bait-up where there was fish activity can pay off. Fish rolling over the bait can reveal a potential hotspot. Tim has referred to this as the fish "marking the spot" - they have found the bait, are attracted to it, but they may not start to eat it straight away. I've observed this myself on here and elsewhere, and have learned enough to know that if fish roll over the baited areas that eventually I'll catch a fish in that spot and so I leave a hookbait there despite the temptation to move it if the action isn't instant. I've sometimes had to wait three nights for that spot to start producing on the Mangrove. Incidentally, I've always baited up with fresh baits each night until the action comes rather than leaving the swim alone. The reason? I always fish with a fresh hookbait (and stringer) each night and so it is important to have identical baits out there alongside the older baits.

The other way of finding hotspots is by trial and error. I guess a likely spot and locate the line of it against a far bank feature which can be identified at night. This could be a gap in the trees, a landscape feature or whatever, from where I stand to cast. I sometimes chalk around my feet so I

Two landing nets. Necessary on the Mangrove due to the runs which can occur at the same time.

stand in exactly the same place each time. Out goes the marker float beyond the possible spot and it is pulled towards it. When the lead is on the possible spot, before allowing the float to rise, I mark the line a couple of inches above the reel with nail varnish, Tippex or a permanent marker. I can then find the exact spot again for re-baiting for the following night if I need to. A strong isotope taped to the float at night provides an easy target for re-casting, although as I said earlier, I've been shying away from using markers at night, preferring to trust to instinct that the bait is in the same spot. We get quite light nights on the Mangrove as there isn't all that pollution floating about up there, so it is usually possible to see the bait land.

I either get a run or I don't. If I do, it is likely to be a spot from which I'll get another. If I don't get a run I may still have found a productive spot but I may need to give it time. I generally give each spot a two night trial unless I see fish activity over the bait in which case I leave it alone. It's important to record in the memory the conditions under which a particular spot produced at a certain time. I'm blessed with a retentive memory which startles others at times in relation to the detail I can recall. I can remember every fish I ever caught and from which spot - and everyone elses too! If you haven't got a good memory, make diary notes to see if any patterns emerge in a particular swim.

Incidentally, I have not found the need to resort to back-leads when fishing the open water and have fished tight lines all of the time, although initially, this was through fear of the fish making progress towards the pads when hooked without me knowing. This shows though, how unpressured the Mangrove fish are due to the small number of members - if it was anywhere else I would feel the need to use backleads. This is the only water in the last ten years I've fished where you still get line bites!

Choice of bait for my Mangrove campaign was a formality. The old Premier Aminos had been used heavily for three seasons on the water, so it was the natural choice to use, despite the fact that all of the bait fish must have been caught on it several times over. This fact never worries me - because nutritional baits get better or they are not really nutritional - although I always look to improve on the bait that has been used heavily if I can. A new oil - an orange-coloured Scottish McSalmon oil - had been highly rated by Geoff Bowers, and I decided to use this and I wanted to avoid synthetic liquid flavours as I was sure that these had been extensively used on the water. Various natural flavours on powdered carriers we'd been playing about with, and in trials down south a powdered cream additive had been found particularly effective, and I incorporated this at 20 gm per kilo.

Another additive I've included, is an amino acid compound incorporating the much whispered about betaine. This additive is completely natural as it is derived from plant sources. It is used (under another name) in commercial aquaculture in food pellets to stimulate salmon to feed in freshwater conditions. Betaine, which is similar to the amino acid glycine, naturally occurs in Green Lipped Mussel extract and other marine molluscs, and had been known to me for some time, but as I could only obtain it in its pure state I wasn't sure of the correct dosages to use. Green Lipped Mussel is a known fish catcher in its own right - but levels recommended by many bait firms are as low as a couple of grams per kilo which I don't think is sufficient for the betaine content to be the main attractor trigger. But it is an extract not dissimilar in strength to some liver extracts which have been used at much higher levels successfully. Geoff Bowers is certainly convinced that Green Lipped is used at too low a level in carp baits, and I can confirm that a number of anglers have had very recent spectacular success on the southern pits with Green Lipped as the sole attractor at 1-2 ounces per kilo. This level is still safe too - though a little expensive! I am sure marine extracts - Green Lipped, Krill, Anchovy etc are going to be the real biggie in fishmeals in the near future as are other natural sources of betaine. I thought about the Green Lipped concept before fishing the Mangrove, but so far have stuck to my thoroughly proven line-up of attractors. The betaine proportion of the amino additive I've been using on the Mangrove is quite low but the remaining ingredients are also terrific fish attractors too. The additive contains betaine, alanine, isoleucine, leucine, valine, glycine, serine, phenylalanine, histidine, methionine, tyrosine, threonine and glutamic acid. Importantly, the additive is water soluble. This was added at a teaspoon per 6 eggs. There is a major role for amino acids in boiled baits. Although undoubtedly, some amino acids may be destroyed in the boiling process, sufficient of the best ones survive at the centre of the boilie to still leech out and assist in attraction. I also think that particular aminos come into play at certain times in the bait's gradual breakdown in the water. I can't definitely prove that - but I'm sufficiently convinced by my experiences to suggest that it may be the case.

What is certainly the case is that the use of pre-digested fishmeals (and other forms of pre-digested animal protein) significantly enhances the attractiveness and digestibility of the bait. Baits with a significant proportion of these sorts of ingredients causes bait breakdown completely within 24-48 hours, depending on water temperature and how active nuisance fish are. This gives the bait a tremendous advantage over more traditional fishmeals because the chemical signal given off by the attractors are much stronger. One or two have said to me, that a hard boilie that breaks down to being a soft one fairly quickly is a disadvantage and that it is better to use a hard bait

The bleakness of the Fallen Tree swim in winter.

that stays out there for days until it is eaten. I disagree. The level of attraction is stronger with a breaking-down bait, and I know the exact length of life of any bait out in front of me. This makes it easier to gauge the amount of bait to introduce to top-up in relation to the time I have available and to the possible number of fish out in front of me. I always tend to bait heavily initially if I have at least a couple of nights at my disposal. With a heavy fishmeal bait that lasts for so much longer, it can be very easy to overbait initially - it is easy to put bait in - but impossible to get it out again. You can't overbait with a bait that has broken down in 24 hours in the warm summer months, if you've got 48 hours or more to fish. A dissolving bait means too, that you can constantly maintain a constant level of attraction. The pre-digested meal increases the food value of the bait and it goes more quickly through the fishes gut than coarse fishmeal ingredients.

The bait went off with a bang from day one - as I expected it to - and everything with fins in the Mangrove couldn't get enough of it. My Mangrove results have exceeded my wildest expectations. First season captures included 35 twenties and 5 thirties - the most thirties anyone has ever caught from this water in a single season.

The fifth Mangrove thirty caught in my very first season, the superb Linear.

I've got to the stage in my life when I haven't got time to roll masses of bait and I no longer have the inclination to roll it on the bank. So I pay someone I trust to roll it for me. As an old purist in terms of bait I wasn't altogether happy with this but my initial reservations have all been laid to rest.

Interestingly enough, all of my Mangrove carp have been caught on bottom baits - a few of the ready rolled baits which have been allowed to harden for a few hours and then soaked in oil. I haven't used a pop-up, a buoyant or critically balanced bait at all, and I think I would have caught far fewer fish if I had done. Looking

Ambition achieved - an English thirty pound common. Caught from Fallen Tree.

back at my own previous approach to silt rigs that is quite surprising. For ten years on the silt lakes I used pop-ups and buoyant baits exclusively, because I felt I needed to because of soft silt. In the last few seasons, virtually all of my fish have been caught on bottom baits which must at certain times have been partly sunk into the silt or out of sight. Thinking about it logically, that is where the fish feed and where they also find the free offerings. Logically too, it shows that we can become so obsessed with our own complex human ideas about the rig that we think we ought to be using that we sometimes forget that carp are - in the great scheme of things - very simple creatures.

. . . .

When you fish the Mangrove a madness creeps up on you. It is a wonderful place and a million miles removed from the big fish circuit I have fished on for so long. You become addicted to the place, the lack of fishing pressure, the tranquillity and the hospitality (not to mention the good food and drink) on offer in the nearby village. There is no place like it. I find it hard to think about fishing anywhere else at the moment and friends fishing elsewhere have already made remarks like, "We won't hear of him again, he's retired onto that Mangrove" and so on. I have to admit that they may have a point.

Is there a cure for my Mangrove fever? Tim says I've just got to fish it out of my system and if I do I'll enjoy going there and still enjoy going elsewhere. He may be right, for I suspect that that is how he came through the fever, for he too, was once similarly afflicted.

What a lovely addiction!